Workshop on Multilingual Information Access (MIA 2022)

AA001799

Online
15 July 2022

ISBN: 978-1-7138-5635-1

Printed from e-media with permission by:

Curran Associates, Inc.
57 Morehouse Lane
Red Hook, NY 12571

Some format issues inherent in the e-media version may also appear in this print version.

Printed with permission by Curran Associates, Inc. (2022)

Association for Computational Linguistics
209 N. Eighth Street
Stroudsburg, Pennsylvania 18360

Phone: 1-570-476-8006
Fax: 1-570-476-0860

acl@aclweb.org

Additional copies of this publication are available from:

Curran Associates, Inc.
57 Morehouse Lane
Red Hook, NY 12571 USA
Phone: 845-758-0400
Fax: 845-758-2633
Email: curran@proceedings.com
Web: www.proceedings.com

MIA 2022

The Workshop on Multilingual Information Access (MIA)

Proceedings of the Workshop

July 15, 2022

Order copies of this and other ACL proceedings from:

Association for Computational Linguistics (ACL)
209 N. Eighth Street
Stroudsburg, PA 18360
USA
Tel: +1-570-476-8006
Fax: +1-570-476-0860
acl@aclweb.org

Organizing Committee

Organizing Committee

Akari Asai, University of Washington
Eunsol Choi, University of Texas at Austin
Jonathan H. Clark, Google Research
Junjie Hu, University of Wisconsin-Madison
Chia-Hsuan Lee, University of Washington
Jungo Kasai, University of Washington
Shayne Longpre, MIT
Ikuya Yamada, Studio Ousia and RIKEN
Rui Zhang, Penn State University

Program Committee

Senior Program Committee

C. M. Downey, University of Washington
Mehrad Moradshahi, Stanford University
Mihaela Bornea, IBM, International Business Machines
Mihir Kale, Carnegie Mellon University
Ryokan Ri, The University of Tokyo, Tokyo Institute of Technology
Zhucheng Tu, Apple
Akari Asai, Paul G. Allen School of Computer Science & Engineering, University of Washington
Akiko Eriguchi, Microsoft
Chia-Hsuan Lee, University of Washington, Seattle
He Bai, University of Waterloo
Jessica Ouyang, University of Texas at Dallas
Jonathan H. Louis, Google
Mikio Nakano, Honda Research Institute
Rebecca J. Passonneau, Penn State University
Gabriel Skantze, KTH
Manfred Stede, Universität Potsdam
David Traum, University of Southern California
Koichiro Yoshino, Nara Institute of Science and Technology

Program Committee

Sean Andrist, Microsoft Research, United States
Masahiro Araki, Kyoto Institute of Technology, Japan
Ron Artstein, USC Institute for Creative Technologies, United States
Yoav Artzi, Cornell University, United States
Timo Baumann, Universität Hamburg, Germany
Frederic Bechet, Aix Marseille Universite - LIS/CNRS, France
Steve Beet, Aculab plc, United Kingdom
Jose Miguel Benedi, Universitàt Politècnica de València, Spain
Luciana Benotti, Universidad Nacional de Cordoba, Argentina
Yonatan Bisk, Carnegie Mellon University, United States
Nate Blaylock, Cerence, United States
Dan Bohus, Microsoft Research, United States
Johan Boye, KTH, Sweden
Chloé Braud, IRIT - CNRS, France
Hendrik Buschmeier, Bielefeld University, Germany
Andrew Caines, University of Cambridge, United Kingdom
Christophe Cerisara, Université de Lorraine, CNRS, LORIA, France
Senthil Chandramohan, Microsoft, United States
Lin Chen, Head of AI, Cambia Health Solutions, United States
Paul Crook, Facebook, United States
Heriberto Cuayahuitl, University of Lincoln, United Kingdom
Nina Dethlefs, University of Hull, United Kingdom
David DeVault, University of Southern California, United States
Barbara Di Eugenio, University of Illinois at Chicago, United States
Jens Edlund, KTH Speech, Music and Hearing, Sweden

Maxine Eskenazi, Carnegie Mellon University, United States
Keelan Evanini, Educational Testing Service, United States
Mauro Falcone, Fondazione Ugo Bordoni, Italy
Michel Galley, Microsoft Research, United States
Milica Gasic, Heinrich Heine University Duesseldorf, Germany
Kallirroi Georgila, University of Southern California, ICT, United States
Alborz Geramifard, Facebook AI, United States
Debanjan Ghosh, Educational Testing Service, United States
Jonathan Ginzburg, Université Paris-Diderot (Paris 7), France
Joakim Gustafson, KTH, Sweden
Ivan Habernal, Technische Universität Darmstadt, Germany
Helen Hastie, Heriot-Watt University, United Kingdom
Michael Heck, Heinrich Heine University, Germany
Behnam Hedayatnia, Amazon, United States
Ryuichiro Higashinaka, NTT Media Intelligence Labs., Japan
Takuya Hiraoka, NEC Central Research Laboratories, Japan
Thomas Howard, University of Rochester, United States
David M. Howcroft, Heriot-Watt University, United Kingdom
Ruihong Huang, Texas A&M University, United States
Michimasa Inaba, The University of Electro-Communications, Japan
Koji Inoue, Kyoto University, Japan
Filip Jurcicek, Apple Inc., United Kingdom
Tatsuya Kawahara, Kyoto University, Japan
Chris Kedzie, Columbia University, United States
Simon Keizer, Toshiba Research Europe Ltd, United Kingdom
Chandra Khatri, Senior AI Research Scientist, Uber AI, United States
Alexander Koller, Saarland University, Germany
Kazunori Komatani, Osaka University, Japan
Ivana Kruijff-Korbayova, DFKI, Germany
Kornel Laskowski, Carnegie Mellon University, United States
Fabrice Lefevre, Avignon Univ., France
Oliver Lemon, Heriot-Watt University, United Kingdom
Junyi Jessy Li, University of Texas at Austin, United States
Pierre Lison, Norwegian Computing Centre, Norway
Bing Liu, Facebook, United States
Eduardo Lleida Solano, University of Zaragoza, Spain
Ramon Lopez-Cozar, University of Granada, Spain
Nurul Lubis, Heinrich Heine University, Germany
Ross Mead, Semio, United States
Teruhisa Misu, Honda Research Institute USA, United States
Seungwhan Moon, Facebook Conversational AI, United States
Raymond Mooney, University of Texas at Austin, United States
Elena Musi, University of Liverpool, United Kingdom
Satoshi Nakamura, Nara Institute of Science and Technology and RIKEN AIP Center, Japan
Vincent Ng, University of Texas at Dallas, United States
Douglas O'Shaughnessy, INRS-EMT (Univ. of Quebec), Canada
Alexandros Papangelis, Uber AI, United States
Cecile Paris, CSIRO, Australia
Nanyun Peng, University of Southern California, United States
Laura Perez-Beltrachini, School of Informatics, University of Edinburgh, United Kingdom
Paul Piwek, The Open University, United Kingdom

Heather Pon-Barry, Mount Holyoke College, United States
Andrei Popescu-Belis, HEIG-VD / HES-SO, Switzerland
Abhinav Rastogi, Google Research, United States
Ehud Reiter, University of Aberdeen, United Kingdom
Norbert Reithinger, DFKI GmbH, Germany
Antonio Roque, Tufts University, United States
Carolyn Rose, Carnegie Mellon University, United States
Clayton Rothwell, Infoscitex Corp., United States
Sakriani Sakti, Nara Institute of Science and Technology (NAIST) / RIKEN AIP, Japan
Ruhi Sarikaya, Amazon, United States
David Schlangen, University of Potsdam, Germany
Ethan Selfridge, Interactions LLC, United States
Georg Stemmer, Intel Corp., Germany
Matthew Stone, Rutgers University, United States
Svetlana Stoyanchev, Toshiba Europe, United Kingdom
Kristina Striegnitz, Union College, United States
Pei-Hao Su, PolyAI, United Kingdom
Hiroaki Sugiyama, NTT Communication Science Labs., Japan
António Teixeira, DETI/IEETA, University of Aveiro, Portugal
Takenobu Tokunaga, Tokyo Institute of Technology, Japan
Bo-Hsiang Tseng, University of Cambridge, United Kingdom
Gokhan Tur, Amazon Alexa AI, United States
Stefan Ultes, Mercedes-Benz AG, Germany
David Vandyke, Apple, United Kingdom
Hsin-Min Wang, Academia Sinica, Taiwan
Yi-Chia Wang, Uber AI, United States
Nigel Ward, University of Texas at El Paso, United States
Jason D Clark, Apple, United States
Jungo Kasai, Paul G. Allen School of Computer Science & Engineering, University of Washington
Sebastian Ruder, Google
Shayne Longpre, Massachusetts Institute of Technology
Tom Sherborne, University of Edinburgh
Tom Kwiatkowski, Google
Wei Wang, Apple AI/ML
Xinyan Yu, Department of Computer Science, University of Washington
Xutan Peng, University of Sheffield

Table of Contents

Program

Friday, July 15, 2022

09:15 - 09:00	*Opening Remark*
10:15 - 09:15	*Invited talks for the model track*
11:00 - 10:15	*Model panels*
12:00 - 11:00	*Poster session*
13:00 - 12:00	*Lunch break*
13:45 - 13:00	*Shared task session*
14:00 - 13:45	*Best paper talk*
15:00 - 14:00	*Invited talks for the resource track*
15:15 - 15:00	*Break*
16:00 - 15:15	*Resource panels*
16:15 - 16:00	*Closing session*

Geographical Distance Is The New Hyperparameter: A Case Study Of Finding The Optimal Pre-trained Language For English-isiZulu Machine Translation.

Muhammad Umair Nasir[1], **Innocent Amos Mchechesi**[2]

[1] Ominor AI, [2] University of the Witwatersrand, South Africa

Abstract

Stemming from the limited availability of datasets and textual resources for low-resource languages such as isiZulu, there is a significant need to be able to harness knowledge from pre-trained models to improve low resource machine translation. Moreover, a lack of techniques to handle the complexities of morphologically rich languages has compounded the unequal development of translation models, with many widely spoken African languages being left behind. This study explores the potential benefits of transfer learning in an English-isiZulu translation framework. The results indicate the value of transfer learning from closely related languages to enhance the performance of low-resource translation models, thus providing a key strategy for low-resource translation going forward. We gathered results from 8 different language corpora, including one multi-lingual corpus, and saw that isiXhosa-isiZulu outperformed all languages, with a BLEU score of 8.56 on the test set which was better from the multi-lingual corpora pre-trained model by 2.73. We also derived a new coefficient, *Nasir's Geographical Distance Coefficient (NGDC)* which provides an easy selection of languages for the pre-trained models. NGDC also indicated that isiXhosa should be selected as the language for the pre-trained model.

1 Introduction

Neural machine translation aims to automate the translation of text or speech from one language to another utilising neural networks (Nyoni and Bassett, 2021). Consequently, the performance of neural machine translation (NMT) models is highly dependent on the availability of large parallel corpora to provide sufficient training data. Low-resource languages which are under-represented in internet sources lack suitable training corpora and therefore suffer from limited development, obtaining poor translation performance. This phenomenon is exacerbated by a lack of content creators, dataset curators and language specialists, resulting in barriers at many stages in the translation process (Lakew et al., 2020; Zoph et al., 2016; Sennrich and Zhang, 2019).

Therefore, due to the historical focus on dominant languages such as English in the development of neural machine translation (NMT) models, low-resource and morphologically complex languages remain a challenge for current translation systems (Haddow et al., 2021; Koehn and Knowles, 2017). Due to limited resources in terms of both computational expense and available datasets, it is vital to be able to leverage knowledge from current pre-trained models to provide more effective solutions. Therefore, in this investigation, the effects of transfer learning from closely related languages, as well as comparison with high-resourced languages for pre-trained scenario, is explored in the context of English to Zulu translation.

Furthermore, this study derives the Nasir's Geographical Distance coefficient. *Geographical Distance (GD)* (Holman et al., 2007) has been studied for various scientific research areas (Bei et al., 2021; Krajsa and Fojtova, 2011; Riginos and Nachman, 2001) as it provides deep insights in many aspects. We will also use GD as a hyperparameter for an attempt to get a language for a pre-trained model in an effective and with a $O(n)$ complexity. Although there are many ways to find GD, we will use literal approximation of distance in kilometers and suggest the techniques in future directions.

1.1 Background

Previous studies have indicated poor translation performance for the isiZulu languages due to its morphological complexity and limited available data (Martinus and Abbott, 2019). The challenging nature of English-isiZulu translation is highlighted in a benchmark of five low-resource African languages by Martinus and Abbott (2019), where isiZulu obtains a much poorer BLEU score in

Proceedings of the Workshop on Multilingual Information Access (MIA), pages 1 - 8
July 15, 2022

comparison to other evaluated languages. The study suggests that the collection of higher quality datasets for isiZulu would greatly benefit translation performance.

Furthermore, the challenges associated with the morphological complexity of Nguni languages such as isiZulu are tackled in a study by Moeng et al. (2021). The investigation explores the use of supervised sequence-to-sequence models to tokenize isiZulu, isiXhosa, isiNdebele and siSwati sentences, demonstrating promising results for improved segmentation of morphologically complex Nguni languages.

A notable study by Nyoni and Bassett (2021) compares the use of zero-shot learning, transfer learning and multi-lingual learning on three Bantu languages, namely isiZulu, isiXhosa and chiShona. The results indicate that multi-lingual learning where a many-to-many model was trained using three different language pairs, English-isiZulu, English-isiXhosa and isiXhosa-isiZulu led to optimal results on their custom dataset.

In addition, the study found that transfer learning from a closely related Bantu language is highly effective for low resource translation models, with statistically significant results being obtained when transfer learning to isiZulu using the pretrained English-to-isiXhosa model (Nyoni and Bassett, 2021). In contrast, transfer learning from the English-to-Shona model did not yield any statistically significant improvement, indicating the role of morphological similarity in the transfer learning process.

There has been a lot of work in providing assistance to low-resourced languages for machine translation focus of the area. Neubig and Hu (2018) trained multilingual models as seed models and then continued training on low-resourced language. Sennrich et al. (2015) looks into training monolingual data with automatic back-translation (Edunov et al., 2018; Caswell et al., 2019; Edunov et al., 2019) to improve scores through only a monolingual data. Another work that utilizes back-translation for effecctive NMT training is done by Dou et al. (2020). Koneru et al. (2022) proposes a cost-effective training procedure to increase the performance of models on NMT tasks, utilizing a small number of annotated sentences and dictionary entries. Park et al. (2020) looked into decoding strategies for low-resourced languages in an attempt to improve training. Nguyen and Chiang (2017) looked into related languages to a target language for low-resourced languages to prove effectiveness of similar languages.

Similarly, this study aims to investigate whether transfer learning from a morphologically similar language will be effective on the novel, high-quality Umsuka English-isiZulu parallel corpus and if so, how does it perform when we use high-resourced mono- and multi-lingual corpora. This study will also derive a formula which will ease the way for selecting a language for a pre-trained model.

2 Methodology

This investigation evaluates several models pretrained on different language pairs, both low- and high-resourced, on a recently release English-Zulu parallel corpus. The dataset utilized to fine-tune and benchmark the models is discussed below.

2.1 Dataset

The Umsuka English-isiZulu Parallel Corpus (Mabuya et al., 2021) provides a novel, high-quality parallel dataset for machine translation, containing English sentences sampled from both News Crawl datasets which were then translated into isiZulu, and isiZulu sentences from the NCHLT monolingual corpus and UKZN isiZulu National monolingual corpus, which were then translated into English. Each translation was performed twice, by two differing translators, due to the high morphological complexity of the isiZulu language. This also serves the purpose of considering one translation as a reference and the other as target. This can be validated as both have been translated by human annotators and are different from each other. The dataset is publicly available from the Zenodo platform[1].

2.2 Models

The three models tested are based on the MarianMT model (Junczys-Dowmunt et al., 2018) which is constructed using a Transformer architecture. Each model is pretrained on a different set of language pairs from the Helsinki Corpus.

MarianMT (Junczys-Dowmunt et al., 2018) is a toolkit for neural machine translation written in C++ with over 1000 models trained on different language pairs from OPUS[2], available at the Hug-

[1]`https://zenodo.org/record/5035171#.YZvn1fFBy3J`

[2]`https://opus.nlpl.eu/`

gingFace Model Hub[3]. Each model is based on a Transformer encoder-decoder structure with 6 layers in each component (Junczys-Dowmunt et al., 2018). From the available models, 8 pre-trained models were selected[4], representing pre-training on a closely related language, pre-training on a more distantly related language within the same family and pre-training on multiple unrelated languages, with less and more data, respectively. Since each model was based on the same architecture, this allowed for a controlled comparison of the language pairs used for pre-training, as any discrepancies due to architectural differences were discounted.

Since isiXhosa and isiZulu are both part of the Nguni branch of Bantu languages, isiXhosa is closely related to isiZulu in the Bantu language family tree (Nyoni and Bassett, 2021). As well as Shona, or chiShona, is selected as it is also a part of Southern Bantu language group (Nyoni and Bassett, 2021). Another Bantu language, Kiswahili was explored to determine the effects of transfer learning from another language within the Bantu family which is not as closely related to the target isiZulu language. While isiZulu is classified as a Southern Bantu and Nguni language, Kiswahili is part of the Northeast Bantu and Sabaki languages (Nurse et al., 1993).

Twi, or Akan-kasa, is spoken in Ghana, has been selected to have a representation from Western Africa and to explore the effects a dialect of the Akan language on fine-tuning isiZulu. Luganda is selected as a representation from Niger-Congo family of languages and is spoken in East-African Country of Uganda. This will able us to explore the fine-tuning regime in Niger-Congo languages.

Arabic and French are selected as they are morphologically very different and are considered to be high-resourced (Ali et al., 2014; Besacier et al., 2014). We explore effects of fine-tuning high-resourced languages with different morphologies. As the notion of having more and multi-lingual data will be better for fine-tuning, we select a corpus of Romance languages, which is created by joining 48 Romance languages including French, Italian, Spanish, Walloon, Catalan, Occitan, Romansh etc. We include Romance languages so that we can cover the aspect of big multi-lingual corpora being fine-tuned on low-resourced isiZulu and to prove our hypothesis.

[3]https://huggingface.co/

[4]https://github.com/umair-nasir14/NGDC

2.3 Implementation Reproducibility

We believe all experiments must be *Reproducible*. To achieve this we are open-sourcing our code on GitHub (added in the footnote previously).

3 Results

Each model was benchmarked on the test set using the BLEU(Papineni et al., 2002) score as tabulated in Table 1 below. It can be observed that the optimal model is given by the MarianMT model pre-trained on the English-Xhosa dataset. This confirms our hypothesis that transfer learning from a geographically distant language would result in poor performance. Here GD is in Kilometers (Km) and corpus size is in Number Of Sentences in millions (M).

In Fig. 1 below, we can observe that the MarianMT model pre-trained on the English-Xhosa dataset outperforms all other models by a good margin, obtaining a final BLEU score of 8.56. This result suggests that the morphological similarities between the isiZulu and isiXhosa languages plays a strong role in the benefits attained through fine-tuning.

Following identification of the optimal model, the MarianMT model pre-trained on the En-Xh dataset was further fine-tuned for 75 epochs on Umsuka dataset, giving a final optimal BLEU score of 17.61 on training set and 13.73 on test.

4 Analysis

We now present an analysis of the results in light of both the underlying theory and previous literature. In order to further understand the effects of pre-training on different languages, the datasets used for pre-training of the MarianMT models were inspected. Notably, although the number of sentences in English-Xhosa dataset is in order of magnitudes less than Romance languages corpus but still performs better. This justifies our hypothesis and opens up a path to effective fine-tuning through the knowladge of morphologies and not by adding multiple languages into a single corpus. Arabic and French having approximately 5 and 23 times more data also suggests the above mentioned hypothesis that with closer GD and lesser data is much better, in many ways, than larger data and farther GD.

Other Bantu languages that were selected, Kiswahili and chiShona performed almost similar to Arabic and French with order of magnitudes of lesser data which suggests that even if they are

Language(s)	BLEU(Val)	BLEU(Test)	Corpus Size(NOS)	GD(KM)
isiXhosa	10.20	8.56	20.7	1000
Romance	7.76	5.83	1232.7	13094.4
Arabic	5.76	3.07	102.8	5205
French	5.42	3.91	479.1	13094
Kiswahili	5.28	3.97	9.1	3783.1
chiShona	4.32	2.83	0.1	1584
Twi	1.91	1.34	0.047	7962
Luganda	0.94	0.55	0.039	4883.7

Table 1: BLEU scores, GD and corpora size

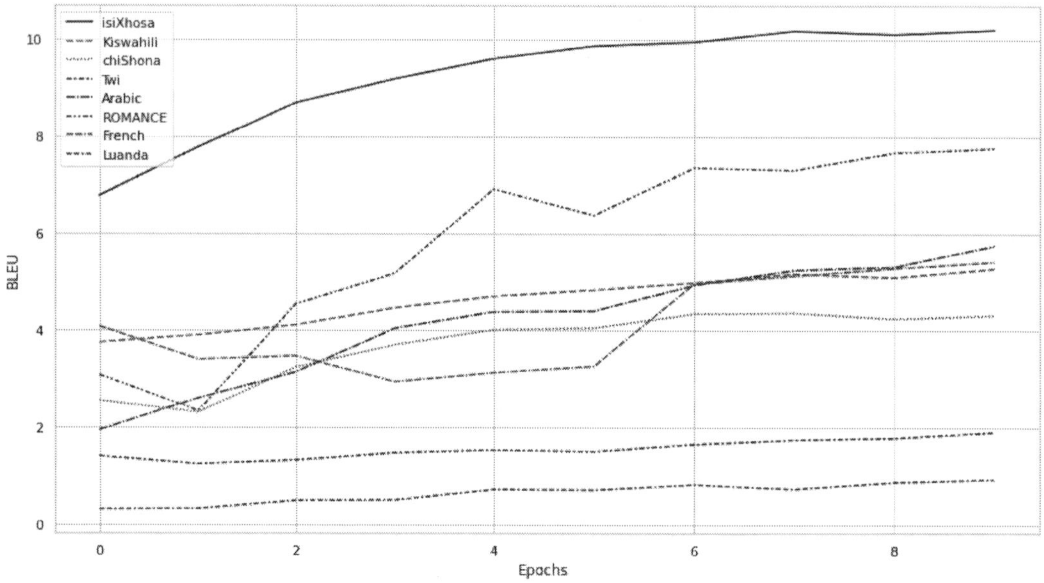

Figure 1: BLEU scores per epoch according to different pre-training languages, indicates high performance of morphologically similar isiXhosa, which outperforms a model trained on a very large corpora and rest of corpora.

not as similar to isiZulu, the distance being very close to where isiZulu is spoken tends to have a great impact. We speak similar languages in neighbouring cities and countries which should have an effect on the model and so the result suggests. Twi and Luganda, having very less data and higher GD, gives us very poor results.

From Table 1, we also observe that distance between the target language and the language from a pre-trained model is a very important factor. Alone, to a good extent it can serve the purpose of choosing the language of pre-trained model but we want to look one step deeper as one can argue that Romance languages corpora, French and Arabic perform relatively better but the distances are larger. Thus we also look into Size of Corpus (Table 1). Which forces us to think about deriving a relationship that involves both distance and the size. This will be explained in the upcoming sub-section.

4.1 Nasir's Geographical Distance Coefficient

In Figure 2 we can observe that there is a sensible relationship between BLEU scores and distance, and as a rule of thumb there should always be a relationship with corpus size (Lin et al., 2019). With further analysis we can deduce that neither distance alone nor corpus size alone can be taken for granted when selecting a language for pre-trained model. Thus, we derive a formula which takes into account both distance and corpus size in account. This formula is intended to be used before training to know which language corpora to select.

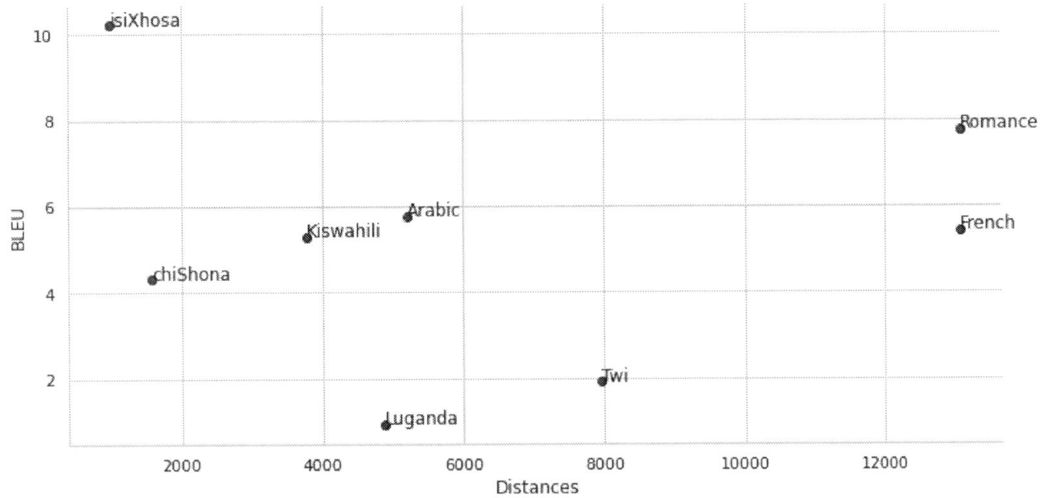

Figure 2: Relationship between BLEU scores and distance (KM) of places where languages are spoken from the place where isiZulu is spoken.

$$z = \frac{cD}{(1-c)S}$$

$$\delta = \begin{cases} 1, & \text{if } D \geq D_{max} \\ \frac{exp(z)}{1+exp(z)}, & \text{otherwise} \end{cases}$$

where D is the distance between language to fine-tune and language of the pre-trained model, S is the size of corpus, c is the weight coefficient, set to 0.4, which could act as hyperparameter. D_{max} is also hyperparameter to be tuned when it is being used in different languages in different parts of the world. δ is the coefficient we are introducing, *Nasir's Geographical Distance Coefficient (NGDC)*. The goal here is to minimize NGDC.

Table 2, Figures 3 and 4 shows the results and effectiveness of our introduced NPC. We can observe that without imposing penalty we have Romance languages, Arabic and French as desired pre-trained model languages along with isiXhosa and Kiswahili, which makes absolute sense as some have more data and others are near to target language but we want to have morphologically closer languages which will get better results. It would also be better if lesser carbon footprint is left and lesser training resources are used. Thus, with the penalty we only get isiXhosa and Kiswahili as desired ones, which will eventually be better in all perspectives.

5 Impact Statement

The potential impacts of this investigation can be explored in light of the possible contributions, risks and societal impact.

5.1 Applications and Benefits

The study poses potential benefits to further research into low-resource languages as it motivates careful choice of the pre-trained model used for transfer learning in order to improve performance on low resource languages. This could provide a vital tool to improve the efficiency and performance of low resource translation pipelines, especially in resource-constrained environments. In addition, this principle could be applied more broadly to other language groups with morphologically similar languages.

Moreover, effective transfer learning provides the additional advantage of promoting decreased computational expense since prior knowledge from previously trained networks can be leveraged effectively. This could work to mitigate the substantial detrimental environmental impact stemming from the intensive GPU training required to train neural machine translation models. This is critical to ensure sustainable development of machine translation models by minimising resource waste.

5.2 Limitations and Drawbacks

It should be noted that any conclusions drawn from the study are based on the BLEU score as the sole

Language(s)	BLEU	NGDC(With Penalty)	NGDC(Without Penalty)
isiXhosa	10.20	0.5080	0.5080
Romance	7.76	1.0000	0.5007
Arabic	5.76	1.0000	0.5084
French	5.42	1.0000	0.5045
Kiswahili	5.28	0.5688	0.5688
chiShona	4.32	0.9999	0.9999
Twi	1.91	1.0000	1.0000
Luganda	0.94	1.0000	1.0000

Table 2: NGDC with and without Penalty.

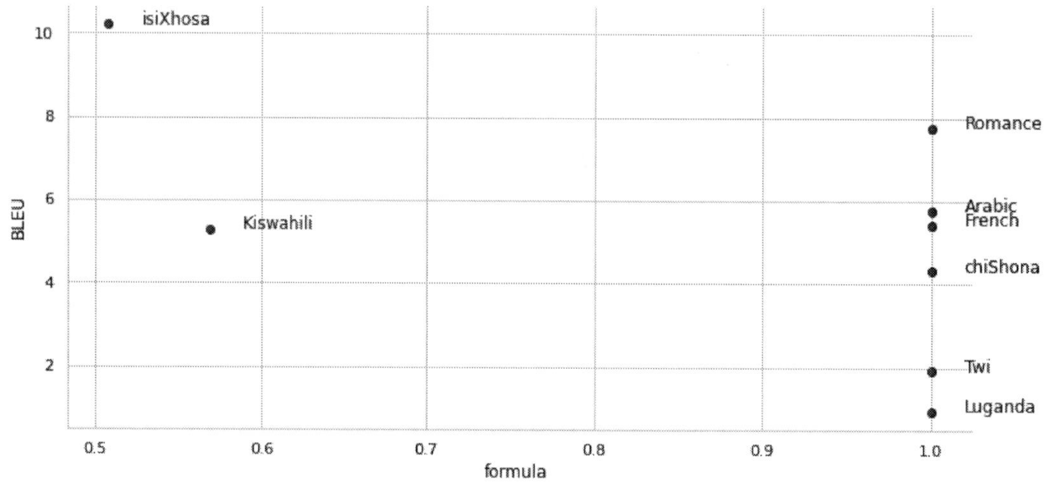

Figure 3: NGDC with Penalty

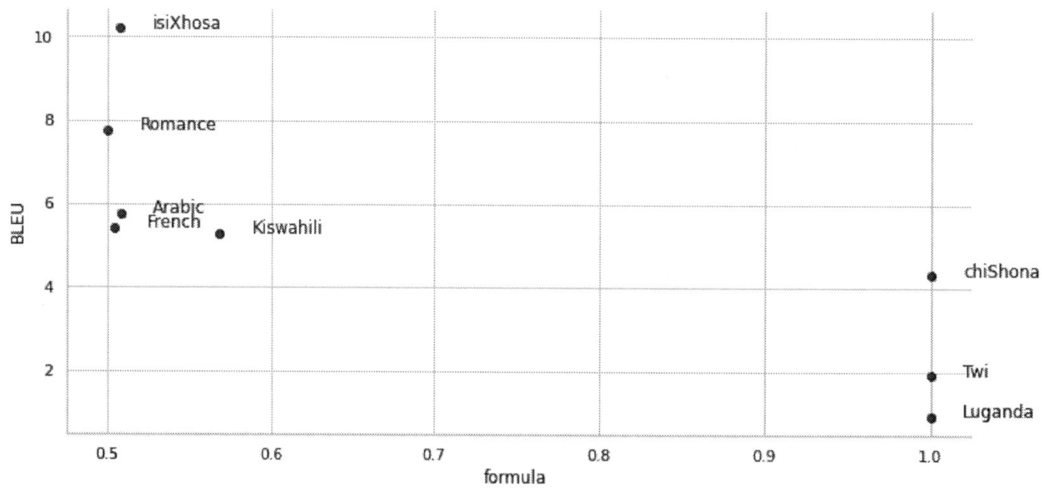

Figure 4: NGDC without Penalty

evaluation metric. This may provide a limited view of the true translation performance as it is based on n-gram similarity and does not necessarily measure whether the meaning of a sentence has been captured. A further improvement could be to conduct a similar study with additional expertise from a linguistic specialist to verify whether the output of the translation models is valid.

5.3 Social Impact

Societal impacts of low resource neural machine translation include furthering accessibility of information to under-represented languages and working to close the digital divide between high-resource and low-resource languages. Machine translation is an essential component of applications ranging from voice-assisted smart-phone applications that provide healthcare to rural communities to ensuring multi-lingual access to educational materials. Therefore it is vital that machine translation technology is accessible and functional for low-resource languages to be able to build valuable tools which could have a beneficial societal impact.

6 Conclusion and Future Directions

English-isiZulu translation has historically obtained poor results on translation benchmarks due to a lack of high-quality training data and appropriate tokenization schemes able to handle the agglutinative structure of isiZulu sentences. In this investigation, the challenges of isiZulu translation in terms of both morphological complexity and a lack of textual resources are explored using the recently released Umsuka English-isiZulu Parallel Corpus. In order to investigate the effects of the impact of the pre-trained model selected for transfer learning, several models were fine-tuned and benchmarked on the Umsuka dataset.

MariantMT models pre-trained on English-Xhosa, English-Swahili, English-Shona, English-Twi, English-Luganda, English-Arabic, English-French and English-Multilingual Romance languages, respectively. The study found that the pre-trained English-Xhosa model attained the optimal results with a handsome margin. Thus, the results indicate that transfer learning is particularly effective when languages are within the same sub-family while transfer learning is less effective when the model is pre-trained on a more distantly related language, no matter the size of the data to an extreme extent. We have also introduced a novel *Nasir's Geographical Distance Coefficient* which will help researchers find a language for pre-trained model effectively and will result in using less resources.

Therefore, this study motivates careful choice of the pre-trained model used for transfer learning, utilising existing knowledge of language family trees, to promote improved performance of low resource translation. In addition, we have open-sourced[5] our best model which was fine-tuned for 75 epochs using the original MarianMT model pre-trained on the English-Xhosa language pair, obtaining a final BLEU score of 17.61 on train while 13.73 on test set. We have also gathered all model cards for the models that were used for further experimentation.

This study yeilds promising future directions as the experiment was done on only 8 corpora. We suggest to increase the number and observe the derivation of the result. We also suggest to combine Bantu language as one multi-lingual corpora and observe the result. The experiment has been done on a novel Umsuka parallel corpora, the study should extend to more common benchmarks. This study should extend to different low-resourced languages of different continents of our world. We have derived a formula that takes into the account just the distance and the size of corpora, a promising research would be to derive a formula that takes morphologies and/or phonologies and fives a distance based on that. With NGDC at hand, it motivates to create a framework where one enters a target language, a D_{max} and a value for weight coefficient c and gets desirable models to train on. There are many precise ways of finding GD, such as Lambert's formula (Lambert, 1942) and Vincenty's formula (Vincenty, 1975) which may enhance NGDC's performance. It also opens up ways to introduce morphology in the formula, which we expect it to improve the overall selection of the models.

References

Ahmed Ali, Hamdy Mubarak, and Stephan Vogel. 2014. Advances in dialectal arabic speech recognition: A study using twitter to improve egyptian asr. In *Proceedings of the 11th International Workshop on Spoken Language Translation: Papers*.

Eva Bei, Mikołaj Zarzycki, Val Morrison, and Noa Vilchinsky. 2021. Motivations and willingness to provide care from a geographical distance, and the impact of distance care on caregivers' mental and physical health: A mixed-method systematic review protocol. *BMJ open*, 11(7):e045660.

Laurent Besacier, Etienne Barnard, Alexey Karpov, and Tanja Schultz. 2014. Introduction to the special issue on processing under-resourced languages.

[5] `https://huggingface.co/MUNasir/umsuka-en-zu`

Isaac Caswell, Ciprian Chelba, and David Grangier. 2019. Tagged back-translation. *arXiv preprint arXiv:1906.06442*.

Zi-Yi Dou, Antonios Anastasopoulos, and Graham Neubig. 2020. Dynamic data selection and weighting for iterative back-translation. *arXiv preprint arXiv:2004.03672*.

Sergey Edunov, Myle Ott, Michael Auli, and David Grangier. 2018. Understanding back-translation at scale. *arXiv preprint arXiv:1808.09381*.

Sergey Edunov, Myle Ott, Marc'Aurelio Ranzato, and Michael Auli. 2019. On the evaluation of machine translation systems trained with back-translation. *arXiv preprint arXiv:1908.05204*.

Barry Haddow, Rachel Bawden, Antonio Valerio Miceli Barone, Jindřich Helcl, and Alexandra Birch. 2021. Survey of low-resource machine translation. *arXiv preprint arXiv:2109.00486*.

Eric W Holman, Christian Schulze, Dietrich Stauffer, and Søren Wichmann. 2007. On the relation between structural diversity and geographical distance among languages: observations and computer simulations.

Marcin Junczys-Dowmunt, Roman Grundkiewicz, Tomasz Dwojak, Hieu Hoang, Kenneth Heafield, Tom Neckermann, Frank Seide, Ulrich Germann, Alham Fikri Aji, Nikolay Bogoychev, et al. 2018. Marian: Fast neural machine translation in c++. *arXiv preprint arXiv:1804.00344*.

Philipp Koehn and Rebecca Knowles. 2017. Six challenges for neural machine translation. *arXiv preprint arXiv:1706.03872*.

Sai Koneru, Danni Liu, and Jan Niehues. 2022. Cost-effective training in low-resource neural machine translation. *arXiv preprint arXiv:2201.05700*.

Ondrej Krajsa and Lucie Fojtova. 2011. Rtt measurement and its dependence on the real geographical distance. In *2011 34th International Conference on Telecommunications and Signal Processing (TSP)*, pages 231–234. IEEE.

Surafel M Lakew, Matteo Negri, and Marco Turchi. 2020. Low resource neural machine translation: A benchmark for five african languages. *arXiv preprint arXiv:2003.14402*.

Walter D Lambert. 1942. The distance between two widely separated points on the surface of the earth. *Journal of the Washington Academy of Sciences*, 32(5):125–130.

Yu-Hsiang Lin, Chian-Yu Chen, Jean Lee, Zirui Li, Yuyan Zhang, Mengzhou Xia, Shruti Rijhwani, Junxian He, Zhisong Zhang, Xuezhe Ma, et al. 2019. Choosing transfer languages for cross-lingual learning. *arXiv preprint arXiv:1905.12688*.

Rooweither Mabuya, Jade Abbott, and Vukosi Marivate. 2021. Umsuka english - isizulu parallel corpus.

Laura Martinus and Jade Z Abbott. 2019. A focus on neural machine translation for african languages. *arXiv preprint arXiv:1906.05685*.

Tumi Moeng, Sheldon Reay, Aaron Daniels, and Jan Buys. 2021. Canonical and surface morphological segmentation for nguni languages. *arXiv preprint arXiv:2104.00767*.

Graham Neubig and Junjie Hu. 2018. Rapid adaptation of neural machine translation to new languages. *arXiv preprint arXiv:1808.04189*.

Toan Q Nguyen and David Chiang. 2017. Transfer learning across low-resource, related languages for neural machine translation. *arXiv preprint arXiv:1708.09803*.

Derek Nurse, Thomas J Hinnebusch, and Gérard Philipson. 1993. *Swahili and Sabaki: A linguistic history*, volume 121. Univ of California Press.

Evander Nyoni and Bruce A Bassett. 2021. Low-resource neural machine translation for southern african languages. *arXiv preprint arXiv:2104.00366*.

Kishore Papineni, Salim Roukos, Todd Ward, and Wei-Jing Zhu. 2002. Bleu: a method for automatic evaluation of machine translation. In *Proceedings of the 40th annual meeting of the Association for Computational Linguistics*, pages 311–318.

Chanjun Park, Yeongwook Yang, Kinam Park, and Heuiseok Lim. 2020. Decoding strategies for improving low-resource machine translation. *Electronics*, 9(10):1562.

C Riginos and MW Nachman. 2001. Population subdivision in marine environments: the contributions of biogeography, geographical distance and discontinuous habitat to genetic differentiation in a blennioid fish, axoclinus nigricaudus. *Molecular ecology*, 10(6):1439–1453.

Rico Sennrich, Barry Haddow, and Alexandra Birch. 2015. Improving neural machine translation models with monolingual data. *arXiv preprint arXiv:1511.06709*.

Rico Sennrich and Biao Zhang. 2019. Revisiting low-resource neural machine translation: A case study. *arXiv preprint arXiv:1905.11901*.

Thaddeus Vincenty. 1975. Direct and inverse solutions of geodesics on the ellipsoid with application of nested equations. *Survey review*, 23(176):88–93.

Barret Zoph, Deniz Yuret, Jonathan May, and Kevin Knight. 2016. Transfer learning for low-resource neural machine translation. *arXiv preprint arXiv:1604.02201*.

An Annotated Dataset and Automatic Approaches for Discourse Mode Identification in Low-resource Bengali Language

Salim Sazzed
Old Dominion University
Norfolk, VA, USA
ssazz001@odu.edu

Abstract

The modes of discourse aid in comprehending the convention and purpose of various forms of languages used during communication. In this study, we introduce a discourse mode annotated corpus for the low-resource Bengali (also referred to as Bengali) language. The corpus consists of sentence-level annotation of three discourse modes, *narrative*, *descriptive*, and *informative* of the text excerpted from a number of Bengali novels. We analyze the annotated corpus to expose various linguistic aspects of discourse modes, such as class distributions and average sentence lengths. To automatically determine the mode of discourse, we apply CML (classical machine learning) classifiers with n-gram based statistical features and a fine-tuned BERT (Bidirectional Encoder Representations from Transformers) based language model. We observe that fine-tuned BERT-based model yields better results than CML classifiers. Our created discourse mode annotated dataset, the first of its kind in Bengali, and the evaluation, provide baselines for the automatic discourse mode identification in Bengali and can assist various downstream natural language processing tasks.

1 Introduction

Discourse is the notion of conversation that is expressed through language. Based on Webber et al. (2012), discourse indicates the relationship between states, events, or beliefs manifested within one or multiple sentences in a given mode of communication. Understanding discourse structures and identifying relationships between various modes can help downstream natural language processing tasks including text summarization (Li et al., 2016), question answering (Verberne et al., 2007), anaphora resolution (Hirst, 1981), and machine translation (Li et al., 2014).

The modes of discourse, also referred to as rhetorical modes, represent the variety, conventions, and purposes of the dominant types of language used in communication (both oral and written). The discourse modes have high importance while writing composition because they attribute to several factors that would affect the quality and coherence of a text. The combination and interaction of various discourse modes make a text organized and unified (Smith, 2003). To give an example, the writer may start an expressing an event through narration, then provide details regarding using descriptive modes and establish ideas with argument. Discourse modes have also importance in rhetorical research as they are closely related to rhetoric (Connors, 1981) that provides guidelines for effectively expressing content.

Researchers categorized modes of discourse into various categories (Rozakis, 2003; Song et al., 2017; Dhanwal et al., 2020). Based on Rozakis (2003), discourse modes can be classified into four categories, *narration*, *description*, *exposition*, and *argument*. Narration mode primarily focuses on governing the progression of the story by presenting and connecting events; *exposition* mode instructs or explains; the *argument* aims to provide a convincing or persuasive statement; *description* tries to provide detailed mentions of characters, objects, and scenery, in a figurative language. Song et al. (2017) categorized the mode of discourse into five categories, *narration*, *exposition*, *description*, *argument* and *emotion* expressing sentences in narrative essays, while Dhanwal et al. (2020) annotated discourse mode of short story into *argumentative*, *narrative*, *descriptive*, *dialogic*

Proceedings of the Workshop on Multilingual Information Access (MIA), pages 9 - 15

and *informative* categories. Although a piece of text can be labeled as a specific mode of discourse, it is not uncommon to have text snippets with multiple modes of discourse Song et al. (2017) where one of them possesses the dominant role.

Although discourse structure and mode have a significant role in various downstream natural language processing tasks, research in this area is largely unexplored in Bengla. Although Bengali is the 7th most spoken language in the world [1], NLP resources are scarcely available except few areas such as sentiment analysis (Sazzed and Jayarathna, 2019; Sazzed, 2020) or inappropriate textual content detection (Sazzed, 2021a,b,c). Regarding discourse analysis, only a limited number of works performed research (Chatterjee and Chakraborty, 2019; Banerjee, 2010; Sarkar and Chatterjee, 2013; Das and Stede, 2018; Das et al., 2020). However, to the best of our knowledge, no study related to automatic discourse mode identification has been carried out yet. Thus, in this study, we introduce an annotated dataset and present a set of techniques for the automatic identification of discourse modes.

Following the rough guidelines provided by Smith (2003) and Dhanwal et al. (2020) for discourse mode annotation, we manually categorize a dataset of 3310 sentences from Bengali Novels into various discourse modes. The sentences are annotated in three modes of discourse, *narrative*, *descriptive* and *informative*. For automatic identification of the discourse mode, we extract word n-gram based features from the text and then employ several classical machine learning (CML) classifiers such as logistic regression (LR), support vector machine (SVM), random forest (RF). In addition, the transformer-based multilingual BERT language model is leveraged and fine-tuned for discourse mode determination. We observe that the multilingual BERT model yields better performance than the CML classifiers, although the difference is not substantial compared to LR or SVM.

1.1 Contributions

The main contributions of this study can be summarized as follows-

- We create a Bengali discourse mode corpus by collecting and annotating texts from a number of Bengali novels. Currently, no discourse mode annotated dataset is available in Bengali; therefore, a key contribution of this study is the development of such a resource that is publicly available for researchers [2].
- We analyze the annotated corpus to reveal attributes of text representing various discourse modes.
- We employ CML classifiers with n-gram based statistical features and a fine-tuned pre-trained language model for automatically identifying various modes of discourse.

2 Data Annotation and Collection

The data collection process starts with identifying a set of novels from Bengali literature. We select six 20th-century Bengali novels গোলমেলে লোক, পথের পাঁচালি, আরণ্যক,পটাশগড়ের জঙ্গ,নন্দিত নরকে, হিমু) written by three famous Bengali novelists, *'Shirshendu Mukhopadhyay'*, *'Bibhutibhushan Bandyopadhyay'*, and *'Humayun Ahmed'*. Unlike English, the electronic versions (i.e., eBooks) of Bengali books are hardly available as eBooks are not popular among Bengali readers. Moreover, we notice that most of the eBooks available in PDF format were created by scanning images of the print versions; therefore, they are not suitable for text extraction. We find a website that provides a set of Bengali fiction in EPUB format. From there, we manually download the above-stated six Bengali novels and extract the text for annotation.

Three native Bengali speakers with university-level education perform the annotation. Annotating the mode of discourse in a piece of text (i.e., sentence) is often challenging since a sentence may have multiple modes, or the distinction is often not obvious. Thus annotators are provided a set of online

[1] https://www.babbel.com/en/magazine/the-10-most-spoken-languages-in-the-world

[2] https://github.com/sazzadcsedu/DiscourseBangla.git

resources and guidelines from a number of publications.

The discourse modes are selected based on the existing works of Song et al. (2017) and Dhanwal et al. (2020). Song et al. (2017) categorized modes of discourse into five categories, *narration*, *exposition*, *description*, *argument* and *emotion* in narrative essays, while Dhanwal et al. (2020) annotated discourse modes into *argumentative*, *narrative*, *descriptive*, *dialogic* and *informative* categories. As our annotated content (i.e., excerpted sentences of Bengali novels) are more similar to the content (i.e., short stories) of Dhanwal et al. (2020), our annotated discourse modes are more similar to their annotation. However, we notice that the presence of the argumentative mode in a fictional novel is rare as instead of establishing any opinion, a novel tells a story in chronological order. Besides, it is observed that the dialogic category itself does not comprise any new mode. Instead, it echoes the narrative or descriptive or other modes from a third-person point of view; thus, we do not include it as a separate mode.

2.1 Discourse Modes

In this study, the following three discourse modes are considered for annotation.

Narrative: Narrative sentences relate to entities performing particular actions, often in chronological order as a part of storytelling.

Bengali: সর্বজয়া ছেলের কাণ্ড দেখিয়া অবাক হইয়া রহিল

English Translation: "Sarvajaya was surprised to see the boy's actions"

Descriptive: Descriptive statements illustrate specific entities with some kind of description so that reader can imagine this in his mind. It enables readers to visualize characters, settings, and actions. For example, it tells how entities look, sound, feel, taste, and smell.

Bengali: একমাথা ঝাঁকড়া ঝাঁকড়া চুল, ভারি শান্ত, সুন্দর চোখমুখ, কুচকুচে কালো গায়ের রং ।

English Translation: "She has curly hair, heavy, calm, beautiful eyes, and a sleek black complexion"

Informative: Informative sentences provide information regarding entities or circumstances.

Bengali: এটা পটাশগড়ের এক রাজা বানিয়েছিল ।

English Translation: It was made by a king of Potashgarh.

2.2 Annotation Task

The annotation guidelines consist of the formal and informal descriptions of three different types of discourse modes, examples of various modes with the explanation, and examples of co-occurrence of various modes with mode dominance. Although the annotation is performed at the sentence level, the annotators are instructed to consider the surrounding sentences to get a better idea about the context of the sentence for better annotation. In case of the presence of multiple modes in a sentence, the annotators are asked to determine the most dominant discourse mode based on the provided guidelines and their own judgment and label accordingly.

2.3 Annotation and Dataset Statistics

The final dataset consists of 3310 sentences annotated by the three annotators, where two annotators label all the sentences and the third annotator acts only if there is any disagreement between the first two annotators for any case. Note that to include varied types of events and description sentences are randomly selected from the various sections of the novels by annotators (around 50% by each of the annotators). We observe an annotator agreement of 0.78 based on a Cohen's kappa (Cohen, 1960) for the label assignment between the first two annotators.

Table 1: Statistics of various discourse modes in the annotated corpus

Classifier	#Sentence	#Words/ Sentence
Narrative	2282	14.62
Descriptive	782	23.43
Informative	246	11.73

Table 1 depicts the distributions of various modes of discourse in the annotated dataset. As shown in Table 1, the annotated dataset is class imbalanced. We notice that the most dominant mode in the novels is *narrative* since the progression of a novel involves a lot of narrative events. Overall, almost 70% of the sentences in the annotated corpus represent narrative mode. The descriptive mode has 782 instances, while the informative mode is less prevalent and has only 246 samples.

We observe that the most frequently co-occurring modes are *narrative* and *descriptive*, as often chronological events are described with some details. We find that over 20% of narrative sentences convey description to some extent. This observation is consistent with the findings of Song et al. (2017). In the presence of multiple discourse modes within the same sentence, it is often challenging to identify the dominant one.

As seen by Table 1, the average sentence lengths of different discourse modes vary to some extent. For example, the lengths of the sentences representing the descriptive mode are much higher than the other two modes. A higher length of descriptive sentences is expected since they elucidate particular entities or events with some details.

3 Machine Learning Based Approaches

3.1 Classical ML Classifier

We employ four classical supervised ML classifiers: logistic regression (LR), support vector machine (SVM), random forest (RF), and extra trees (ET) for determining the modes of the discourse of sentences. For SVM, we apply all three types of kernels, linear, polynomial, and Gaussian radial basis function (RBF). We find the linear kernel performs best for our classification problem (reported results).

The word n-gram features are utilized as input for the CML classifiers. An n-gram is a contiguous sequence of n items from a piece of text. We extract the word-level unigrams and bigrams from the text, compute corresponding tf-idf scores, and then feed those values to the CML classifiers.

For the CML classifiers, the default parameter settings of the scikit-learn (Pedregosa et al., 2011) library are used. A class-balanced weight is set for all CML classifiers.

3.2 Deep Learning Based Classifier

The transformer-based pre-trained contextual embedding such as BERT (Devlin et al., 2019) and RoBERTa (Liu et al., 2019) have achieved state-of-the-art results in various text classification tasks with limited labeled data. As these language models have been trained with a large amount of unlabelled data, they possess contextual knowledge; thus, fine-tuning them utilizing a small amount of problem-specific labeled data can attain satisfactory results.

BERT utilizes the transformer architecture to learn contextual relationships between words (or sub-words) in a piece of text. Before feeding text sequences into BERT, 15% of the words in each sequence are replaced with a [MASK] token. The BERT model then tries to infer the original value of the masked words utilizing the contextual meaning provided by the surrounding non-masked words present in the sequence.

The multilingual BERT (M-BERT) (Devlin et al., 2019) is the multilingual version of BERT, which was pre-trained with the Wikipedia content of 104 languages (Bengali is one of them). It consists of twelve-layer transformer blocks where each block contains twelve head self-attention layers and 768 hidden layers that result in approximately 110 million parameters.

3.2.1 Fine Tuning

We fine-tune M-BERT for categorizing sentences into the three classes, *narrative, descriptive, informative*. Since this is a classification task, we utilize the classification module of the M-BERT. The hugging face library (Wolf et al., 2019) is used to fine-tune M-BERT.

Since the initial layers of M-BERT only learn very general features, we keep them untouched. Only the last layer of the M-BERT is fine-tuned for our binary-level classification task. We only add one layer on top of the M-BERT for classification that acts as a classifier. We tokenize and feed our input training data to fine-tune M-BERT model; Afterward, the fine-tuned model is used for classifying the testing data.

A mini-batch size of 8 and a learning rate of $4*10^{-5}$ are used. The validation and training split ratio is set to 80% and 20%. The model is optimized using the Adam optimizer (Kingma and Ba, 2014), and the loss parameter is set to sparse-categorical-cross-entropy. The model is trained for 3 epochs with early

Table 2: Performance of various approaches for discourse mode prediction

Type	Classifier	Narrative	Descriptive	Informative
		F1/Acc.	**F1/Acc.**	**F1/Acc.**
CML	LR	0.8857/0.9708	0.6796 /0.5896	0.064/0.0333
	SVM	0.8739/0.9787	0.6126/0.4909	0.0328/0.0167
	RF	0.8433/0.9911	0.3773/0.2416	0.0165/0.0083
	ET	0.8458/0.9938	0.4/0.2571	0.0328/0.0167
DL	Multilingual BERT	0.912/0.957	0.66/0.6875	0.0468/0.024

Table 3: An example of the confusion matrix yielded by the LR classifier

Class	Narrative	Descriptive	Informative
Narrative	2213	69	0
Descriptive	337	438	7
Informative	184	50	12

stopping enabled.

3.3 Evaluation Settings

To evaluate the performances of various approaches, 5-fold cross-validation is applied. The 5-fold cross-validation split the dataset into 5-mutually independent subsets. It consists of 5 iterations; in each iteration, one of the new subsets is used as a testing set, and the other two subsets are used as a training set.

The F1 score and accuracy of all three classes are reported separately. The F1 score of each class is computed based on its precision and recall scores. Let c represents a particular class and c' refer to all other classes. The TP, FP, and FN for the class c are defined as follows-
TP = both true label and prediction refer a sentence to class c
FP = true label of a sentence is class c', while prediction says it is class c
FN = true label marks a sentence as class c, while prediction refers to it class c'

4 Results and Discussion

Table 2 provides the F1 scores and accuracy of various CML-based classifiers and transformers-based M-BERT model for discourse mode identification.

The results reveal that all the four CML classifiers, LR, SVM, RF, and ET, yield high performance for the narrative class prediction; they achieve F1 scores between 0.84-0.89 and an accuracy of around 97%. For the descriptive class prediction, LR and SVM perform better than the RF and ET; they obtain f1 scores over 0.60 compared to 0.4 scores of decision tree-based classifiers. However, we observe that for informative class prediction all the classifiers perform poorly.

We observe that the performances of CML classifiers are affected by the class distribution of the dataset. Since the narrative class contains close to 70% of the instances in the dataset, the classifiers are biased towards it (Table 3). All the CML classifiers fail to provide an acceptable level of performance for the minor *informative* class even after using class-balanced weights. We also employ SMOTE (Chawla et al., 2002) oversampling techniques for class balancing; however, we do not notice any noticeable performance improvement using SMOTE.

The transformer-based multilingual language model yield slightly better performance than the CML classifiers. For the dominant *narrative* class, it attains an f1 score of 0.912. For other classes, it obtains similar f1 scores of the LR and SVM, around 0.67 and 0.05, respectively. It is noticed that all the classifiers perform poorly for the minor *informative* class prediction.

The results suggest that the transformer-based multilingual BERT model can be effective for discourse mode classification in Bengali text. Although we do not notice significant improvement compared to CML classifiers in this study, it could be attributed to limited labeled data. With more labeled data incorporated, the improvement could be higher (transformer-based models have shown state-of-the-art performances for various NLP tasks across languages). Low resource language such as Bengali suffers from data annotation issues, as there are not enough resources to create a large labeled dataset. Thus, incorporating a pre-trained model can help address the scarcity of annotated data in the Bengali language to some extent.

5 Summary and Future Work

In this study, we introduce a corpus consisting of sentences level annotation of various modes of discourse. The corpus consists of excerpted text from Bengali novels annotated with three different discourse modes: *narrative*, *descriptive* and *informative*. We provide details of the annotation procedure, such as annotation guidelines and annotator agreements, and investigate the characteristics of various discourse modes. Finally, we employ CML and deep learning-based classification approaches for automatic discourse mode identification. We observe that transformer-based fine-tuned language models yield the best performance. Our future work will expand the size of the corpus and demonstrate the usefulness of discourse mode annotated data for downstream tasks such as automated essay scoring and sentiment analysis in the low-resource Bengali language.

References

Sanjoy Banerjee. 2010. Context in communication: analysis of bengali spoken discourse.

Rajoshree Chatterjee and Jayshree Chakraborty. 2019. Analyzing discourse coherence in bengali elementary choras (children's nursery rhymes). *Rupkatha Journal on Interdisciplinary Studies in Humanities*, 11(3).

Nitesh V Chawla, Kevin W Bowyer, Lawrence O Hall, and W Philip Kegelmeyer. 2002. Smote: synthetic minority oversampling technique. *Journal of artificial intelligence research*, 16:321–357.

Jacob Cohen. 1960. A coefficient of agreement for nominal scales. *Educational and psychological measurement*, 20(1):37–46.

Robert J Connors. 1981. The rise and fall of the modes of discourse. *College Composition and Communication*, 32(4):444–455.

Debopam Das and Manfred Stede. 2018. Developing the bangla rst discourse treebank. In *Proceedings of the Eleventh International Conference on Language Resources and Evaluation (LREC 2018)*.

Debopam Das, Manfred Stede, Soumya Sankar Ghosh, and Lahari Chatterjee. 2020. Dimlex-bangla: A lexicon of bangla discourse connectives. In *Proceedings of the 12th Language Resources and Evaluation Conference*, pages 1097–1102.

Jacob Devlin, Ming-Wei Chang, Kenton Lee, and Kristina Toutanova. 2019. Bert: Pre-training of deep bidirectional transformers for language understanding.

Swapnil Dhanwal, Hritwik Dutta, Hitesh Nankani, Nilay Shrivastava, Yaman Kumar, Junyi Jessy Li, Debanjan Mahata, Rakesh Gosangi, Haimin Zhang, Rajiv Shah, et al. 2020. An annotated dataset of discourse modes in hindi stories. In *Proceedings of the 12th Language Resources and Evaluation Conference*, pages 1191–1196.

Graeme Hirst. 1981. Discourse-oriented anaphora resolution in natural language understanding: A review. *American journal of computational linguistics*, 7(2):85–98.

Diederik P Kingma and Jimmy Ba. 2014. Adam: A method for stochastic optimization. *arXiv preprint arXiv:1412.6980*.

Junyi Jessy Li, Marine Carpuat, and Ani Nenkova. 2014. Assessing the discourse factors that influence the quality of machine translation. In *Proceedings of the 52nd Annual Meeting of the Association for Computational Linguistics (Volume 2: Short Papers)*, pages 283–288.

Junyi Jessy Li, Kapil Thadani, and Amanda Stent. 2016. The role of discourse units in near-extractive summarization. In *Proceedings of the 17th Annual Meeting of the Special Interest Group on Discourse and Dialogue*, pages 137–147.

Yinhan Liu, Myle Ott, Naman Goyal, Jingfei Du, Mandar Joshi, Danqi Chen, Omer Levy, Mike Lewis, Luke Zettlemoyer, and Veselin Stoyanov. 2019. Roberta: A robustly optimized bert pretraining approach. *arXiv preprint arXiv:1907.11692*.

F. Pedregosa, G. Varoquaux, A. Gramfort, V. Michel, B. Thirion, O. Grisel, M. Blondel, P. Prettenhofer, R. Weiss, V. Dubourg, J. Vanderplas, A. Passos, D. Cournapeau, M. Brucher, M. Perrot, and E. Duchesnay. 2011. Scikit-learn: Machine learning in Python. *Journal of Machine Learning Research*, 12:2825–2830.

Laurie Rozakis. 2003. *The complete idiot's guide to grammar and style*. Penguin.

Abhishek Sarkar and Pinaki Sankar Chatterjee. 2013. Identification of rhetorical structure relation from discourse marker in bengali language understanding.

Salim Sazzed. 2020. Cross-lingual sentiment classification in low-resource bengali language. In *Proceedings of the sixth workshop on noisy user-generated text (W-NUT 2020)*, pages 50–60.

Salim Sazzed. 2021a. Abusive content detection in transliterated bengali-english social media corpus. In *Proceedings of the Fifth Workshop on Computational Approaches to Linguistic Code-Switching*, pages 125–130.

Salim Sazzed. 2021b. Identifying vulgarity in bengali social media textual content. *PeerJ Computer Science*, 7:e665.

Salim Sazzed. 2021c. A lexicon for profane and obscene text identification in bengali. In *Proceedings of the International Conference on Recent Advances in Natural Language Processing (RANLP 2021)*, pages 1289–1296.

Salim Sazzed and Sampath Jayarathna. 2019. A sentiment classification in bengali and machine translated english corpus. In *2019 IEEE 20th international conference on information reuse and integration for data science (IRI)*, pages 107–114. IEEE.

Carlota S Smith. 2003. *Modes of discourse: The local structure of texts*, volume 103. Cambridge University Press.

Wei Song, Dong Wang, Ruiji Fu, Lizhen Liu, Ting Liu, and Guoping Hu. 2017. Discourse mode identification in essays. In *Proceedings of the 55th Annual Meeting of the Association for Computational Linguistics (Volume 1: Long Papers)*, pages 112–122.

Suzan Verberne, Lou Boves, Nelleke Oostdijk, and Peter-Arno Coppen. 2007. Evaluating discourse-based answer extraction for why-question answering. In *Proceedings of the 30th annual international ACM SIGIR conference on Research and development in information retrieval*, pages 735–736.

Bonnie Webber, Markus Egg, and Valia Kordoni. 2012. Discourse structure and language technology. *Natural Language Engineering*, 18(4):437–490.

Thomas Wolf, Lysandre Debut, Victor Sanh, Julien Chaumond, Clement Delangue, Anthony Moi, Pierric Cistac, Tim Rault, Rémi Louf, Morgan Funtowicz, et al. 2019. Huggingface's transformers: State-of-the-art natural language processing. *arXiv preprint arXiv:1910.03771*.

Pivot Through English: Reliably Answering Multilingual Questions without Document Retrieval

Ivan Montero[♠] **Shayne Longpre**[♣]
Ni Lao[♣] **Andrew J. Frank**[♣] **Christopher DuBois**[♣]

[♠]Paul G. Allen School of Computer Science & Engineering, University of Washington
[♣]Apple Inc.
ivamon@cs.washington.edu
{slongpre, ni_lao, a_frank, cdubois}@apple.com

Abstract

Existing methods for open-retrieval question answering in lower resource languages (LRLs) lag significantly behind English. They not only suffer from the shortcomings of non-English document retrieval, but are reliant on language-specific supervision for either the task or translation. We formulate a task setup more realistic to available resources, that circumvents document retrieval to reliably transfer knowledge from English to lower resource languages. Assuming a strong English question answering model or database, we compare and analyze methods that pivot through English: to map foreign queries to English and then English answers back to target language answers. Within this task setup we propose Reranked Multilingual Maximal Inner Product Search (RM-MIPS), akin to semantic similarity retrieval over the English training set with reranking, which outperforms the strongest baselines by 2.7% on XQuAD and 6.2% on MKQA. Analysis demonstrates the particular efficacy of this strategy over state-of-the-art alternatives in challenging settings: low-resource languages, with extensive distractor data and query distribution misalignment. Circumventing retrieval, our analysis shows this approach offers rapid answer generation to many other languages off-the-shelf, without necessitating additional training data in the target language.

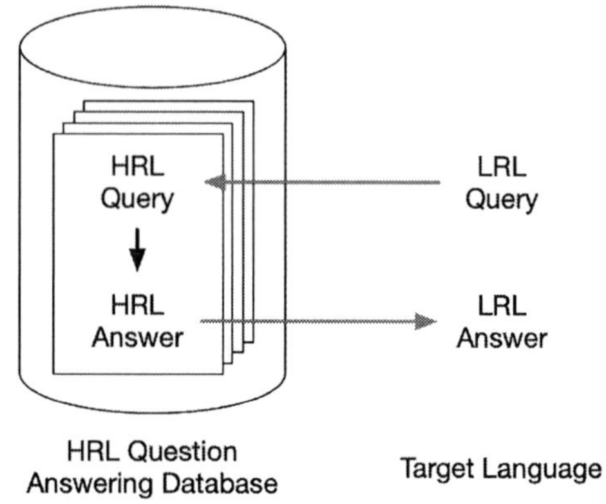

Figure 1: **Cross-Lingual Pivots (XLP):** We introduce the "Cross Lingual Pivots" task, formulated as a solution to multilingual question answering that circumvents document retrieval in low resource languages (LRL). To answer LRL queries, approaches may leverage a question-answer system or database in a high resource language (HRL), such as English.

1 Introduction

Open-Retrieval question answering (ORQA) has seen extensive progress in English, significantly outperforming systems in lower resource languages (LRLs). This advantage is largely driven by the scale of labelled data and open source retrieval tools that exist predominantly for higher resource languages (HRLs) — usually English.

To remedy this discrepancy, recent work leverages English supervision to improve multilingual systems, either by simple translation or zero shot transfer (Asai et al., 2018; Cui et al., 2019; Charlet et al., 2020). While these approaches have helped generalize reading comprehension models to new languages, they are of limited practical use without reliable information retrieval in the target language, which they often implicitly assume.

In practice, we believe this assumption can be challenging to meet. A new document index can be expensive to collect and maintain, and an effective retrieval stack typically requires language-specific labelled data, tokenization tools, manual heuristics, and curated domain blocklists (Fluhr et al., 1999; Chaudhari, 2014; Lehal, 2018). Consequently, we discard the common assumption of robust non-English document retrieval, for a more realistic one: that there exists a high-quality English database of query-answer string pairs. We motivate and explore the Cross-Lingual Pivots (**XLP**) task (Section 2), which we contend will accelerate progress in LRL question answering by reflecting these practical considerations. This pivot task is

Proceedings of the Workshop on Multilingual Information Access (MIA), pages 16 - 28
July 15, 2022 ©2022 Association for Computational Linguistics

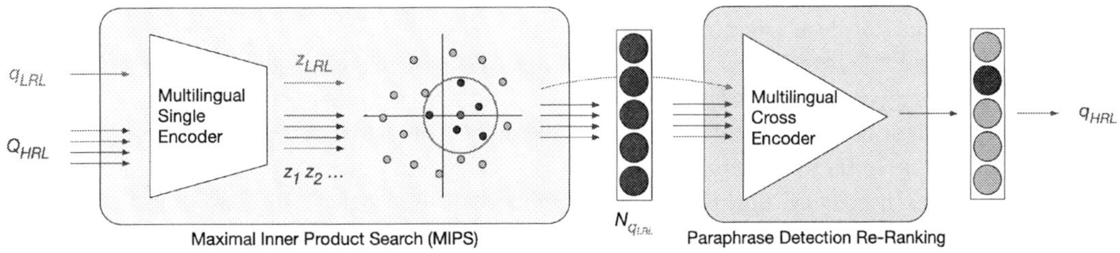

Figure 2: **Reranked Multilingual Maximal Inner Product Search (RM-MIPS):** For the Cross-Lingual Pivots task, we propose an approach that maps the LRL query to a semantically equivalent HRL query, finds the appropriate HRL answer, then uses knowledge graph or machine translation to map the answer back to the target LRL. Specifically, the first stage (in blue) uses multilingual single encoders for fast maximal inner product search (MIPS), and the second stage (in red) reranks the top k candidates using a more expressive multilingual cross-encoder that takes in the concatenation of the LRL query and candidate HRL query.

similar to "translate test" and "MT-in-the-middle" paradigms (Hajič et al., 2000; Zitouni and Florian, 2008; Schneider et al., 2013; Mallinson et al., 2017) except for the availability of the high-resource language database, which allows for more sophisticated pivot approaches. Figure 1 illustrates a generalized version of an XLP, where LRL queries may seek knowledge from any HRL with its own database.

For this task we combine and compare state-of-the-art methods in machine translation ("translate test") and cross-lingual semantic similarity, in order to map LRL queries to English, and then English answers back to the LRL target language. In particular we examine how these methods are affected by certain factors: (a) whether the language is high, medium or low resource, (b) the magnitude of data in the HRL database, and (c) the degree of query distribution alignment between languages (i.e., the number of LRL queries that have matches in the HRL database).

Lastly we propose an approach to this task, motivated by recent dense nearest neighbour (kNN) models in English which achieve strong results in QA by simply searching for similar questions in the training set (or database in our case) (Lewis et al., 2020). We leverage nearest neighbor semantic similarity search followed by cross-encoder reranking (see Figure 2), and refer to the technique as Reranked Multilingual Maximal Inner Product Search (**RM-MIPS**). Not only does this approach significantly improve upon "Translate Test" (the most common pivot technique) and state-of-the-art paraphrase detection baselines, our analysis demonstrates it is more robust to lower resource languages, query distribution misalignment, and the size of the English database.

By circumventing document retrieval and task-specific supervision signals, this straightforward approach offers reliable answer generation to many of the languages present in pretraining, off-the-shelf. Furthermore, it can be re-purposed to obtain reliable training data in the target language, with fewer annotation artifacts, and is complementary to a standard end-to-end question answering system. We hope this analysis complements existing multilingual approaches, and facilitates adoption of more practical (but effective) methods to improve knowledge transfer from English into other languages.

We summarize our contributions as:

- XLP: We explore a more realistic task setup for practically expanding Multilingual OR-QA to lower resource languages.
- Comprehensive analysis of factors affecting XLP: (I) types of approaches (translation, paraphrasing) (II) language types, (III) database characteristics, and (IV) query distribution alignment.
- RM-MIPS: A flexible approach to XLP that beats strong (or state-of-the-art) baselines.

2 Task: Cross-Lingual Pivots

The Open-Retrieval Question Answering (ORQA) task evaluates models' ability to answer information-seeking questions. In a multilingual setting, the task is to produce answers in the same language as the query. In some cases, queries may only find answers, or sufficient evidence, in a different language, due to *informational asymmetries* (Group, 2011; Callahan and Herring, 2011). To address this, Asai et al. (2020) propose

Cross-Lingual Open-Retrieval Question Answering (XORQA), similar to the Cross-Lingual Information Retrieval (CLIR) task, where a model needs to leverage intermediary information found in other languages, in order to serve an answer in the target language. In practice, this intermediary language tends to be English, with the most ample resources and training data.

Building on these tasks, we believe there are other benefits to pivoting through high resource languages that have so far been overlooked, and consequently limited research that could more rapidly improve non-English QA. These two benefits are (I) large query-answer databases have already been collected in English, both in academia (Joshi et al., 2017) and in industry (Kwiatkowski et al., 2019), and (II) it is often very expensive and challenging to replicate robust retrieval and passage reranking stacks in new languages (Fluhr et al., 1999; Chaudhari, 2014; Lehal, 2018). [1] As a result, the English capabilities of question answering systems typically exceed those for non-English languages by large margins (Lewis et al., 2019; Longpre et al., 2020; Clark et al., 2020).

We would note that prior work suggests even without access to an English query-answer database, translation methods with an English document index and retrieval outperforms LRL retrieval for open-retrieval QA (see the end-to-end XOR-FULL results in Asai et al. (2020)). This demonstrates the persistent weakness of non-English retrieval, and motivates alternatives approaches such as cross-lingual pivots.

To remedy this disparity, we believe attending to these two considerations would yield a more realistic task setup. Like multilingual ORQA, or XORQA, the task of XLPs is to produce an answer $\hat{a}_{LRL}$ in the same "Target" language as question q_{LRL}, evaluated by Exact Match of F1 token-overlap with the real answer a_{LRL}. Instead of assuming access to a LRL document index or retrieval system (usually provided by the datasets), we assume access to an English database D_{HRL} which simply maps English queries to their English answer text. Leveraging this database, and circumventing LRL retrieval, we believe progress in this task will greatly accelerate multilingual capabilities of real question answering assistants.

3 Re-Ranked Multilingual Maximal Inner Product Search

For the first stage of the XLP task, our goal is to find an equivalent English query for a LRL query: "Query Matching". Competing approaches include Single Encoders and Cross Encoders, described further in section 4.2. Single Encoders embed queries independently into a latent vector space, meaning each query q_{EN} from the English database Q_{EN} can be pre-embedded offline. At inference time, the low resource query q_{LRL} is embedded, then maximal inner product search (MIPS) finds the approximate closest query q_{EN} among all Q_{EN} by cosine similarity. By comparison, Cross Encoders leverage cross-attention between q_{LRL} and candidate match q_{EN} at inference time, thus requiring $O(|Q_{EN}|)$ forward passes at inference time to find the best paraphrase. While usually more accurate this is computationally infeasible for a large set of candidates.

We propose a method that combines both Single Encoders and Cross Encoders, which we refer to as Reranked Mulilingual Maximal Inner Product Search (RM-MIPS). The process, shown in Figure 2, first uses a multilingual sentence embedder with MIPS to isolate the top-k candidate similar queries, then uses the cross encoder to rerank the candidate paraphrases. This approach reflects the Retrieve and Read paradigm common in OR-QA, but applies it to a multilingual setting for semantic similarity search.

The model first queries the English database using the Multilingual Single Encoder $\mathrm{SE}(q_i) = z_i$ to obtain the k-nearest English query neighbors $\mathcal{N}_{q_{LRL}} \subseteq Q_{EN}$ to the given query q_{LRL} by cosine similarity.

$$\mathcal{N}_{q_{LRL}} = \underset{\{q_1,\ldots,q_k\}\subseteq Q_{EN}}{\arg\max} \sum_{i=1}^{k} \mathrm{sim}(z_{LRL}, z_i)$$

Then, it uses the Multilingual Cross Encoder $\mathrm{CE}(q_1, q_2)$ to score the remaining set of queries $\mathcal{N}_{q_{LRL}}$ to obtain the final prediction.

$$\textbf{RM-MIPS}(q_{LRL}) = \underset{q_{EN}\in\mathcal{N}_{q_{LRL}}}{\arg\max}\ \mathrm{CE}(q_{EN}, q_{LRL})$$

[1] While it is straightforward to adapt question answering "reader" modules with zero-shot learning (Charlet et al., 2020), retrieval can be quite challenging. Not only is the underlying document index costly to expand and maintain for a new language (Chaudhari, 2014), but supervision signals collected in the target language are particularly important for dense retrieval and reranking systems which both serve as bottlenecks to downstream multilingual QA (Karpukhin et al., 2020). Additionally, real-world QA agents typically require human curated, language-specific infrastructure for retrieval, such as regular expressions, custom tokenization rules, and curated website blocklists.

RM-MIPS(q_{LRL}) proposes an equivalent English query q_{EN}, whose English answer can be pulled directly from the database.

	XQuAD	MKQA
High	es, de, ru, zh	de, es, fr, it, ja, pl, pt, ru, zh_cn
Medium	ar, tr, vi	ar, da, fi, he, hu, ko, nl, no, sv, tr, vi
Low	el, hi, th	km, ms, th, zh_hk, zh_tw

Table 1: We evaluate cross-lingual pivot methods by language groups, divided into high, medium, and low resource according to Wikipedia coverage Wu and Dredze (2020). Note that due to greater language diversity, MKQA contains lower resource languages than XQuAD.

4 Experiments

We compare systems that leverage an English QA database to answer questions in lower resource languages. Figure 1 illustrates a cross-lingual pivot (XLP), where the task is to map an incoming query from a low resource language to a query in the high resource language database (LRL → HRL, discussed in 4.2), and then a high resource language answer to a low resource language answer (HRL → LRL, discussed in 4.3).

4.1 Datasets

We provide an overview of the question answering and paraphrase datasets relevant to our study.

4.1.1 Question Answering

To assess cross-lingual pivots, we consider multilingual OR-QA evaluation sets that (a) contain a diverse set of language families, and (b) have "parallel" questions across all of these languages. The latter property affords us the opportunity to change the distributional overlap and analyze its effect (5.3).

XQuAD Artetxe et al. (2019) human translate 1.2k SQuAD examples (Rajpurkar et al., 2016) into 10 other languages. We use all of SQuAD 1.1 (100k+) as the associated English database, such that only 1% of database queries are represented in the LRL evaluation set.

MKQA Longpre et al. (2020) human translate 10k examples from the Natural Questions (Kwiatkowski et al., 2019) dataset to 25 other languages. We use the rest of the Open Natural Questions training set (84k) as the associated English database, such that only 10.6% of the database queries are represented in the LRL evaluation set[2].

4.1.2 Paraphrase Detection

To detect paraphrases between LRL queries and HRL queries we train multilingual sentence embedding models with a mix of the following paraphrase datasets.

PAWS-X Yang et al. (2019b) machine translate 49k examples from the PAWS (Zhang et al., 2019) dataset to six other languages. This dataset provides both positive and negative paraphrase examples.

Quora Question Pairs (QQP) Sharma et al. (2019) provide English question pair examples from Quora; we use the 384k examples from the training split of Wang et al. (2017). This dataset provides both positive and negative examples of English paraphrases.

4.2 Query Matching Baselines: LRL Query → HRL Query

We consider a combination of translation techniques and cross-lingual sentence encoders to find semantically equivalent queries across languages. We select from pretrained models which report strong results on similar multilingual tasks, or fine-tune representations for our task using publicly available paraphrase datasets (4.1.2).[3]. Each fine-tuned model receives basic hyperparameter tuning over the learning rate and the ratio of training data from PAWS-X and QQP.[4]

NMT + MIPS We use a many-to-many, Transformer-based (Vaswani et al., 2017), encoder-decoder neural machine translation system, trained on the OPUS multilingual corpus covering 100 languages (Zhang et al., 2020). To match the translation to an English query, we use the Universal Sentence Encoder (USE) (Cer et al., 2018) to perform maximal inner product search (MIPS).

Pretrained Single Encoders We consider pretrained multilingual sentence encoders for sentence retrieval. We explore mUSE[5] (Yang et al., 2019a), LASER (Artetxe and Schwenk, 2019), and m-SentenceBERT as the Single Encoder (Reimers and Gurevych, 2019).

[2]Open Natural Questions train set found here: `https://github.com/google-research-datasets/natural-questions/tree/master/nq_open`

[3]Retriever-Reader models do not fit in the Cross-Lingual Pivots task due to requiring document retrieval, but assuming perfect cross-lingual retrieval/reading, these systems would perform as well as *Perfect LRL → HRL* in Tables 2 and 3

[4]We used an optimal learning rate of 1e-5, and training data ratio of 75% PAWS-X and 25% QQP.

[5]mUSE was only trained on the following 16 languages: ar, ch_cn, ch_tw, en, fr, de, it, ja, ko da, pl, pt, es, th, tr ru

MKQA + Natural Questions	LRL → HRL (Acc.)				LRL → HRL → LRL (F1)			
Language Groups	All	High	Medium	Low	All	High	Medium	Low
NMT + MIPS	74.4 ± 15.8	78.8 ± 13.3	78.3 ± 10.0	57.7 ± 19.0	65.8 ± 16.3	70.7 ± 14.5	69.9 ± 11.0	47.8 ± 17.0
mUSE	71.8 ± 21.2	**88.2** ± 4.4	57.8 ± 20.4	73.2 ± 19.6	62.8 ± 18.3	**77.8** ± 8.9	52.6 ± 16.9	58.2 ± 15.8
LASER	74.2 ± 15.0	70.0 ± 14.6	82.6 ± 8.5	63.3 ± 16.8	65.4 ± 15.4	62.8 ± 14.3	73.6 ± 9.4	52.0 ± 16.6
Single Encoder (XLM-R)	73.0 ± 6.8	72.6 ± 3.7	73.4 ± 8.3	72.6 ± 7.3	63.2 ± 8.1	63.9 ± 4.9	65.4 ± 8.9	57.1 ± 8.0
RM-MIPS (mUSE)	78.2 ± 12.5	86.9 ± 3.1	71.9 ± 12.5	76.7 ± 14.0	68.1 ± 12.4	76.3 ± 8.0	64.9 ± 11.3	60.4 ± 12.7
RM-MIPS (LASER)	80.1 ± 9.4	79.5 ± 7.8	**83.7** ± 5.6	73.1 ± 13.6	69.4 ± 11.2	70.0 ± 9.3	74.1 ± 7.3	57.8 ± 13.2
RM-MIPS (XLM-R)	**83.5** ± 5.2	84.9 ± 2.7	**83.7** ± 5.7	**80.7** ± 6.1	**72.0** ± 9.3	74.7 ± 7.6	**74.2** ± 7.7	**62.7** ± 9.5
Perfect LRL → HRL	-	-	-	-	90.1 ± 7.3	91.8 ± 7.1	92.4 ± 4.2	81.9 ± 7.5

Table 2: **MKQA results by language group with MKQA + Natural Questions as the HRL Database**: (left) the accuracy for the LRL → HRL Query Matching stage; (right) the F1 scores for the End-to-End XLP task, using WikiData translation for Answer Translation; and (bottom) the F1 score only for Wikidata translation, assuming Query Matching (LRL → HRL) was perfect. Macro standard deviation are computed for language groups (±). The difference between all method pairs are significant.

XQuAD + SQuAD	LRL → HRL (Acc.)				LRL → HRL → LRL (F1)			
Language Group	All	High	Medium	Low	All	High	Medium	Low
NMT + MIPS	77.7 ± 14.4	78.4 ± 21.4	76.5 ± 4.7	78.0 ± 8.0	24.5 ± 12.0	28.8 ± 17.3	24.5 ± 3.3	18.7 ± 3.8
mUSE	68.0 ± 38.5	**94.5** ± 3.0	66.4 ± 34.5	34.2 ± 40.7	21.1 ± 15.8	**31.9** ± 15.6	20.3 ± 9.8	7.3 ± 7.8
LASER	46.7 ± 24.9	54.7 ± 24.3	63.9 ± 1.6	18.8 ± 10.9	15.2 ± 11.6	20.1 ± 14.1	19.9 ± 2.3	4.1 ± 2.3
Single Encoder (XLM-R)	81.4 ± 6.2	85.1 ± 1.9	79.4 ± 9.4	78.6 ± 2.2	24.3 ± 10.8	29.1 ± 14.4	24.5 ± 5.3	17.7 ± 3.0
RM-MIPS (mUSE)	72.0 ± 34.0	**94.4** ± 2.5	75.1 ± 25.4	39.1 ± 37.8	22.4 ± 14.7	**31.8** ± 15.4	23.7 ± 6.0	8.5 ± 6.9
RM-MIPS (LASER)	69.2 ± 23.7	77.5 ± 14.8	85.4 ± 3.0	41.9 ± 21.8	21.2 ± 12.3	26.7 ± 14.3	26.0 ± 3.1	9.2 ± 4.0
RM-MIPS (XLM-R)	**92.2** ± 2.4	93.4 ± 1.7	**90.4** ± 2.7	**92.3** ± 1.4	**27.2** ± 10.8	31.5 ± 15.2	**27.4** ± 3.1	**21.2** ± 2.8
Perfect LRL → HRL	-	-	-	-	46.6 ± 13.1	51.0 ± 15.5	51.2 ± 5.0	36.3 ± 8.4

Table 3: **XQuAD results by language group with XQuAD + SQuAD as the HRL Database**: (left) the accuracy for the LRL → HRL Query Matching stage; (right) the F1 scores for the End-to-End XLP task, using machine translation to translate answers from HRL → LRL; and (bottom) the F1 score only for Wikidata translation, assuming Query Matching (LRL → HRL) was perfect. Macro standard deviations are computed for language groups (±). The difference between all method pairs are significant.

Finetuned Single Encoders We finetune transformer encoders to embed sentences, per Reimers and Gurevych (2019). We use the softmax loss over the combination of $[x; y; |x - y|]$ from Conneau et al. (2017a) and mean pool over the final encoder representations to obtain the final sentence representation. We use XLM-R Large as the base encoder (Conneau et al., 2019).

Cross Encoders We finetune XLM-R Large (Conneau et al., 2019) which is pretrained using the multilingual masked language modelling (MLM) objective.[6] For classification, a pair of sentences are given as input for classification, taking advantage of cross-attention between sentences.

4.3 Answer Translation: HRL Answer → LRL Answer

Once we've found an English (HRL) query using RM-MIPS, or one of our "Query Matching" baselines, we can use the English database to lookup the English answer. Our final step is to generate an equivalent answer in the target (LRL) language.

We explore straightforward methods of answer generation, including basic neural machine translation (NMT), and WikiData entity translation.

Machine Translation For NMT we use our many-to-many neural machine translation as described in Section 4.2.

WikiData Entity Translation We propose our WikiData entity translation method for QA datasets with primarily entity type answers that would likely appear in the WikiData knowledge graph (Vrandečić and Krötzsch, 2014).[7] This method uses a named entity recognizer (NER) with a WikiData entity linker to find an entity (Honnibal and Montani, 2017). [8] We train our own entity linker on the public WikiData entity dump according to spaCy's instructions. If a WikiData entity is found, its structured metadata often contains the equivalent term in the target language, localized to the relevant script/alphabet. For our implementation, when a WikiData entity is not found, or its translation is not available in the target language, we simply return

[6] We use the pretrained Transformer encoder implementations in the Huggingface library (Wolf et al., 2019).

[7] `https://www.wikidata.org`

[8] `https://github.com/explosion/spaCy`

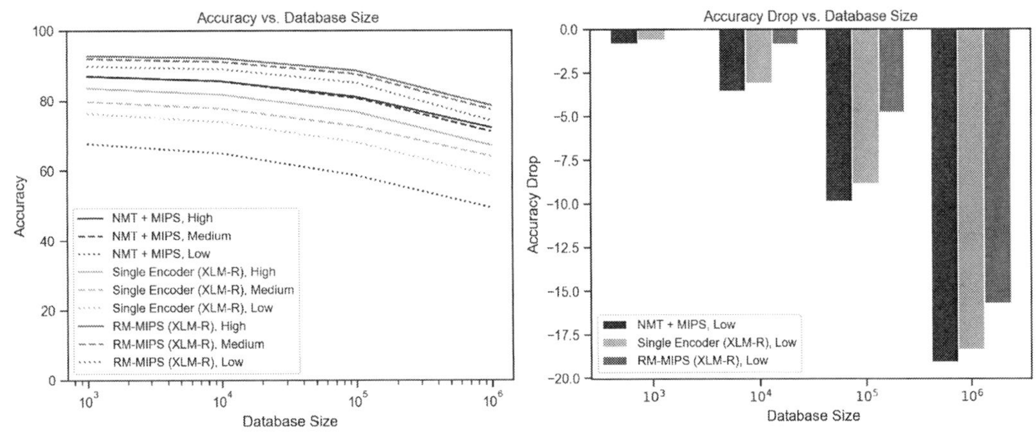

Figure 3: **Effect of Database Size on LRL $\rightarrow$ HRL.** Left: Query Matching accuracy of the strongest methods on different language groups as the amount of "unaligned" queries in the English database increases. Right: The accuracy drop of the different methods on low resource languages as the amount of queries in the English database increases beyond the original parallel count.

the English answer.

For XQuAD end-to-end experiments we find straightforward machine translation works best, whereas for MKQA, which contains more short, entity-type answers, we find WikiData Entity Translation works best. We report results using these simple methods and leave more sophisticated combinations or improvements to future work.

5 Results

5.1 End-To-End (E2E) Results

We benchmark the performance of the cross-lingual pivot methods on XQuAD and MKQA. To simulate a realistic setting, we add all the English questions from SQuAD to the English database used in the XQuAD experiments. Similarly we add all of Natural Questions queries (not just those aligned across languages) in the MKQA experiments. For each experiment we group the languages into high, medium, and low resource, as shown in Table 1, according to Wu and Dredze (2020). Tables 2 and 3 present the mean performance by language group, for query matching (LRL $\rightarrow$ HRL), and end-to-end results (LRL $\rightarrow$ HRL $\rightarrow$ LRL), query matching and answer translation in sequence.

Among the models, RM-MIPS typically outperforms baselines, particularly on lower resource languages. We find the reranking component in particular offers significant improvements over the non-reranked sentence encoding approaches in low resource settings, where we believe sentence embeddings are most inconsistent in their performance. For instance, RM-MIPS (LASER) outperforms LASER by 5.7% on the Lowest resource E2E MKQA task, and 4.0% across all languages. The margins are even larger between RM-MIPS (mUSE) and mUSE as well as RM-MIPS (XLM-R) and XLM-R.

For certain high resource languages, mUSE performs particularly strongly, and for XQuAD languages, LASER performs poorly. Accordingly, the choice of sentence encoder (and its language proportions in pretraining) is important in optimizing for the cross-lingual pivot task. The modularity of RM-MIPS offers this flexibility, as the first stage multiligual encoder can be swapped out: we present results for LASER, mUSE, and XLM-R.

Comparing query matching accuracy (left) and end-to-end F1 (right) in Tables 2 and 3 measures the performance drop due to answer translation (HRL $\rightarrow$ LRL, see section 4.3 for details). We see this drop is quite small for MKQA as compared to XQuAD. Similarly, the "Perfect LRL $\rightarrow$ HRL" measures the Answer Translation stage on all queries, showing XQuAD's machine translation for answers is much lower than MKQA's Wikidata translation for answers. This observation indicates that (a) Wikidata translation is particularly strong, and (b) cross-lingual pivot techniques are particularly useful for datasets with frequent entity, date, or numeric-style answers, that can be translated with Wikidata, as seen in MKQA. Another potential factor in the performance difference between MKQA and XQuAD is that MKQA contains naturally occurring questions, whereas XQuAD does not. Despite the lower mean end-to-end perfor-

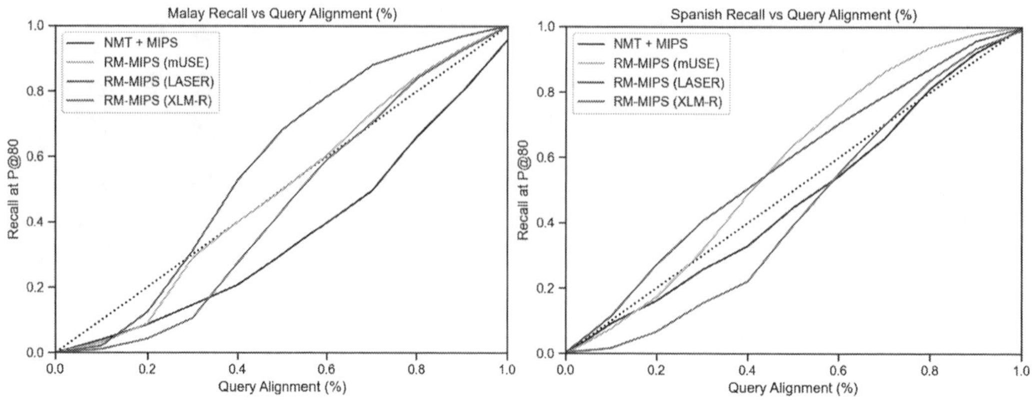

Figure 4: **Effects of Query Alignment on MKQA end-to-end Performance:** At a target precision of 80%, the end-to-end Malay (left) and Spanish (right) recall are plotted for each degree of query alignment. The query alignment axis indicates the percentage of 10k queries with parallel matches retained in the English database.

mance for XQuAD, this cross-lingual pivot can still be used alongside traditional methods, and can be calibrated for high precision/low coverage by abstaining from answering questions that are Wikidata translatable.

One other noteable advantage of paraphrase-based pivot approaches, is that no LRL-specific annotated training data is required. A question answering system in the target language requires in-language annotated data, or an NMT system from English. Traditional NMT "translate test" or "MT-in-the-middle" (Asai et al., 2018; Hajič et al., 2000; Schneider et al., 2013) approaches also require annotated parallel data to train. RM-MIPS and our other paraphrase baselines observe monolingual corpora at pre-training time, and only select language pairs during fine-tuning (those present in PAWS-X), and yet these models still perform well on XLP even for non-PAWS-X languages.

5.2 Database Size

To understand the impact of database size on the query matching process, we assemble a larger database with MSMARCO (800k), SQuAD (100k), and Open-NaturalQuestions (90k). Note that none of the models are explicitly tuned to MKQA, and since MSMARCO and Open-NQ comprise natural user queries (from the same or similar distribution), we believe these are challenging "distractors". In Figure 3 we plot accuracy of the most performant models from Tables 2 and 3 on each of the high, medium, and low resource language groups over different sizes of database on MKQA. We report the initial stage query matching (LRL $\rightarrow$ HRL) to isolate individual model matching performance. We observe that RM-MIPS degrades less quickly with database size than competing methods, and that it degrades less with the resourcefulness of the language group.

5.3 Query Alignment

In some cases, incoming LRL queries may not have a corresponding semantic match in the HRL database. To assess the impact of this, we vary the percentage of queries that have a corresponding match by dropping out their parallel example in the English database (in increments of 10%). In Figures 4 we report the median end-to-end recall scores over five different random seeds, at each level of query alignment (x-axis). At each level of answer query alignment we recompute a No Answer confidence threshold for a target precision of 80%. Due to computational restraints, we select one low resource (Malay) and one high resource language (Spanish) to report results on. We find that even calibrated for high precision (a target of 80%) the cross-lingual pivot methods can maintain proportional, and occasionally higher, coverage to the degree of query misalignment. RM-MIPS methods in particular can *outperform* proportional coverage to alignment (the dotted black line on the diagonal) by sourcing answers from similar queries in the database to those dropped out. Consequently, a practitioner can maintain high precision and respectable recall by selecting a threshold for any degree of query misalignment observed in their test distribution.

The primary limitation of RM-MIPS, or other pivot-oriented approaches, is that their performance is bounded by the degree of query alignment. However, QA systems still fail to replicate their English answer coverage in LRLs (Longpre et al., 2020), and so we expect pivot techniques to remain essential until this gap narrows completely.

6 Related Work

Cross-Lingual Modeling Multilingual BERT (Devlin et al., 2019), XLM (Lample and Conneau, 2019), and XLM-R (Conneau et al., 2019) use masked language modeling (MLM) to share embeddings across languages. Artetxe and Schwenk (2019) introduce LASER, a language-agnostic sentence embedder trained using many-to-many machine translation. Yang et al. (2019a) extend Cer et al. (2018) in a multilingual setting by following Chidambaram et al. (2019) to train a multitask dual-encoder model (mUSE). These multilingual encoders are often used for semantic similarity tasks. Reimers and Gurevych (2019) propose finetuning pooled BERT token representations (Sentence-BERT), and Reimers and Gurevych (2020) extend with knowledge distillation to encourage vector similarity among translations. Other methods improve multilingual transfer via language alignment (Roy et al., 2020; Mulcaire et al., 2019; Schuster et al., 2019) or combining machine translation with multilingual encoders (Fang et al., 2020; Cui et al., 2019; Mallinson et al., 2018).

Multilingual Question Answering Efforts to explore multilingual question answering include MLQA (Lewis et al., 2019), XQuAD (Artetxe et al., 2019), MKQA (Longpre et al., 2020), TyDi (Clark et al., 2020), XORQA (Asai et al., 2020) and MFAQ (De Bruyn et al., 2021).

Prior work in multilingual QA achieves strong results combining neural machine translation and multilingual representations via **Translate-Test**, **Translate-Train**, or **Zero Shot** approaches (Asai et al., 2018; Cui et al., 2019; Charlet et al., 2020; Stepanov et al., 2013; He et al., 2013; Dong et al., 2017). This work focuses on *extracting* the answer from a multilingual passage (Cui et al., 2019; Asai et al., 2018), assuming passages are provided.

Improving Low Resource With High Resource Efforts to improve performance on low-resource languages usually explore language alignment or transfer learning. Chung et al. (2017) find supervised and unsupervised improvements in transfer learning when finetuning from a language specific model, and Lee and Lee (2019) leverage a GAN-inspired discriminator (Goodfellow et al., 2014) to enforce language-agnostic representations. Aligning vector spaces of text representations in existing models (Conneau et al., 2017b; Schuster et al., 2019; Mikolov et al., 2013) remains a promising direction. Leveraging high resource data has also been studied in sequence labeling (Xie et al., 2018; Plank and Agić, 2018; Schuster et al., 2019) and machine translation (Johnson et al., 2017; Zhang et al., 2020).

Paraphrase Detection The paraphrase detection task determines whether two sentences are semantically equivalent. Popular paraphrase datasets include Quora Question Pairs (Sharma et al., 2019), MRPC (Dolan and Brockett, 2005), and STS-B (Cer et al., 2017). The adversarially constructed PAWS dataset Zhang et al. (2019) was translated to 6 languages, offering a multilingual option, PAWS-X Yang et al. (2019b). In a multilingual setting, an auxiliary paraphrase detection (or nearest neighbour) component, over a datastore of training examples, has been shown to greatly improve performance for neural machine translation (Khandelwal et al., 2020).

7 Conclusion

In conclusion, we formulate a task to cross-lingual open-retrieval question answering more realistic to the constraints and challenges faced by practitioners expanding their systems' capabilities beyond English. Leveraging access to a large English training set our method of query retrieval followed by reranking greatly outperforms strong baseline methods. Our analysis compares multiple methods of leveraging this English expertise and concludes our two-stage approach transfers better to lower resource languages, and is more robust in the presence of extensive distractor data and query distribution misalignment. Circumventing retrieval, this approach offers fast online or offline answer generation to many languages straight off-the-shelf, without necessitating additional training data in the target language.

We hope this analysis will promote creative methods in multilingual knowledge transfer, and the cross-lingual pivots task will encourage researchers to pursue problem formulations better informed by the needs of existing systems. In particular, leveraging many location and culturally-specific query knowledge bases, with cross-lingual pivots across many languages is an exciting extension of this work.

References

Mikel Artetxe, Sebastian Ruder, and Dani Yogatama. 2019. On the cross-lingual transferability of monolingual representations. *arXiv preprint arXiv:1910.11856*.

Mikel Artetxe and Holger Schwenk. 2019. Massively multilingual sentence embeddings for zero-shot cross-lingual transfer and beyond. *Transactions of the Association for Computational Linguistics*, 7:597–610.

Akari Asai, Akiko Eriguchi, Kazuma Hashimoto, and Yoshimasa Tsuruoka. 2018. Multilingual extractive reading comprehension by runtime machine translation. *arXiv preprint arXiv:1809.03275*.

Akari Asai, Jungo Kasai, Jonathan H Clark, Kenton Lee, Eunsol Choi, and Hannaneh Hajishirzi. 2020. Xor qa: Cross-lingual open-retrieval question answering. *arXiv preprint arXiv:2010.11856*.

Ewa S. Callahan and Susan C. Herring. 2011. Cultural bias in wikipedia content on famous persons. *Journal of the American Society for Information Science and Technology*, 62(10):1899–1915.

Daniel Cer, Mona Diab, Eneko Agirre, Inigo Lopez-Gazpio, and Lucia Specia. 2017. Semeval-2017 task 1: Semantic textual similarity multilingual and crosslingual focused evaluation. *Proceedings of the 11th International Workshop on Semantic Evaluation (SemEval-2017)*.

Daniel Cer, Yinfei Yang, Sheng-yi Kong, Nan Hua, Nicole Limtiaco, Rhomni St John, Noah Constant, Mario Guajardo-Cespedes, Steve Yuan, Chris Tar, et al. 2018. Universal sentence encoder for english. In *Proceedings of the 2018 Conference on Empirical Methods in Natural Language Processing: System Demonstrations*, pages 169–174.

Delphine Charlet, Geraldine Damnati, Frederic Bechet, Gabriel Marzinotto, and Johannes Heinecke. 2020. Cross-lingual and cross-domain evaluation of machine reading comprehension with squad and CALOR-quest corpora. In *Proceedings of the 12th Language Resources and Evaluation Conference*, pages 5491–5497, Marseille, France. European Language Resources Association.

Swapnil Chaudhari. 2014. Cross lingual information retrieval. *Center for Indian Language Technology*.

Muthu Chidambaram, Yinfei Yang, Daniel Cer, Steve Yuan, Yunhsuan Sung, Brian Strope, and Ray Kurzweil. 2019. Learning cross-lingual sentence representations via a multi-task dual-encoder model. In *Proceedings of the 4th Workshop on Representation Learning for NLP (RepL4NLP-2019)*, pages 250–259.

Yu-An Chung, Hung-Yi Lee, and James Glass. 2017. Supervised and unsupervised transfer learning for question answering. *arXiv preprint arXiv:1711.05345*.

Jonathan H Clark, Eunsol Choi, Michael Collins, Dan Garrette, Tom Kwiatkowski, Vitaly Nikolaev, and Jennimaria Palomaki. 2020. Tydi qa: A benchmark for information-seeking question answering in typologically diverse languages. *arXiv preprint arXiv:2003.05002*.

Alexis Conneau, Kartikay Khandelwal, Naman Goyal, Vishrav Chaudhary, Guillaume Wenzek, Francisco Guzmán, Edouard Grave, Myle Ott, Luke Zettlemoyer, and Veselin Stoyanov. 2019. Unsupervised cross-lingual representation learning at scale. *arXiv preprint arXiv:1911.02116*.

Alexis Conneau, Douwe Kiela, Holger Schwenk, Loïc Barrault, and Antoine Bordes. 2017a. Supervised learning of universal sentence representations from natural language inference data. In *Proceedings of the 2017 Conference on Empirical Methods in Natural Language Processing*, pages 670–680.

Alexis Conneau, Guillaume Lample, Marc'Aurelio Ranzato, Ludovic Denoyer, and Hervé Jégou. 2017b. Word translation without parallel data. *arXiv preprint arXiv:1710.04087*.

Yiming Cui, Wanxiang Che, Ting Liu, Bing Qin, Shijin Wang, and Guoping Hu. 2019. Cross-lingual machine reading comprehension. In *Proceedings of the 2019 Conference on Empirical Methods in Natural Language Processing and the 9th International Joint Conference on Natural Language Processing (EMNLP-IJCNLP)*, pages 1586–1595.

Maxime De Bruyn, Ehsan Lotfi, Jeska Buhmann, and Walter Daelemans. 2021. Mfaq: a multilingual faq dataset. *arXiv preprint arXiv:2109.12870*.

Jacob Devlin, Ming-Wei Chang, Kenton Lee, and Kristina Toutanova. 2019. Bert: Pre-training of deep bidirectional transformers for language understanding. In *Proceedings of the 2019 Conference of the North American Chapter of the Association for Computational Linguistics: Human Language Technologies, Volume 1 (Long and Short Papers)*, pages 4171–4186.

Bill Dolan and Chris Brockett. 2005. Automatically constructing a corpus of sentential paraphrases. In *Third International Workshop on Paraphrasing (IWP2005)*.

Li Dong, Jonathan Mallinson, Siva Reddy, and Mirella Lapata. 2017. Learning to paraphrase for question answering. *arXiv preprint arXiv:1708.06022*.

Yuwei Fang, Shuohang Wang, Zhe Gan, Siqi Sun, and Jingjing Liu. 2020. Filter: An enhanced fusion method for cross-lingual language understanding. *arXiv preprint arXiv:2009.05166*.

Christian Fluhr, Robert E Frederking, Doug Oard, Akitoshi Okumura, Kai Ishikawa, and Kenji Satoh. 1999. Multilingual (or cross-lingual) information retrieval. *Proceedings of the Multilingual Information Management: Current Levels and Future Abilities*.

Ian Goodfellow, Jean Pouget-Abadie, Mehdi Mirza, Bing Xu, David Warde-Farley, Sherjil Ozair, Aaron Courville, and Yoshua Bengio. 2014. Generative adversarial nets. In *Advances in neural information processing systems*, pages 2672–2680.

Miniwatts Marketing Group. 2011. Internet world stats: Usage and population statistics. *Miniwatts Marketing Group*.

Jan Hajič, Jan Hric, and Vladislav Kuboň. 2000. Machine translation of very close languages. In *Proceedings of the Sixth Conference on Applied Natural Language Processing*, ANLC '00, page 7–12, USA. Association for Computational Linguistics.

Xiaodong He, Li Deng, Dilek Hakkani-Tur, and Gokhan Tur. 2013. Multi-style adaptive training for robust cross-lingual spoken language understanding. In *2013 IEEE International Conference on Acoustics, Speech and Signal Processing*, pages 8342–8346. IEEE.

Matthew Honnibal and Ines Montani. 2017. spaCy 2: Natural language understanding with Bloom embeddings, convolutional neural networks and incremental parsing. To appear.

Melvin Johnson, Mike Schuster, Quoc V Le, Maxim Krikun, Yonghui Wu, Zhifeng Chen, Nikhil Thorat, Fernanda Viégas, Martin Wattenberg, Greg Corrado, et al. 2017. Google's multilingual neural machine translation system: Enabling zero-shot translation. *Transactions of the Association for Computational Linguistics*, 5:339–351.

Mandar Joshi, Eunsol Choi, Daniel S Weld, and Luke Zettlemoyer. 2017. Triviaqa: A large scale distantly supervised challenge dataset for reading comprehension. *arXiv preprint arXiv:1705.03551*.

Vladimir Karpukhin, Barlas Oğuz, Sewon Min, Patrick Lewis, Ledell Wu, Sergey Edunov, Danqi Chen, and Wen tau Yih. 2020. Dense passage retrieval for open-domain question answering.

Urvashi Khandelwal, Angela Fan, Dan Jurafsky, Luke Zettlemoyer, and Mike Lewis. 2020. Nearest neighbor machine translation. *arXiv preprint arXiv:2010.00710*.

Tom Kwiatkowski, Jennimaria Palomaki, Olivia Redfield, Michael Collins, Ankur Parikh, Chris Alberti, Danielle Epstein, Illia Polosukhin, Jacob Devlin, Kenton Lee, et al. 2019. Natural questions: A benchmark for question answering research. *Transactions of the Association for Computational Linguistics*, 7:453–466.

Guillaume Lample and Alexis Conneau. 2019. Cross-lingual language model pretraining. *arXiv preprint arXiv:1901.07291*.

Chia-Hsuan Lee and Hung-Yi Lee. 2019. Cross-lingual transfer learning for question answering. *arXiv preprint arXiv:1907.06042*.

Manpreet Lehal. 2018. Challenges in cross language information retrieval.

Patrick Lewis, Barlas Oğuz, Ruty Rinott, Sebastian Riedel, and Holger Schwenk. 2019. Mlqa: Evaluating cross-lingual extractive question answering. *arXiv preprint arXiv:1910.07475*.

Patrick Lewis, Pontus Stenetorp, and Sebastian Riedel. 2020. Question and answer test-train overlap in open-domain question answering datasets. *arXiv preprint arXiv:2008.02637*.

Shayne Longpre, Yi Lu, and Joachim Daiber. 2020. Mkqa: A linguistically diverse benchmark for multilingual open domain question answering.

Jonathan Mallinson, Rico Sennrich, and Mirella Lapata. 2017. Paraphrasing revisited with neural machine translation. In *Proceedings of the 15th Conference of the European Chapter of the Association for Computational Linguistics: Volume 1, Long Papers*, pages 881–893.

Jonathan Mallinson, Rico Sennrich, and Mirella Lapata. 2018. Sentence compression for arbitrary languages via multilingual pivoting. In *Proceedings of the 2018 Conference on Empirical Methods in Natural Language Processing*, pages 2453–2464.

Tomas Mikolov, Quoc V Le, and Ilya Sutskever. 2013. Exploiting similarities among languages for machine translation. *arXiv preprint arXiv:1309.4168*.

Phoebe Mulcaire, Jungo Kasai, and Noah A Smith. 2019. Polyglot contextual representations improve crosslingual transfer. In *Proceedings of the 2019 Conference of the North American Chapter of the Association for Computational Linguistics: Human Language Technologies, Volume 1 (Long and Short Papers)*, pages 3912–3918.

Barbara Plank and Željko Agić. 2018. Distant supervision from disparate sources for low-resource part-of-speech tagging. In *Proceedings of the 2018 Conference on Empirical Methods in Natural Language Processing*, pages 614–620, Brussels, Belgium. Association for Computational Linguistics.

Pranav Rajpurkar, Jian Zhang, Konstantin Lopyrev, and Percy Liang. 2016. Squad: 100,000+ questions for machine comprehension of text. In *Proceedings of the 2016 Conference on Empirical Methods in Natural Language Processing*, pages 2383–2392.

Nils Reimers and Iryna Gurevych. 2019. Sentence-bert: Sentence embeddings using siamese bert-networks. In *Proceedings of the 2019 Conference on Empirical Methods in Natural Language Processing and the 9th International Joint Conference on Natural Language Processing (EMNLP-IJCNLP)*, pages 3973–3983.

Nils Reimers and Iryna Gurevych. 2020. Making monolingual sentence embeddings multilingual using knowledge distillation. *arXiv preprint arXiv:2004.09813*.

Uma Roy, Noah Constant, Rami Al-Rfou, Aditya Barua, Aaron Phillips, and Yinfei Yang. 2020. Lareqa: Language-agnostic answer retrieval from a multilingual pool. *arXiv preprint arXiv:2004.05484*.

Nathan Schneider, Behrang Mohit, Chris Dyer, Kemal Oflazer, and Noah A. Smith. 2013. Supersense tagging for Arabic: the MT-in-the-middle attack. In *Proceedings of the 2013 Conference of the North American Chapter of the Association for Computational Linguistics: Human Language Technologies*, pages 661–667, Atlanta, Georgia. Association for Computational Linguistics.

Tal Schuster, Ori Ram, Regina Barzilay, and Amir Globerson. 2019. Cross-lingual alignment of contextual word embeddings, with applications to zero-shot dependency parsing. In *Proceedings of the 2019 Conference of the North American Chapter of the Association for Computational Linguistics: Human Language Technologies, Volume 1 (Long and Short Papers)*, pages 1599–1613.

Lakshay Sharma, Laura Graesser, Nikita Nangia, and Utku Evci. 2019. Natural language understanding with the quora question pairs dataset. *arXiv preprint arXiv:1907.01041*.

Evgeny A Stepanov, Ilya Kashkarev, Ali Orkan Bayer, Giuseppe Riccardi, and Arindam Ghosh. 2013. Language style and domain adaptation for cross-language slu porting. In *2013 IEEE Workshop on Automatic Speech Recognition and Understanding*, pages 144–149. IEEE.

Ashish Vaswani, Noam Shazeer, Niki Parmar, Jakob Uszkoreit, Llion Jones, Aidan N Gomez, Łukasz Kaiser, and Illia Polosukhin. 2017. Attention is all you need. In *Proceedings of the 31st International Conference on Neural Information Processing Systems*, pages 6000–6010.

Denny Vrandečić and Markus Krötzsch. 2014. Wikidata: A free collaborative knowledgebase. *Commun. ACM*, 57(10):78–85.

Zhiguo Wang, Wael Hamza, and Radu Florian. 2017. Bilateral multi-perspective matching for natural language sentences. In *Proceedings of the 26th International Joint Conference on Artificial Intelligence*, pages 4144–4150.

Thomas Wolf, Lysandre Debut, Victor Sanh, Julien Chaumond, Clement Delangue, Anthony Moi, Pierric Cistac, Tim Rault, R'emi Louf, Morgan Funtowicz, and Jamie Brew. 2019. Huggingface's transformers: State-of-the-art natural language processing. *ArXiv*, abs/1910.03771.

Shijie Wu and Mark Dredze. 2020. Are all languages created equal in multilingual BERT? In *Proceedings of the 5th Workshop on Representation Learning for NLP*, pages 120–130, Online. Association for Computational Linguistics.

Jiateng Xie, Zhilin Yang, Graham Neubig, Noah A. Smith, and Jaime Carbonell. 2018. Neural cross-lingual named entity recognition with minimal resources. In *Proceedings of the 2018 Conference on Empirical Methods in Natural Language Processing*, pages 369–379, Brussels, Belgium. Association for Computational Linguistics.

Yinfei Yang, Daniel Cer, Amin Ahmad, Mandy Guo, Jax Law, Noah Constant, Gustavo Hernandez Abrego, Steve Yuan, Chris Tar, Yun-Hsuan Sung, et al. 2019a. Multilingual universal sentence encoder for semantic retrieval. *arXiv preprint arXiv:1907.04307*.

Yinfei Yang, Yuan Zhang, Chris Tar, and Jason Baldridge. 2019b. Paws-x: A cross-lingual adversarial dataset for paraphrase identification. In *Proceedings of the 2019 Conference on Empirical Methods in Natural Language Processing and the 9th International Joint Conference on Natural Language Processing (EMNLP-IJCNLP)*, pages 3678–3683.

Biao Zhang, Philip Williams, Ivan Titov, and Rico Sennrich. 2020. Improving massively multilingual neural machine translation and zero-shot translation. *arXiv preprint arXiv:2004.11867*.

Yuan Zhang, Jason Baldridge, and Luheng He. 2019. Paws: Paraphrase adversaries from word scrambling. In *Proceedings of the 2019 Conference of the North American Chapter of the Association for Computational Linguistics: Human Language Technologies, Volume 1 (Long and Short Papers)*, pages 1298–1308.

Imed Zitouni and Radu Florian. 2008. Mention detection crossing the language barrier. In *Proceedings of the 2008 Conference on Empirical Methods in Natural Language Processing*, pages 600–609, Honolulu, Hawaii. Association for Computational Linguistics.

A Reproducibility

A.1 Experimental Setup

Computing Infrastructure. For all of our experiments, we used a computation cluster with 4 NVIDIA Tesla V100 GPUs, 32GB GPU memory and 256GB RAM.

Implementation We used Python 3.7, PyTorch 1.4.0, and Transformers 2.8.0 for all our experiments. We obtain our datasets from the citations specified in the main paper, and link to the repositories of all libraries we use.

Hyperparameter Search For our hyper parameter searches, we perform a uniformly random search over learning rate and batch size, with ranges specified in Table 4, optimizing for the development accuracy. We find the optimal learning rate and batch size pair to be $1e-5$ and 80 respectively.

Evaluation For query matching, we use scikit-learn [9] to calculate the accuracy. For end-to-end performance, we use the MLQA evaluation script to obtain the F1 score of the results[10].

Datasets We use the sentences in each dataset as-is, and rely on the pretrained tokenizer for each model to perform preprocessing.

A.2 Model Training

Query Paraphrase Dataset We found the optimal training combination of the PAWS-X and QQP datasets by training XLM-R classifiers on training dataset percentages of $(100\%, 0\%)$, $(75\%, 25\%)$, and $(50\%, 50\%)$ of (PAWS-X, QQP) – with the PAWS-X percentage entailing the entirety of the PAWS-X dataset – and observe the performance on matching multilingual XQuAD queries. We shuffle the examples in the training set, and restrict the input examples to being (English, LRL) pairs. We perform a hyperparameter search as specified in Table 5 for each dataset composition, and report the test results in Table 4.

A.3 Cross Encoder

We start with the pretrained `xlm-roberta-large` checkpoint in Huggingface's transformers[11] library and perform a hyperparameter search with the parameters specified in Table 1 by using a modified version of Huggingface's text classification training pipeline for GLUE.

The cross encoder was used in all the RM-MIPS methods. In particular, it was used in the RM-MIPS (mUSE), RM-MIPS (LASER), and RM-MIPS (XLM-R) rows of tables in the main paper.

[9] `https://scikit-learn.org/stable/`

[10] `https://github.com/facebookresearch/MLQA`

[11] `https://github.com/huggingface/transformers`

(PAWS-X, QQP)	XQuAD
$(100\%, 0\%)$	0.847
$(75\%, 25\%)$	**0.985**
$(50\%, 50\%)$	0.979

Table 4: **XLM-R Query Paraphrase Performance On Different Query Compositions.** The performance of XLM-Roberta on matching XQuAD test queries when finetuned on different training set compositions of PAWS-X and QQP.

MODEL PARAMETERS	VALUE/RANGE
Fixed Parameters	
Model	XLM-Roberta Large
Num Epochs	3
Dropout	0.1
Optimizer	Adam
Learning Rate Schedule	Linear Decay
Max Sequence Length	128
Tuned Parameters	
Batch Size	[8, 120]
Learning Rate	$[9e-4, 1e-6]$
Extra Info	
Model Size (# params)	$550M$
Vocab Size	250,002
Trials	30

Table 5: **Cross Encoder Hyperparameter Selection And Tuning Ranges** The hyper parameters we chose and searched over for XLM-Roberta large on the query paraphrase detection datasets.

B Full Results Breakdowns

B.1 LRL→HRL Results

See Table 6 and 7 for the non-aggregated LRL→HRL language performances of each method on MKQA and XQuAD respectively.

B.2 LRL→HRL→LRL Results

See Table 8 and 9 for the non-aggregated LRL→HRL→LRL language performances of each method on MKQA and XQuAD respectively.

	ar	zh_{cn}	da	de	es	fi	fr	he	zh_{hk}	hu	it	ja	km
NMT + MIPS	69.2	48.0	89.8	87.5	86.5	76.0	87.6	74.3	42.5	79.1	86.6	62.0	45.4
mUSE	80.0	83.2	51.7	90.9	91.7	37.6	91.5	33.5	80.8	40.7	91.6	80.0	35.6
LASER	81.5	62.8	88.6	52.0	79.9	81.6	78.5	85.5	64.0	69.1	80.4	39.3	40.2
Single Encoder (XLM-R)	58.0	76.3	84.8	74.6	73.3	65.5	74.1	67.8	77.0	66.9	69.0	71.4	59.0
RM-MIPS (mUSE)	77.6	81.2	77.2	88.8	88.9	59.9	88.8	44.1	81.2	64.1	88.4	81.2	50.6
RM-MIPS (LASER)	77.2	77.7	89.2	66.9	84.7	84.8	84.4	83.3	78.1	77.5	84.7	64.2	48.2
RM-MIPS (Ours)	72.6	80.7	90.1	86.8	87.0	82.7	87.2	80.6	81.0	81.4	85.5	79.5	72.4

	ko	ms	nl	no	pl	pt	ru	sv	th	tr	zh_{tw}	vi
NMT + MIPS	54.2	86.0	88.8	87.2	81.9	87.4	81.9	87.2	75.0	79.6	39.7	76.0
mUSE	73.7	87.6	92.0	50.3	84.9	93.3	87.2	50.3	88.6	87.0	73.2	38.6
LASER	68.6	92.5	93.1	92.4	73.7	85.2	78.1	92.8	62.1	75.2	57.9	79.9
Single Encoder (XLM-R)	72.3	76.4	79.1	81.3	70.6	65.7	78.8	83.8	79.4	68.7	71.2	78.6
RM-MIPS (mUSE)	74.7	89.9	90.9	75.6	87.3	89.8	87.1	76.0	86.8	86.6	75.0	64.4
RM-MIPS (LASER)	73.1	89.5	90.2	89.7	81.9	86.7	84.3	89.8	77.0	82.3	72.5	84.0
RM-MIPS (XLM-R)	75.2	89.0	89.8	88.8	85.6	85.5	86.1	90.0	85.4	83.6	75.5	85.9

Table 6: **MKQA + Natural Questions Per-Language LRL→HRL Results.** The accuracy scores for each method on query matching.

	ar	de	el	es	hi	ru	th	tr	vi	zh
NMT + MIPS	71.7	90.8	86.7	95.2	79.9	85.7	67.4	82.9	74.8	41.8
mUSE	87.4	96.4	7.5	98.1	3.4	93.2	91.6	94.1	17.8	90.3
LASER	61.7	33.1	3.7	86.2	28.6	70.4	24.2	65.3	64.7	29.2
Single Encoder (XLM-R)	66.8	85.1	81.7	87.8	77.6	85.0	76.6	81.9	89.4	82.3
RM-MIPS (mUSE)	90.4	96.3	14.8	97.3	10.1	93.2	92.6	95.7	39.3	91.0
RM-MIPS (LASER)	81.6	59.9	11.1	95.5	59.1	88.3	55.5	89.0	85.7	66.2
RM-MIPS (XLM-R)	86.6	94.2	94.1	95.5	92.0	93.0	90.7	92.5	92.1	90.8

Table 7: **XQuAD + SQuAD Per-Language LRL→HRL Results.** The accuracy scores for each method on query matching.

	ar	zh_{cn}	da	de	es	fi	fr	he	zh_{hk}	hu	it	ja	km
NMT + MIPS	60.0	41.7	85.8	83.8	82.4	72.0	83.7	63.3	41.2	74.5	82.5	60.1	44.8
mUSE	68.6	62.7	50.1	87.2	87.4	37.2	87.5	31.9	68.7	40.0	87.2	74.9	35.0
LASER	70.1	49.5	84.6	50.8	76.3	77.3	75.3	72.8	56.2	65.0	76.8	39.1	38.1
Single Encoder (XLM-R)	50.9	57.5	81.0	71.7	70.2	62.0	70.9	58.6	65.8	63.1	66.0	68.0	54.9
RM-MIPS (mUSE)	66.9	61.3	74.4	85.2	84.8	58.0	84.9	39.9	68.8	61.5	84.1	75.8	46.0
RM-MIPS (LASER)	66.7	59.0	85.0	64.6	80.7	80.3	80.6	71.0	66.3	72.7	80.6	61.7	45.3
RM-MIPS (Ours)	62.8	60.8	85.9	83.3	83.1	78.4	83.3	68.7	68.6	76.6	81.5	74.4	64.4

	ko	ms	nl	no	pl	pt	ru	sv	th	tr	zh_{tw}	vi
NMT + MIPS	47.5	81.1	85.3	80.2	77.6	83.3	72.6	84.1	62.9	74.7	35.2	70.6
mUSE	63.0	82.7	88.5	48.4	80.4	88.9	77.2	49.4	72.2	81.7	55.6	37.7
LASER	59.1	87.4	89.7	85.1	70.0	81.2	69.4	89.5	53.7	70.7	45.7	74.4
Single Encoder (XLM-R)	62.5	72.2	76.0	75.2	67.0	62.5	70.1	80.8	66.3	64.6	54.1	73.1
RM-MIPS (mUSE)	64.2	84.8	87.3	70.6	82.5	85.3	77.1	73.9	70.7	81.2	56.6	61.3
RM-MIPS (LASER)	63.1	84.4	86.7	81.8	77.3	82.4	74.7	86.6	64.3	77.1	55.1	78.2
RM-MIPS (XLM-R)	64.7	84.0	86.3	81.6	81.0	81.3	76.3	86.9	69.9	78.6	56.8	79.9

Table 8: **MKQA + Natural Questions Per-Language LRL→HRL→LRL WikiData Results.** The F1 scores for end-to-end performance of each method on every language when using WikiData translation

	ar	de	el	es	hi	ru	th	tr	vi	zh
NMT + MIPS	35.3	55.5	39.2	68.2	32.9	30.7	17.8	42.1	45.6	19.0
mUSE	40.8	58.2	4.4	70.0	1.6	33.4	23.4	47.0	11.8	33.6
LASER	29.9	22.7	1.5	61.8	10.8	24.2	6.4	33.0	38.6	12.7
Single Encoder (XLM-R)	31.3	52.9	37.3	63.9	30.9	30.1	18.6	42.0	52.7	30.6
RM-MIPS (mUSE)	42.6	58.1	7.8	69.6	4.2	33.4	23.2	47.5	26.1	33.8
RM-MIPS (LASER)	38.3	38.2	5.7	68.3	22.9	31.1	13.7	44.5	50.7	26.3
RM-MIPS (XLM-R)	40.9	57.3	42.1	68.7	36.7	33.0	22.9	45.7	54.5	33.6

Table 9: **XQuAD + SQuAD Per-Language LRL→HRL→LRL NMT Results.** The F1 scores for end-to-end performance of each method on every language when using NMT translation

Cross-Lingual QA as a Stepping Stone for Monolingual Open QA in Icelandic

Vésteinn Snæbjarnarson
Miðeind ehf
University of Iceland
vesteinn@mideind.is

Hafsteinn Einarsson
University of Iceland
hafsteinne@hi.is

Abstract

It can be challenging to build effective open question answering (open QA) systems for languages other than English, mainly due to a lack of labeled data for training. We present a data efficient method to bootstrap such a system for languages other than English. Our approach requires only limited QA resources in the given language, along with machine-translated data, and at least a bilingual language model. To evaluate our approach, we build such a system for the Icelandic language and evaluate performance over trivia style datasets. The corpora used for training are English in origin but machine translated into Icelandic. We train a bilingual Icelandic/English language model to embed English context and Icelandic questions following methodology introduced with DensePhrases (Lee et al., 2021). The resulting system is an open domain cross-lingual QA system between Icelandic and English. Finally, the system is adapted for Icelandic only open QA, demonstrating how it is possible to efficiently create an open QA system with limited access to curated datasets in the language of interest.

1 Introduction

Open QA systems are question-answering systems that suggest answers to questions by searching through a text corpus. Such systems have improved significantly in recent years, which can, to a large extent, be attributed to transformer-based vector representations of text that are well suited for the task (Vaswani et al., 2017). The most successful systems have been trained with a focus on English using large datasets such as Natural Questions (Kwiatkowski et al., 2019) (>320k questions), and SQuAD (Okazawa, 2021) (>150k questions). In some cases, questions have been generated from text using large generative neural networks (Alberti et al., 2019). For most languages, such large datasets do not exist, and the generative models do not perform as well as for English which constitutes the bulk of the training data. For this reason, we investigate what performance can be reached in QA for Icelandic, a language with low QA resources. In that investigation, we study the question of whether English QA data can aid QA system development through the use of machine translation.

In this paper, we present a method to bootstrap an Open QA system for Icelandic where just a few thousand labelled data entries are available. We adapt the DensePhrases (Lee et al., 2021) method by applying a bilingual language model, and machine-translated data, in a cross-lingual manner to create a monolingual Open QA system for Icelandic, the first of its kind built exclusively for the language. An overview of the build process is shown step by step in Figure 1.

2 Related work

2.1 Reading comprehension and Open QA

Open-domain question answering methods look for answers to a given question in a given text corpus (for a recent survey, see (Zhu et al., 2021)). These methods can be contrasted with reading comprehension (RC) style methods that identify an answer to a question within a single document. The RC methods are useful when an answer is sought in a given text, often referred to as the context. Open QA methods are open in the sense that the questions they can handle are open ended given a large enough underlying corpus. Open QA can be thought of as a generalization of reading comprehension since the answer is typically retrieved from a large collection of text instead of a single document. We note that most open QA methods are extractive, meaning that the suggested answer is found verbatim within a given document. There are also QA methods that provide an answer without explicitly searching through a corpus. For example, the answer can be generated based on knowledge embedded in learned parameters of a system such

Proceedings of the Workshop on Multilingual Information Access (MIA), pages 29 - 36
July 15, 2022 ©2022 Association for Computational Linguistics

as GPT-3 (Brown et al., 2020). While promising, the non-extractive methods are not considered in this paper.

Open QA methods solve a common issue in information retrieval where it is not known in what document an answer lies. The simpler reading comprehension methods can be used as components in open QA systems by combining them with a *retriever* component. BM25 (Robertson et al., 1995), a TF-IDF variant, is an example of a commonly used retriever that ranks context based on term frequencies that are shared with the question and their overall commonality. The top documents found by the retriever can then be fed to the reading comprehension component along with the question. The reading comprehension component can, for example, be a fine-tuned variant of a neural language model such as BERT (Devlin et al., 2019). The reading comprehension component is trained to predict the start and end location of an answer span or report whether an answer is not found within the given context by training on a dataset of context and question pairs.

2.2 Fast retrieval and DensePhrases

In recent years, efforts in improving open QA have focused on speeding up the lookup of documents, for example, by taking advantage of neural methods. Such a speedup has been realized by embedding documents and questions as dense vector representations such that lookup can be based on fast similarity search where the inner product of the question vector and document vector is used as a proxy for their similarity (Karpukhin et al., 2020; Lee et al., 2019; Lin et al., 2021). The embedding function can be trained such that a given question will, with a good chance, lead to the correct document being the highest ranked in the similarity search. The embedding function can also be trained end-to-end by basing the loss function on the performance of looking up the answer. A downside of these methods, in particular the end-to-end systems, is that they can be expensive to train since the document embeddings need to be updated often as a result of updates to the embedding function (Guu et al., 2020), which can be particularly expensive when many documents need to be embedded repeatedly throughout the training process. Some mitigations have been suggested; as is the case in DensePhrases (Lee et al., 2021), which is the foundation of our approach.

In DensePhrases, segments from documents are first embedded using a phrase model (and fixed), then a query model is trained to embed questions such that the inner product of question embeddings and correct context embeddings are maximized. For an incorrect pairing, the model is trained such that the inner product is minimized instead.

Fast databases intended for lookup with maximum inner product search (MIPS) (Johnson et al., 2019) enable systems such as DensePhrases to provide answers from massive datasets in subsecond time, making them excellent candidates for production-grade QA systems where an answer and its source can be reported.

2.3 Multilingual and cross-lingual QA

In cross-lingual QA, the question and answer are not required to be in the same language, and in multilingual QA the aim is to search for answers in a multilingual corpus. Multilingual QA is not necessarily cross-lingual since the answer can be generated in the same language as the query.

Interest in cross-lingual QA is likely reflected in the growing number of QA datasets in foreign languages (Rogers et al., 2021). For reading comprehension, it has been shown that multilingual LMs such as mBERT fine-tuned in an English reading comprehension task are capable of zero-shot transfer to other languages such as Japanese, French, and Hindi (Siblini et al., 2021; Gupta and Khade, 2020). Multilingual QA has been performed by extending models for English by using machine translation (MT) on the query and answer (Asai et al., 2021a), MT has also been used to adapt an English semantic parsing model for other languages (Sherborne et al., 2020; Moradshahi et al., 2020). Multilingual QA was recently implemented without explicit use of MT by extending the Dense Passage Retriever model from Karpukhin et al. (2020) with a fine-tuned mT5 model as an answer generator (Asai et al., 2021b). The answer generator receives top-scoring multilingual passages along with the question and desired answer language to generate the answer. This flexible approach even generalizes to languages not seen in the QA training process thanks to the diverse training set for crosslingual retrieval. A similar approach with an answer generator has also been applied where passage candidates come from different monolingual corpora, and the question is translated and embedded with several monolingual language models (Muller et al., 2021).

2.4 Icelandic QA data

Currently, a single extractive dataset exists for Icelandic, NQiI (Snæbjarnarson and Einarsson, 2022). It is a small Icelandic dataset containing only ~5k question-context pairs, half of which have no answer. The dataset is sourced from the Icelandic Wikipedia following the methodology introduced in TyDi-QA (Clark et al., 2020). This limited amount of Icelandic QA data is the main reason we translate English QA datasets.

3 Methods

3.1 Translating QA data

In the first step of the process, we use an English-Icelandic translation system (Símonarson et al., 2021) for translating NewsQA (Trischler et al., 2017), SQuAD and Natural Questions (NQ) (Kwiatkowski et al., 2019). We reviewed the translated questions from SQuAD and out of 100 randomly sampled questions we found that 80 were properly translated such that the meaning was fully preserved.

We translate questions, answers and contexts independently and use a fuzzy matching algorithm (see Appendix A) to map translated answers to spans in the translated context. We refer to the fully translated versions of the datasets as NewsQA-IS, SQuAD-IS, and NQ-IS. For the translated versions of the datasets where only the questions are answered as we use NewsQA-ISQ, SQuAD-ISQ, and NQ-ISQ (for an overview, see Table 1).

In DensePhrases, questions are generated for all spans of length 0–20 words in the English Wikipedia using a fine-tuned T5 (Raffel et al., 2020) model. As no such model currently exist that can reliably generate Icelandic, we also translate the generated questions. The spans themselves can not be easily translated as the available models are mostly good at translating well-formed sentences. We refer to this dataset as DP-ISQ. For an overview of all QA datasets used see Table 1.

3.2 Pre-training an Icelandic–English language model

A bilingual language model for Icelandic and English was trained following the base XLM-RoBERTa implementation (Conneau et al., 2020). We refer to this model as LM EN-IS. The Icelandic training data is the same as the one used for IceBERT (Snæbjarnarson et al., 2022). The Books 3 corpus[1] is used as source for English data, it contains around 100GB of data text from a variety of books. The model was trained for 220k updates using a batch size of 8k completing 27 epochs over the data.

3.2.1 Training RC models

After pre-training, the bilingual model (LM EN-IS) is fine-tuned for cross-lingual RC where questions are asked in Icelandic and answered in English (step 3 in Figure 1). We fine-tune using SQuAD-ISQ, NewsQA-ISQ, and NQ-ISQ. We refer to this model as the IS-EN RC model.

The bilingual model (LM EN-IS) is also fine-tuned for an Icelandic only reading comprehension task (step 4 in Figure 1) using the fully translated datasets, NQ-IS, SQuAD-IS and NewsQA-IS along with NQiI. We refer to this model as the IS-IS RC model.

These RC models are later used as a teacher models (Hinton et al., 2015). The IS-EN RC model is distilled in the fifth step and the IS-IS RC model in the sixth step of the build process when fine-tuning the Open QA system. Note that to be compatible with the training of the DensePhrases model, these models do not predict missing answers.

3.2.2 Training cross-lingual DensePhrases

We also fine-tune the bilingual model (LM EN-IS) to train a DensePhrases setup [2]. We use the partially translated DP-ISQ dataset to train the cross-lingual DensePhrases model. The result is a phrase encoder that accepts English and a query encoder that accepts Icelandic. Following the DensePhrases approach, we distil the IS-EN RC model at training time. This distillation step can be beneficial since the comparison in the DensePhrases setup is based on an inner product operation, whereas the RC model was trained in a cross-attention setting. This distillation step improved the EM score by 2 points for the original DensePhrases paper and could be validated through ablation in our low-resource setting as well. We refer to the crosslingual DensePhrases model as DensePhrases-IS-EN

[1]This is similar to (Kobayashi, 2018) and was made available in the issue section of the GitHub repository `https://github.com/soskek/bookcorpus/issues/27`.

[2]With minor adjustments to work with the SentencePiece (Kudo and Richardson, 2018) tokenization used by the bilingual model

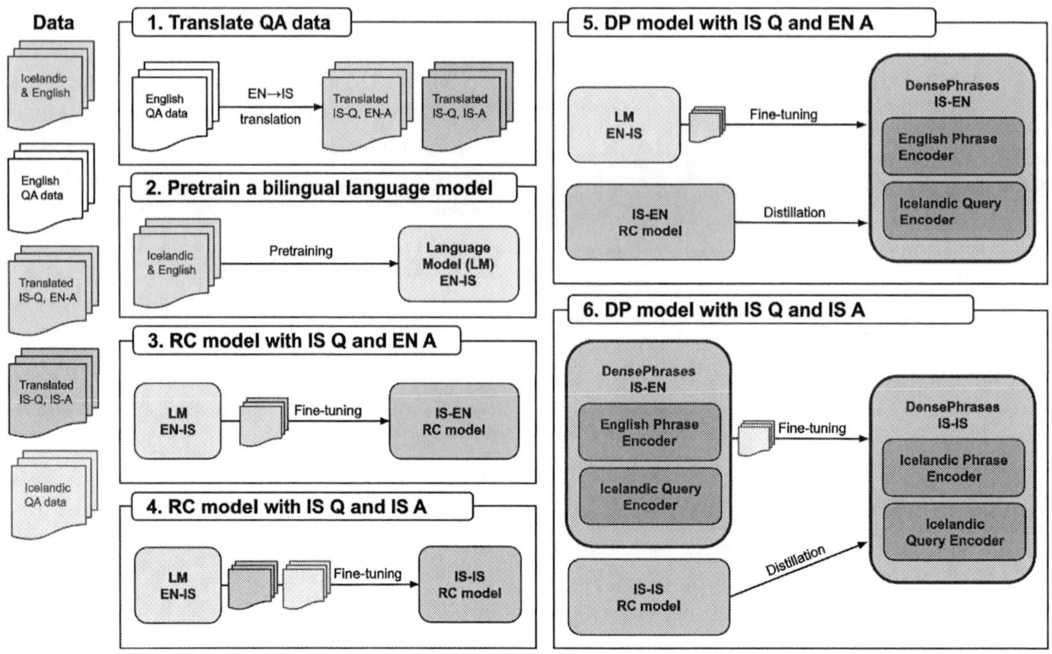

Figure 1: Diagram showing how to train an Icelandic DensePhrases model in six steps.

3.2.3 Training Icelandic only DensePhrases

In the last step of our process, we take the cross-lingual model DensePhrases-IS-EN and fine-tune it on NQiI to develop a fully Icelandic Open QA system. In this final step, we also distil the IS-IS RC model from the fourth step of the build process. We refer to the final Icelandic only model as DensePhrases-IS.

4 Results

4.1 Reading comprehension model performance

A comparison of RC performance is shown in 2. The table includes performance for the English model RoBERTa and untranslated SQuAD data (for the subset of the data that was successfully translated). Using the bilingual model only leads to a slight drop in performance (-1.7 F1). Translating the data further decreases the performance (-2.7 F1, row 6 in the table) but not catastrophically in any sense. In comparison, fine-tuning on an Icelandic only model (IceBERT) improves performance slightly (+0.6 F1, row 7 in the table). These models are not used in any of the steps shown in Figure 1 but the results validate not only the adequacy of the translation method applied, they also demonstrate that the bilingual model is suitable to be adapted for QA in both Icelandic and English.

All models were trained for 4 epochs, using a learning rate of 3e-5, maximum sequence length of 512 tokens and a document stride of 128.

Performance of the IS-EN RC model is measured on the development set of NQ with translated questions. We fine-tune on NQ-ISQ and SQuAD-ISQ, which refer to the Natural questions and SQuAD datasets with only the questions machine translated into Icelandic (step 3, row 5 in the table). Another RC model was fine-tuned on fully translated QA data along with NQiI (step 4, row 8 in the table). We chose that model for use in the fourth step since it was trained on more data than the models in rows 6 and 7 with a small sacrifice in performance on SQuAD-IS, 70.80 F1 and 69.51 EM. With ~2/3 questions answered exactly, we conclude that the RC models serve well as a teacher models for the DensePhrases training (steps 5 and 6).

4.2 Open QA performance

Performance for the cross-lingual Open QA system (DensePhrases-IS-EN, from step 5) is shown in Table 3 where results are evaluated for the Natural Questions test-dataset, both for the version with machine-translated questions (Is–En) and the original one (En–En). The system still performs well on the English only data. For reference, we note

Original dataset	Transl. dataset	Question transl.	Context transl.	Step
SQuAD	SQuAD-ISQ	✓	✗	3
NewsQA	NewsQA-ISQ	✓	✗	3
NQ	NQ-ISQ	✓	✗	3
SQuAD	SQuAD-IS	✓	✓	4
NewsQA	NewsQA-IS	✓	✓	4
NQ	NQ-IS	✓	✓	4
DensePhrases (generated)	DP-ISQ	✓	✗	5
NQiI	–	✗	✗	6

Table 1: Overview of QA-datasets used in training and how they were translated. The last column refers to steps where the data is used for fine-tuning in Figure 1.

Step	Task	Model	Fine-tuning dataset	F1	EM
-	RC-EN-EN	RoBERTa (EN)	SQuAD	**75.9**	74.3
-	RC-EN-EN	LM EN-IS	SQuAD	74.2	73.0
-	RC-IS-EN	LM EN-IS	NQ-ISQ	74.9	67.1
-	RC-IS-EN	LM EN-IS	SQuAD-ISQ	59.9	50.6
3	RC-IS-EN	LM EN-IS	NQ-ISQ + SQuAD-ISQ	75.8	67.9
-	RC-IS-IS	LM EN-IS	SQuAD-IS	71.5	70.1
-	RC-IS-IS	IceBERT (IS)	SQuAD-IS	**72.1**	70.6
4	RC-IS-IS	LM EN-IS	NewsQA-IS + SQuAD-IS + NQiI	*67.4	64.8

Table 2: Performance in reading comprehension for a mono- and crosslingual setting. RC-X-Y denotes reading comprehension where the question language is X and the answer language is Y. For fine-tuning in the crosslingual setting (RC-IS-EN) in rows 3, 4 and 5, questions have been translated into Icelandic while the context and answers are in English (step 3) whereas the last three rows correspond to fine-tuning on Icelandic only (step 4). The evaluation data in the last row marked with a (*) is from a combination of the datasets used. The best performance on each task is shown in bold.

that the original DensePhrases model (Lee et al., 2021) had an exact match score of 40.9 on NQ and 39.4 on SQuAD when the query-side encoder was fine-tuned for those datasets, respectively.

The Icelandic open QA system (DensePhrases-IS, from step 6) is evaluated on NQiI as well as datasets suitable for open QA in Icelandic, the Gettu betur corpus (4,569 questions with answer) (Ólafur Páll Geirsson, 2013) and Icelandic Trivia Questions[3] (11,610 questions with answers). We note that these datasets are not guaranteed to contain answers that are present in the Icelandic Wikipedia, but serve as a future baseline for Open QA in Icelandic.

Performance results for the model in the sixth step are shown in Table 3. For comparison, a BM25 + IceBERT-QA result is included. The results are not as good as reported for English systems in, e.g. (Karpukhin et al., 2020), which we currently attribute to the small size of the NQiI dataset.

Finally, we embed the Icelandic Wikipedia for use with CORA (Asai et al., 2021b) using the models released with the paper. The NQiI test dataset is used for evaluation. This method significantly outperforms the one presented in this paper as shown in the last row of Table 3 with F1 28.6 and EM 15.0.

5 Discussion and future work

As noted in the literature review, good results have been achieved in multilingual QA using an answer generator to generate an answer in a selected language (Asai et al., 2021b). For a monolingual setting, our approach provides a way to create an Open QA system without an answer generator as in the original DensePhrases approach.

[3]Available online at `https://github.com/sveinn-steinarsson/is-trivia-questions`

Step	Task	Method	Data	EM	F1	EM top 10	F1 top 10
5	Open QA IS-EN	XL-DensePhr.	NQ-ISQ	11.3	15.2	29.6	38.5
5	Open QA EN-EN	XL-DensePhr.	NQ	14.0	18.9	34.7	45.0
6	Open QA IS-IS	XL-DensePhr.	NQiI	9.7	18.8	26.8	44.6
6	Open QA IS-IS	XL-DensePhr.	G.betur	6.0	8.3	14.8	20.6
6	Open QA IS-IS	XL-DensePhr.	Trivia	5.4	6.9	14.6	18.4
-	Open QA IS-IS	BM25 + IB-QA	NQiI	2.4	17.9	2.4	18.1
-	Open QA IS-IS	CORA	NQiI	15.0	**28.6**	-	-

Table 3: Performance for open QA in a cross-lingual Icelandic and English (DensePhrases-IS-EN) setting and in a monolingual IS-IS setting (DensePhrases-IS). In the cross-lingual setting, the performance on NQ is included for reference. All the models are based on the bilingual model (LM EN-IS) except for the last one, which corresponds to using the IceBERT model along with BM25. We highlight in bold the best performance in Open QA on the NQiI dataset.

The model used in the original DensePhrases is SpanBERT (Joshi et al., 2020) whereas we trained a bilingual RoBERTa (Liu et al., 2019) model that has been proven to be successful for Icelandic. For future work, a bilingual SpanBERT model is likely to improve performance as reported in the original paper.

We also evaluated the CORA method on NQiI and it surpassed our method by a significant margin, highlighting the value of training models in a multilingual manner and using a generative model. CORA was not trained specifically on Icelandic QA although it is based on mT5 which was pre-trained on corpora that includes some Icelandic. The result highlights the potential of crosslingual transfer for QA in low-resource languages.

Finally, we emphasize that the quality of the resulting model of the process presented in this paper is affected by multiple factors. For example, it is related to the performance of the translation method but possibly also to language intricacies. A greater amount of training data for Icelandic QA, along with human translated pairs of questions and contexts would cast of light of the penalty incurred from using MT data. We believe the results can be much better with a larger and higher quality target language QA dataset, noting that, e.g. the answer span labelling in the NQiI is somewhat inconsistent. However, we also believe that QA for Icelandic is challenging, and we encourage others to try it out.

6 Conclusion

We have shown how to build an Open QA system from scratch for Icelandic, a language with very limited original QA resources. We first develop a cross-lingual QA system by taking advantage of English QA-data, a well performing translation model, a bilingual language model and the DensePhrases approach. This system is then adapted for monolingual Open QA. The method is not perfect but shows some promising results.

References

Chris Alberti, Daniel Andor, Emily Pitler, Jacob Devlin, and Michael Collins. 2019. Synthetic QA corpora generation with roundtrip consistency. In *Proceedings of the 57th Annual Meeting of the Association for Computational Linguistics*, pages 6168–6173, Florence, Italy. Association for Computational Linguistics.

Akari Asai, Jungo Kasai, Jonathan Clark, Kenton Lee, Eunsol Choi, and Hannaneh Hajishirzi. 2021a. XOR QA: Cross-lingual Open-Retrieval Question Answering. In *Proceedings of the 2021 Conference of the North American Chapter of the Association for Computational Linguistics: Human Language Technologies*, pages 547–564, Online. Association for Computational Linguistics. 00022.

Akari Asai, Xinyan Yu, Jungo Kasai, and Hanna Hajishirzi. 2021b. One Question Answering Model for Many Languages with Cross-lingual Dense Passage Retrieval. *Advances in Neural Information Processing Systems*, 34. 00002.

Tom Brown, Benjamin Mann, Nick Ryder, Melanie Subbiah, Jared D Kaplan, Prafulla Dhariwal, Arvind Neelakantan, Pranav Shyam, Girish Sastry, Amanda Askell, et al. 2020. Language models are few-shot learners. *Advances in neural information processing systems*, 33:1877–1901.

Jonathan H. Clark, Eunsol Choi, Michael Collins, Dan Garrette, Tom Kwiatkowski, Vitaly Nikolaev, and Jennimaria Palomaki. 2020. TyDi QA: A benchmark for information-seeking question answering in typologically diverse languages. *Transactions of the Association for Computational Linguistics*, 8:454–470.

Alexis Conneau, Kartikay Khandelwal, Naman Goyal, Vishrav Chaudhary, Guillaume Wenzek, Francisco Guzmán, Edouard Grave, Myle Ott, Luke Zettlemoyer, and Veselin Stoyanov. 2020. Unsupervised cross-lingual representation learning at scale. In *Proceedings of the 58th Annual Meeting of the Association for Computational Linguistics*, pages 8440–8451, Online. Association for Computational Linguistics.

Jacob Devlin, Ming-Wei Chang, Kenton Lee, and Kristina Toutanova. 2019. BERT: Pre-training of deep bidirectional transformers for language understanding. In *Proceedings of the 2019 Conference of the North American Chapter of the Association for Computational Linguistics: Human Language Technologies, Volume 1 (Long and Short Papers)*, pages 4171–4186, Minneapolis, Minnesota. Association for Computational Linguistics.

Somil Gupta and Nilesh Khade. 2020. BERT Based Multilingual Machine Comprehension in English and Hindi. *arXiv:2006.01432 [cs]*. 00006 arXiv: 2006.01432.

Kelvin Guu, Kenton Lee, Zora Tung, Panupong Pasupat, and Mingwei Chang. 2020. Retrieval Augmented Language Model Pre-Training. In *Proceedings of the 37th International Conference on Machine Learning*, pages 3929–3938. PMLR. 00053 ISSN: 2640-3498.

Geoffrey Hinton, Oriol Vinyals, and Jeff Dean. 2015. Distilling the knowledge in a neural network.

Jeff Johnson, Matthijs Douze, and Hervé Jégou. 2019. Billion-scale similarity search with gpus. *IEEE Transactions on Big Data*, 7(3):535–547.

Mandar Joshi, Danqi Chen, Yinhan Liu, Daniel S. Weld, Luke Zettlemoyer, and Omer Levy. 2020. SpanBERT: Improving pre-training by representing and predicting spans. *Transactions of the Association for Computational Linguistics*, 8:64–77.

Vladimir Karpukhin, Barlas Oguz, Sewon Min, Patrick Lewis, Ledell Wu, Sergey Edunov, Danqi Chen, and Wen-tau Yih. 2020. Dense passage retrieval for open-domain question answering. In *Proceedings of the 2020 Conference on Empirical Methods in Natural Language Processing (EMNLP)*, pages 6769–6781, Online. Association for Computational Linguistics.

Sosuke Kobayashi. 2018. Homemade bookcorpus. `https://github.com/BIGBALLON/cifar-10-cnn`.

Taku Kudo and John Richardson. 2018. SentencePiece: A simple and language independent subword tokenizer and detokenizer for neural text processing. In *Proceedings of the 2018 Conference on Empirical Methods in Natural Language Processing: System Demonstrations*, pages 66–71, Brussels, Belgium. Association for Computational Linguistics.

Tom Kwiatkowski, Jennimaria Palomaki, Olivia Redfield, Michael Collins, Ankur Parikh, Chris Alberti, Danielle Epstein, Illia Polosukhin, Jacob Devlin, Kenton Lee, Kristina Toutanova, Llion Jones, Matthew Kelcey, Ming-Wei Chang, Andrew M. Dai, Jakob Uszkoreit, Quoc Le, and Slav Petrov. 2019. Natural questions: A benchmark for question answering research. *Transactions of the Association for Computational Linguistics*, 7:452–466.

Jinhyuk Lee, Mujeen Sung, Jaewoo Kang, and Danqi Chen. 2021. Learning dense representations of phrases at scale. In *Proceedings of the 59th Annual Meeting of the Association for Computational Linguistics and the 11th International Joint Conference on Natural Language Processing (Volume 1: Long Papers)*, pages 6634–6647, Online. Association for Computational Linguistics.

Kenton Lee, Ming-Wei Chang, and Kristina Toutanova. 2019. Latent retrieval for weakly supervised open domain question answering. In *Proceedings of the 57th Annual Meeting of the Association for Computational Linguistics*, pages 6086–6096, Florence, Italy. Association for Computational Linguistics.

Jimmy Lin, Rodrigo Nogueira, and Andrew Yates. 2021. Pretrained Transformers for Text Ranking: BERT and Beyond. *Synthesis Lectures on Human Language Technologies*, 14(4):1–325. 00103 Publisher: Morgan & Claypool Publishers.

Yinhan Liu, Myle Ott, Naman Goyal, Jingfei Du, Mandar Joshi, Danqi Chen, Omer Levy, Mike Lewis, Luke Zettlemoyer, and Veselin Stoyanov. 2019. Roberta: A robustly optimized BERT pretraining approach. *CoRR*, abs/1907.11692.

Mehrad Moradshahi, Giovanni Campagna, Sina Semnani, Silei Xu, and Monica Lam. 2020. Localizing open-ontology qa semantic parsers in a day using machine translation. In *Proceedings of the 2020 Conference on Empirical Methods in Natural Language Processing (EMNLP)*, pages 5970–5983.

Benjamin Muller, Luca Soldaini, Rik Koncel-Kedziorski, Eric Lind, and Alessandro Moschitti. 2021. Cross-Lingual GenQA: A Language-Agnostic Generative Question Answering Approach for Open-Domain Question Answering. *arXiv:2110.07150 [cs]*. 00000 arXiv: 2110.07150.

Susumu Okazawa. 2021. Swedish translation of squad2.0. `https://github.com/susumu2357/SQuAD_v2_sv`.

Colin Raffel, Noam Shazeer, Adam Roberts, Katherine Lee, Sharan Narang, Michael Matena, Yanqi Zhou, Wei Li, and Peter J. Liu. 2020. Exploring the limits of transfer learning with a unified text-to-text transformer. *Journal of Machine Learning Research*, 21(140):1–67.

Stephen E Robertson, Steve Walker, Susan Jones, Micheline M Hancock-Beaulieu, and Mike Gatford.

1995. Okapi at trec-3. *Nist Special Publication Sp*, 109:109.

Anna Rogers, Matt Gardner, and Isabelle Augenstein. 2021. QA Dataset Explosion: A Taxonomy of NLP Resources for Question Answering and Reading Comprehension. *arXiv:2107.12708 [cs]*. 00008 arXiv: 2107.12708.

Tom Sherborne, Yumo Xu, and Mirella Lapata. 2020. Bootstrapping a crosslingual semantic parser. In *Findings of the Association for Computational Linguistics: EMNLP 2020*, pages 499–517.

Wissam Siblini, Charlotte Pasqual, Axel Lavielle, Mohamed Challal, and Cyril Cauchois. 2021. Multilingual Question Answering from Formatted Text applied to Conversational Agents. *arXiv:1910.04659 [cs]*. 00007 arXiv: 1910.04659.

Haukur Barri Símonarson, Vésteinn Snæbjarnarson, Pétur Orri Ragnarson, Haukur Jónsson, and Vilhjalmur Thorsteinsson. 2021. Miðeind's WMT 2021 submission. In *Proceedings of the Sixth Conference on Machine Translation*, pages 136–139, Online. Association for Computational Linguistics.

Vésteinn Snæbjarnarson, Bergur Tareq Tamimi Einarsson, Ingibjörg Iða Auðunardóttir, Unnar Ingi Sæmundsson, Hildur Bjarnadóttir, Helgi Valur Gunnarsson, and Hafsteinn Einarsson. 2021. NQiI - natural questions in icelandic - v1.0. CLARIN-IS.

Vésteinn Snæbjarnarson and Hafsteinn Einarsson. 2022. Natural questions in icelandic. In *Proceedings of the 13th International Conference on Language Resources and Evaluation (LREC 2022)*, Marseille, France.

Vésteinn Snæbjarnarson, Haukur Barri Símonarson, Pétur Orri Ragnarsson, Svanhvít Lilja Ingólfsdóttir, Haukur Páll Jónsson, Vilhjálmur Þorsteinsson, and Hafsteinn Einarsson. 2022. A warm start and a clean crawled corpus – a recipe for good language models. In *Proceedings of the 13th International Conference on Language Resources and Evaluation (LREC 2022)*, Marseille, France.

Adam Trischler, Tong Wang, Xingdi Yuan, Justin Harris, Alessandro Sordoni, Philip Bachman, and Kaheer Suleman. 2017. NewsQA: A machine comprehension dataset. In *Proceedings of the 2nd Workshop on Representation Learning for NLP*, pages 191–200, Vancouver, Canada. Association for Computational Linguistics.

Ashish Vaswani, Noam Shazeer, Niki Parmar, Jakob Uszkoreit, Llion Jones, Aidan N Gomez, Łukasz Kaiser, and Illia Polosukhin. 2017. Attention is all you need. In *Advances in Neural Information Processing Systems*, volume 30. Curran Associates, Inc.

Fengbin Zhu, Wenqiang Lei, Chao Wang, Jianming Zheng, Soujanya Poria, and Tat-Seng Chua. 2021. Retrieving and reading: A comprehensive survey on open-domain question answering. *CoRR*, abs/2101.00774.

Ólafur Páll Geirsson. 2013. Iceqa: Developing a Question Answering System for Icelandic.

A Answer span alignment

We apply a heuristic matching method to align the translated questions with spans in the translated context. The method does not rely on more complex word alignment methods between the source text and the translated text but is based on translating the answer and looking up the translated answer in the translated answer context using a fuzzy Levenshtein distance.

In our matching method, we search for the translated answer and then the original answer in the translated context. If either is found, we label the matched string as the answer. Otherwise, we apply a fuzzy matching approach. Denote by w_t the number of words in the translated answer. We perform a sliding window search over all contiguous sequences of words in the translated context that contain w_t, $w_t - 1$, $w_t + 1$ many words. We label and return a sequence as the answer in the translated setting if the Levenshtein distance between the translated answer and the sequence exceeds 0.9. If no sequence is sufficiently similar to the translated answer, we repeat this sliding window search using the original answer instead of the translated answer. If neither search was successful, we would discard the translated question-context pair from training in the fourth step.

Only 6,893 questions, 4.8% of the total data, were discarded from the SQuAD dataset using the matching method since an answer span could not be labelled. 11,478 questions, 9.6% of the total, were discarded from the NewsQA dataset. The only publicly released reading-comprehension style Icelandic dataset for QA, Natural Questions in Icelandic (NQiI) (Snæbjarnarson et al., 2021), is also used for training.

Multilingual Event Linking to Wikidata

Adithya Pratapa, Rishubh Gupta, Teruko Mitamura
Language Technologies Institute
Carnegie Mellon University
{vpratapa,rishubhg,teruko}@andrew.cmu.edu

Abstract

We present a task of multilingual linking of events to a knowledge base. We automatically compile a large-scale dataset for this task, comprising of 1.8M mentions across 44 languages referring to over 10.9K events from Wikidata. We propose two variants of the event linking task: 1) multilingual, where event descriptions are from the same language as the mention, and 2) crosslingual, where all event descriptions are in English. On the two proposed tasks, we compare multiple event linking systems including BM25+ (Lv and Zhai, 2011a) and multilingual adaptations of the biencoder and crossencoder architectures from BLINK (Wu et al., 2020). In our experiments on the two task variants, we find both biencoder and crossencoder models significantly outperform the BM25+ baseline. Our results also indicate that the crosslingual task is in general more challenging than the multilingual task. To test the out-of-domain generalization of the proposed linking systems, we additionally create a Wikinews-based evaluation set. We present qualitative analysis highlighting various aspects captured by the proposed dataset, including the need for temporal reasoning over context and tackling diverse event descriptions across languages.[1]

1 Introduction

Language grounding refers to linking concepts (e.g., events/entities) to a context (e.g., a knowledge base) (Chandu et al., 2021). Knowledge base (KB) grounding is a key component of information extraction stack and is well-studied for linking entity references to KBs like Wikipedia (Ji and Grishman, 2011). In this work, we present a new multilingual task that involves linking *event* references to Wikidata KB.[2]

Event linking differs from entity's as it involves taking into account the event participants as well as its temporal and spatial attributes. Nothman et al. (2012) defines event linking as connecting event references from news articles to a news archive consisting of first reports of the events. Similar to entities, event linking is typically restricted to prominent or report-worthy events. In this work, we use a subset of Wikidata as our event KB and link mentions from Wikipedia/Wikinews articles.[3] Figure 1 illustrates our event linking methodology.

Event linking is closely related to the more commonly studied task of cross-document event coreference (CDEC). The goal in CDEC is to understand the identity relationship between event mentions. This identity is often complicated by subevent and membership relations among events (Pratapa et al., 2021). Nothman et al. (2012) proposed event linking as an alternative to coreference that helps ground report-worthy events to a KB. They showed linking helps avoid the traditional bottlenecks seen with the event coreference task. We postulate *linking to be a complementary task to coreference*, where the first mention of an event in a document is typically linked or grounded to the KB and its relationship with the rest of the mentions from the document is captured via coreference. Additionally, due to computational constraints, coreference resolution is often restricted to a small batch of documents. Grounding, however, can be performed efficiently using dense retrieval methods (Wu et al., 2020) and is scalable to any large multi-document corpora.

Grounding event references to a KB has many downstream applications. First, event identity encompasses multiple aspects such as spatio-temporal context and participants. These aspects typically spread across many documents, and KB grounding helps construct a shared global account for each event. Second, grounding is a complementary task to coreference. In contrast to coreference,

[1] https://github.com/adithya7/xlel-wd

[2] www.wikidata.org

[3] We define *mention* as the textual expression that refers to an *event* from the KB.

Proceedings of the Workshop on Multilingual Information Access (MIA), pages 37 - 58
July 15, 2022 ©2022 Association for Computational Linguistics

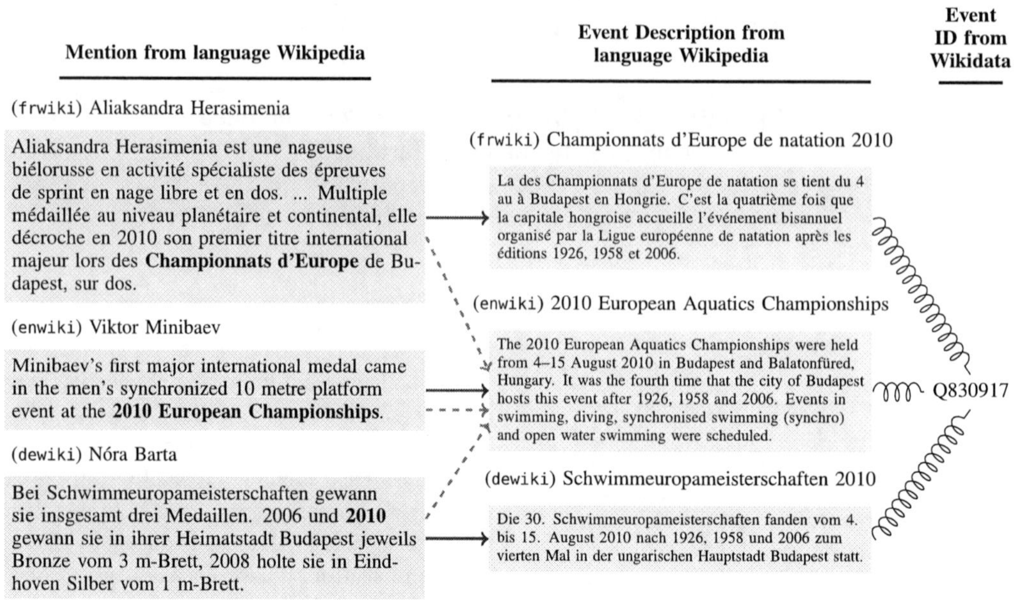

Figure 1: An illustration of multilingual event linking with Wikidata as our interlingua. Mentions from French, English and German Wikipedia (column 1) are linked to the same event from Wikidata (column 3). The title and descriptions for the event Q830917 are compiled from the corresponding language Wikipedias (column 2). The solid blue arrows (⟶) presents our multilingual task, to link `lgwiki` mention to event using `lgwiki` description. The dashed red arrows (- ->) showcases the crosslingual task, to link `lgwiki` mention to event using `enwiki` description.

event grounding formulated as the nearest neighbor search leads to efficient scaling.

For the event linking task, we present a new multilingual dataset that grounds mentions from multilingual Wikipedia/Wikinews articles to the corresponding event in Wikidata. Figure 1 presents an example from our dataset that links mentions from three languages to the same Wikidata item. To construct this dataset, we make use of the hyperlinks in Wikipedia/Wikinews articles. These links connect anchor texts (like '2010 European Championships' or "Championnats d'Europe") in context to the corresponding event Wikipedia page ('2010 European Aquatics Championships' or "Championnats d'Europe de natation 2010"). We further connect the event Wikipedia page to its Wikidata item ('Q830917'), facilitating multilingual grounding of mentions to KB events. We use the title and first paragraph from the language Wikipedia pages as our event descriptions (column 2 in Figure 1).

Such hyperlinks have previously been explored for named entity disambiguation (Eshel et al., 2017), entity linking (Logan et al., 2019) and cross-document coreference of events (Eirew et al., 2021) and entities (Singh et al., 2012). Our work is closely related to the English CDEC work of Eirew et al. (2021), but we view the task as linking instead of coreference. This is primarily due to the fact that most hyperlinked event mentions are prominent and typically cover a broad range of subevents, conflicting directly with the notion of coreference. Additionally, our dataset is multilingual, covering 44 languages, with Wikidata serving as our *interlingua*. Botha et al. (2020) is a related work from entity linking literature that covers entity references from multilingual Wikinews articles to Wikidata.

We use the proposed dataset to develop multilingual event linking systems. We present two variants to the linking task, multilingual and crosslingual. In the multilingual task, mentions from individual language Wikipedia are linked to the events from Wikidata with descriptions taken from the same language (see solid blue arrows (⟶) in Figure 1). The crosslingual task requires systems to use English event description irrespective of the mention language (see dashed red arrows (- ->) in Figure 1). In both tasks, the end goal is to identify the Wikidata ID (e.g. Q830917). Following prior work on entity linking (Logeswaran et al., 2019), we adopt a *zero-shot* approach in all of our experiments. We present results using a retrieve+rank approach based on Wu et al. (2020) that utilizes BERT-based biencoder and crossencoder for our multilingual event linking task. We experiment with two multilingual encoders, mBERT (Devlin et al., 2019) and XLM-RoBERTa (Conneau et al., 2020) and we find biencoder and crossencoder significantly outperform a tf-idf-based baseline, BM25+ (Lv and Zhai, 2011a). Our results indicate the crosslingual task is more challenging than the multilingual task, possibly due to differences in typology of source and target languages. Our key contributions are,

- We propose a new multilingual NLP task that involves linking multilingual text mentions to a knowledge base of events.
- We release a large-scale dataset for the zero-shot multilingual event linking task by compiling mentions from Wikipedia and their grounding to Wikidata. Our dataset captures 1.8M mentions across 44 languages refering to over 10K events. To test out-of-domain generalization, we additionally create a small Wikinews-based evaluation set.
- We present two evaluation setups, multilingual and crosslingual event linking. We show competitive results across languages using a retrieve and rank methodology.

2 Related Work

Our focus task of multilingual event linking shares resemblance with entity/event linking, entity/event coreference and other multilingual NLP tasks.

2.1 Entity Linking

Our work utilizes hyperlinks between Wikipedia pages to identify event references. This idea was previously explored in multiple entity related works, both for dataset creation (Mihalcea and Csomai, 2007; Botha et al., 2020) and data augmentation during training (Bunescu and Paşca, 2006; Nothman et al., 2008). Another related line of work utilized hyperlinks from general web pages to Wikipedia articles for the tasks of cross-document entity coreference (Singh et al., 2012) and named entity disambiguation (Eshel et al., 2017). Sil et al. (2012); Logeswaran et al. (2019) highlighted the need for zero-shot evaluation. We adopt this standard by using a disjoint sets of events for training and evaluation (see subsection 3.2).

2.2 Event Linking

Event linking is important for downstream tasks like narrative understanding. For instance, consider a prominent event like '2020 Summer Olympics'. This event has had a large influx of articles in multiple languages. It is often useful to ground the references to specific prominent subevents in KB. Some examples of such events from Wikidata are "Swimming at the 2020 Summer Olympics – Women's 100 metre freestyle" (Q64513990) and "Swimming at the 2020 Summer Olympics – Men's 100 metre backstroke" (Q64514005). Event linking task while important is albeit less explored. Nothman et al. (2012) linked event-referring expressions from news articles to a news archive. These links are made to the first-reported news article regarding the event. In contrast, we focus on prominent events that have a corresponding Wikidata item. Concurrent to our work, Yu et al. (2021) presents a dataset for linking event mentions to Wikipedia. Similar to our work, they utilize hyperlinks within Wikipedia pages but are restricted to only English. They also create a newswire based evaluation set from NYTimes articles. In contrast, our work utilizes events from Wikidata and covers a larger set of languages. While our work also includes a newswire based evaluation set from Wikinews, it does not explicitly target verb mentions.

2.3 Event Coreference

Event coreference resolution is closely related to event grounding but assumes a stricter notion of identity between mentions (Nothman et al., 2012). Multiple cross-document coreference resolution works made use of Wikipedia (Eirew et al., 2021) and Wikinews (Minard et al., 2016; Pratapa et al., 2021) for dataset collection. Minard et al. (2016) obtained human translations of English Wikinews articles to create a crosslingual event coreference dataset. In contrast, our dataset uses the original multilingual event descriptions written by language Wikipedia contributors (column 2 in Figure 1).

2.4 Multilingual Tasks

A majority of the existing NLP datasets (/systems) cater to a fraction of world languages (Joshi et al., 2020). There is a growing effort on creating more multilingual benchmarks for tasks like natural language inference (XNLI; Conneau et al. (2018)), question answering (TyDi-QA; Clark et al. (2020), XOR QA; Asai et al. (2021)), linking (Mewsli-9; Botha et al. (2020)) as well as comprehensive evaluations (XTREME-R; Ruder et al. (2021)). To the best of our knowledge, our work presents the first benchmark for multilingual event linking.

	Train	Dev	Test	Total
Events	8653	1090	1204	10947
Event Sequences	6758	844	846	8448
Mentions	1.44M	165K	190K	1.8M
Languages	44	44	44	44

Table 1: Dataset Summary

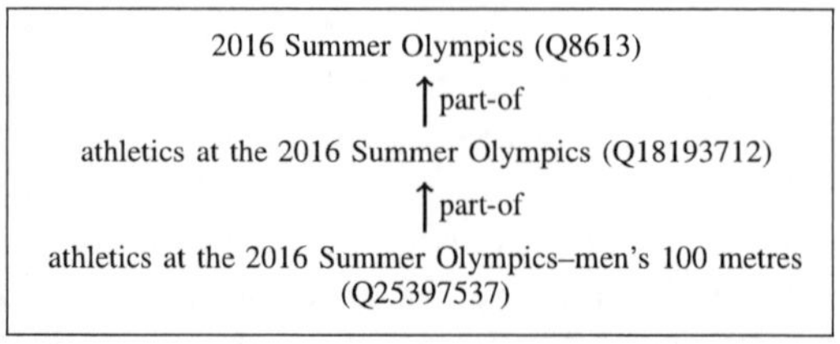

Figure 2: An illustration of event hierarchy in Wikidata.

3 Multilingual Event Linking Dataset

Our data collection methodology is closely related to the zero shot entity linking work of Botha et al. (2020) but we take a top-down approach starting from Wikidata. Eirew et al. (2021) identified event pages from English Wikipedia by processing the infobox elements. However, we found relying on Wikidata for event identification to be more robust. Additionally, Wikidata serves as our *interlingua* that connects mentions from numerous languages.

3.1 Dataset Compilation

To compile our dataset, we follow a three-stage pipeline, 1) identify Wikidata items that correspond to events, 2) for each Wikidata event, collect links to language Wikipedia articles and 3) iterate through all the language Wikipedia dumps to collect mention spans that refer to these events.

Wikidata Event Identification: Events are typically associated with time, location and participants, distinguishing them from entities. To identify events from the large pool of Wikidata (WD) items, we make use of the properties listed on WD.[4] Specifically, we consider a WD item to be a candidate event if it contains the following two properties, temporal[5] and spatial[6]. We perform additional postprocessing on this candidate event set to remove non-events like empires (Roman Empire: Q2277), missions (Surveyor 7: Q774594), TV series (Deception: Q30180283) and historic places (French North Africa: Q352061).[7] Each event in our final set has caused a state change and is grounded in a spatio-temporal context. This distinguishes our set of events from the rest of the items from Wikidata. Following the terminology from Weischedel et al. (2013), these KB events can be characterized as *eventive nouns*.

A Note on WD Hierarchy: WD is a rich structured KB and we observed many instances of hierarchical relationship between our candidate events. See Figure 2 for an example. While this hierarchy adds an interesting challenge to the event grounding task, we observed multiple instances of inconsistency in links. Specifically, we observed references to parent item (Q18193712) even though the child item (Q25397537) was the most appropriate link in context. Therefore, in our dataset, we only include *leaf nodes* as our candidate event set (e.g. Q25397537). This allows us to focus on most atomic events from Wikidata. Expanding the label set to include the hierarchy is an interesting direction for future work.

Wikidata ⇝ Wikipedia: WD items have pointers to the corresponding language Wikipedia articles.[8] We make use of these pointers to identify Wikipedia articles describing our candidate WD events. Figure 1 illustrates this through the coiled pointers (⇝) for the three languages. We make use of the event's Wikipedia article title and its first paragraph as the description for the WD event. Each language version of a Wikipedia article is typically written by independent contributors, so the event descriptions vary across languages.

Mention Identification: Wikipedia articles are often connected through hyperlinks. We iterate through each language Wikipedia and collect anchor texts of hyperlinks to the event Wikipedia pages (column 1 in Figure 1). We retain both the anchor text and the surrounding paragraph (context). Notably, the anchor text can occasionally be a temporal expression or location relevant to the event. In the German mention from Figure 1, the anchor text '2010' links to the event Q830917 (2010 European Aquatics Championships). This event link can be infered by using the context ('Schwimmeuropameisterschaften': European Aquatics Cham-

[4] wikidata.org/wiki/Wikidata:List_of_properties

[5] duration OR point-in-time OR (start-time AND end-time)

[6] location OR coordinate-location

[7] see Table 8 in subsection A.2 of Appendix for the full list of exclusion properties.

[8] https://meta.wikimedia.org/wiki/List_of_Wikipedias

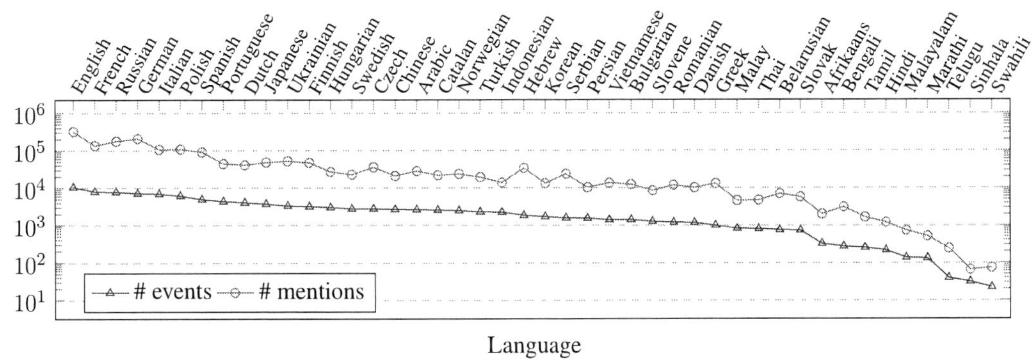

Figure 3: Statistics of events and mentions per language in the proposed dataset. The languages are sorted in the decreasing order of # events. The counts on y-axis are presented in log scale.

pionships). In fact, the neighboring span '2006' refers to a different event from Wikidata (Q612454: 2006 European Aquatics Championships). We use the September 2021 XML dumps of language Wikipedias and the October 2021 dump of Wikidata. We use Wikiextractor tool (Attardi, 2015) to extract text content from the Wikipedia dumps. We retain the hyperlinks in article texts for use in mention identification. Overall, the mentions in our datasets can be categorized into the following types, 1) eventive noun (like the KB event), 2) verbal, 3) location and 4) temporal expression. Such a diversity in the nature of mentions also differentiates the event linking task from the standard named entity linking or disambiguation.

Postprocessing: To link a mention to its event, the context should contain the necessary temporal information. For instance, its important to be able to differentiate between links to '2010 European Aquatics Championships' vs '2012 European Aquatics Championships'. Therefore, we heuristically remove mention (+context) if it completely misses the temporal expressions from the corresponding language Wikipedia title and description. Additionally, we also remove mentions if their contexts are either too short or too long (<100, >2000 characters). We also prune WD events under the following conditions: 1) only contains mentions from a single language, 2) >50% of the mentions match their corresponding language Wikipedia title (i.e., low diversity), 3) very few mentions (<30). Table 1 presents the overall statistics of our dataset. The full list of languages with their event and mention counts are presented in Figure 3. Each WD event on average has mention references from 9 languages indicating the highly multilingual nature of our dataset. See Table 9 in Appendix for details on the geneological information for the chosen languages. We chose our final set of languages by maximizing for the diversity in language typology, language resources (in event-related tasks and general) and the availability of content on Wikipedia. Wikipedia texts and Wikidata KB are available under CC BY-SA 3.0 and CC0 1.0 license respectively. We will release our dataset under CC BY-SA 3.0.

Wikinews ⇝ Wikidata: To test the out-of-domain generalization, we additionally prepare a small evaluation set based on Wikinews articles.[9] Inspired by prior work on multilingual entity linking (Botha et al., 2020), we collect hyperlinks from event mentions in multilingual Wikinews articles to Wikidata. We restrict the set of events to the previously identified 10.9k events from Wikidata (Table 1). We again use Wikiextractor tool to collect raw texts from March 2022 dumps of all language Wikinews. We identify hyperlinks to Wikipedia pages or Wikinews categories that describe the events from Wikidata.

Table 2 presents the overall statistics of our Wikinews-based evaluation set. This set is much smaller in size compared to Wikipedia-based dataset primarily due to significantly smaller footprint of Wikinews.[10] Following the taxonomy from Logeswaran et al. (2019), we present two evaluation settings, cross-domain and zero-shot. Cross-domain evaluation gauges model generalization to unseen domains (newswire). Zero-shot evaluation

[9] `https://www.wikinews.org`

[10] For comparison, English Wikinews contains 21K articles while English Wikipedia contains 6.5M pages.

	Cross-domain	Zero-shot
Events	802	149
Mentions	2562	437
Languages	27	21

Table 2: Summary of Wikinews-based evaluation set. We present two evaluation settings, cross-domain and zero-shot. Zero-shot evaluation set is a subset of cross-domain set as it only includes events from dev and test splits of Wikipedia-based evaluation set (Table 1).

tests on unseen domain and unseen events.[11]

Unlike Wikipedia, Wikinews articles contains meta information such as news article title and publication date that help provide broader context for the document. In section 5, we perform ablations studies to see the impact of this meta information.

Mention Distribution: Following the categories from Logeswaran et al. (2019), we compute mention distributions in the following four buckets, 1) high overlap: mention span is the same as the event title, 2) multiple categories: event title includes an additional disambiguation phrase, 3) ambiguous substring: mention span is a substring of the event title, and 4) low overlap: all other cases. For the Wikipedia-based dataset, the category distribution is 22%, 6%, 14%, and 58%.[12] For the Wikinews-based dataset, the category distribution is 18%, 4%, 6%, and 72%. We also computed the fraction of mentions that are temporal expressions. We used HeidelTime library (Strötgen and Gertz, 2015) for 25 languages and found 6% of the spans in the dev set are temporal expressions.

3.2 Task Definition

Given a mention and a pool of events from a KB, the task is to identify the mention's reference in the KB. For instance, the three mentions from column 1 in Figure 1 are to be linked to the Wikidata event, Q830917. Following Logeswaran et al. (2019), we assume an in-KB evaluation approach, therefore, every mention refers to a valid event from the KB (Wikidata). We collect descriptions for the Wikidata events from all the corresponding language Wikipedias. The article title and the first paragraph constitute the event description. This results in multilingual descriptions for each event (column 2 in Figure 1). We propose two variants of the event linking task, *multilingual* and *crosslingual*, depending on the source and target languages. We define the input mention and event description as source and target respectively. The event label itself (e.g. Q830917) is language-agnostic.

Multilingual Event Linking: Given a mention from language $\mathcal{L}$, the linker searches through the event candidates from the same language $\mathcal{L}$ to identify the correct link. The source and target language are the same in this task. The size of event candidate pool varies across languages (Figure 3), thereby varying the task difficulty.

Crosslingual Event Linking: Given a mention from any language $\mathcal{L}$, the linker searches the entire pool of event candidates to identify the link. Here, we restrict the target language to English, requiring the linker to only make use of the English descriptions for candidate events. Note that, all the events in our dataset have English descriptions.

Creating Splits: The train, dev and test distributions are presented in Table 1. The two tasks, multilingual and crosslingual share the same splits except for the difference in target language descriptions. Following the standard in entity linking literature, we focus on the zero-shot linking, that requires the evaluation and train events to be completely disjoint. Due to prevalence of event sequences in Wikidata, a simple random split is not sufficient.[13] We add an additional constraint that event sequences are disjoint between splits. Systems need to perform temporal and spatial reasoning to distinguish between events within a sequence, making the task more challenging.

4 Modeling

In this section, we present our systems for multilingual and crosslingual event linking to Wikidata. We follow the entity linking system BLINK (Wu et al., 2020) to adapt a retrieve and rank approach. Given a mention, we first use a BERT-based biencoder to retrieve top-k events from the candidate pool. Then, we use a crossencoder to rerank these top-k candidates and identify the best event label. Additionally, following the baselines from entity linking literature, we also experiment with BM25 as a candidate retrieval method.

[11] we consider dev and test events from Table 1 as unseen.

[12] The disambiguation phrase is typically a suffix in the title for English (Logeswaran et al., 2019), but in our multilingual setting, it can be anywhere in the title.

[13] 2008, 2010, 2012 iterations of Aquatics Championships from Figure 1

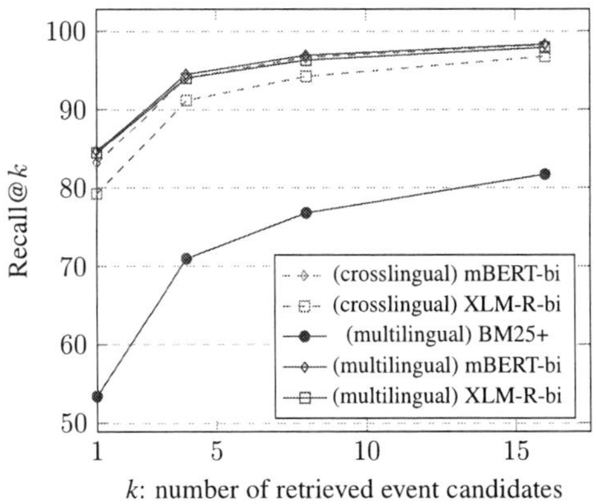

Figure 4: Retrieval performance on dev split.

Model	Multilingual		Crosslingual	
	Dev	Test	Dev	Test
BM25+	53.4	50.1	–	–
mBERT-bi	84.7	84.6	83.2	**83.9**
XLM-R-bi	84.5	84.3	79.3	79.1
mBERT-cross	89.8	**89.3**	81.3	73.9
XLM-R-cross	88.8	87.3	81.0	75.6

Table 3: Event Linking Accuracy. For biencoder models, we report Recall@1.

4.1 BM25

BM25 is a commonly used tf-idf based ranking function and a competitive baseline for entity linking. We explore three variants of BM25, BM25Okapi (Robertson et al., 1994), BM25+ (Lv and Zhai, 2011a) and BM25L (Lv and Zhai, 2011b). We use the implementation of Brown (2020) with mention as query and event description as documents.[14] Since BM25 is a bag-of-words method, we only use in the multilingual task. To create the documents, we use the concatenation of title and description of events. For the query, we experiment with increasing context window sizes of 8, 16, 32, 64 and 128 along with a mention-only baseline.

4.2 Retrieve+Rank

We adapt the standard entity linking architecture (Wu et al., 2020) to the event linking task. This is a two-stage pipeline, a retriever (biencoder) and a ranker (crossencoder).

Biencoder: Using two multilingual transformers, we independently encode the context and event candidates. The input context is constructed as `[CLS]` left context `[MENTION_START]` mention `[MENTION_END]` right context `[SEP]`. Candidate events use a concatenation of event's title and description, `[CLS]` title `[EVT]` description `[SEP]`. In both cases, we use the final layer `[CLS]` token representation as our embedding. For each context, we score the event candidates by taking a dot product between the two embeddings. We follow prior work (Lerer et al., 2019; Wu et al., 2020) to make use of in-batch random negatives during training. At inference, we run a nearest neighbour search to find the top-k candidates.

Model	Multilingual		Crosslingual	
	CD	ZS	CD	ZS
BM25+	53.5	58.6	-	-
mBERT-bi	81.2	76.7	85.4	78.0
XLM-R-bi	82.2	76.7	82.6	76.4
mBERT-cross	90.1	84.4	89.3	76.2
XLM-R-cross	89.7	84.4	88.9	76.0

Table 4: Event linking accuracy on Wikinews test set. CD and ZS indicate cross-domain and zero-shot.

Crossencoder: In our crossencoder, the input constitutes a concatenation of the context and a given event candidate.[15] We take the `[CLS]` token embedding from last layer and pass it through a classification layer. We run crossencoder training only on the top-k event candidates retrieved by the biencoder. During training, we optimize a softmax loss to predict the gold event candidate within the retrieved top-k. For inference, we predict the highest scoring context-candidate tuple from the top-k candidates. We experiment with two multilingual encoders, mBERT (Devlin et al., 2019) and XLM-RoBERTa (Conneau et al., 2020), we refer to the bi- and cross-encoder configurations as mBERT-bi, XLM-RoBERTa-bi and mBERT-cross, XLM-RoBERTa-cross. For crossencoder training and inference, we use the retrieval results from the same BERT-based biencoder.[16]

5 Evaluation

We present our results on the development and test splits of the proposed dataset. In our experi-

[14] To tokenize text across the 44 languages, we used bert-base-multilingual-uncased tokenizer from Huggingface.

[15] `[CLS]` left context `[MENTION_START]` mention `[MENTION_END]` right context `[SEP]` title `[EVT]` description `[SEP]`

[16] see section A.3 in Appendix for other details.

Mention Context: At the 2000 Summer Olympics in Sydney, Sitnikov competed only in two swimming events. ... Three days later, in the **100 m freestyle**, Sitnikov placed fifty-third on the morning prelims. ...
Predicted Label: Swimming at the 2008 Summer Olympics – Men's 100 metre freestyle
Gold Label: Swimming at the 2000 Summer Olympics – Men's 100 metre freestyle

Mention Context: ... war er bei der Oscarverleihung 1935 erstmals für einen Oscar für den besten animierten Kurzfilm nominiert. Eine weitere Nominierung in dieser Kategorie erhielt er **1938** für "The Little Match Girl" (1937).
Predicted Label: The 9th Academy Awards were held on March 4, 1937, ...
Gold Label: The 10th Academy Awards were originally scheduled ... but due to ... were held on March 10, 1938, ..

Mention Context: Ivanova won the silver medal at the 1978 World Junior Championships. She made her senior World debut at the **1979 World Championships**, finishing 18th. Ivanova was 16th at the 1980 Winter Olympics.
Predicted Label: FIBT World Championships 1979
Gold Label: 1979 World Figure Skating Championships

Mention Context: ...攝津號與其姐妹艦河號於1914年10月至11月間參與了青島戰役的最後階段...
Predicted Label: Battle of the Yellow Sea
Gold Label (English): Siege of Tsingtao: The siege of Tsingtao (or Tsingtau) was the attack on the German port of Tsingtao (now Qingdao) ...
Gold Label (Chinese): 青島戰役（，）是第一次世界大戰初期日本進攻國膠州灣殖民地及其首府青島的一場戰役，也是唯一的一場戰役。

Table 5: Examples of errors by the event linking system.

ments, we use bert-base-multilingual-uncased and xlm-roberta-base from Huggingface transformers (Wolf et al., 2020). For the multilingual task, even though the candidate set is partly different between languages, we share the model weights across languages. We believe this weight sharing helps in improving the performance on low-resource languages (Arivazhagan et al., 2019). We follow the standard metrics from prior work on entity linking, both for retrieval and reranking. **Recall@*k*** measures fraction of contexts where the gold event is contained in the top-k retrieved candidates. **Accuracy** measures fraction of contexts where the predicted event candidate matches the gold candidate. We use the unnormalized accuracy score from Logeswaran et al. (2019) that evaluates the overall end-to-end performance (retrieve+rank).

5.1 Results

Figure 4 presents the retrieval results on dev split for both multilingual and crosslingual tasks. The biencoder models significantly outperform the best BM25 configuration, BM25+ (with a context window of 16).[17] The performance is mostly similar for k=8 and k=16 for both biencoder models, therefore, we select k=8 for our crossencoder experiments.[18] Table 3 presents the accuracy scores for the crossencoder models and R@1 scores for retrieval methods. On the multilingual task, mBERT crossencoder model performs the best and significantly better than the corresponding biencoder model. However, on the crosslingual task, mBERT biencoder performs the best. As expected, the crosslingual task is more challenging than the multilingual task. Due to the large number of model parameters, all of our reported results were based on a single training run.

We also measure the cross-domain and zero-shot performance of these systems on the proposed Wikinews evaluation set (section 3.1). As seen in Table 4, we notice good cross-domain but moderate zero-shot transfer. This highlights that unseen events from unseen domains present a considerable challenge. We noticed further gains (4-12%) when the meta information (date and title) is included with the context. Our ablation studies showed that this gain is primarily due to article date.[19]

5.2 Analysis

Performance by Language: Multilingual and crosslingual tasks have three major differences: 1) source & target language, 2) language-specific descriptions can be more informative than English descriptions, and 3) candidate pool varies language (see Figure 3). While the performance is largely the same across languages, we noticed slightly lower crosslingual performance, especially for medium and low-resource languages.[20]

We also perform qualitative analysis of errors made by our mBERT-based biencoder models on multilingual and crosslingual tasks. We summarize

[17] For a detailed comparison of various configurations of BM25 baseline, refer to Figure 5 in Appendix.

[18] see Table 6 in Appendix for Recall@8 scores for all the configurations.

[19] see section A.3 in Appendix for full results.

[20] see Figure 8 and Figure 9 in Appendix

our observations from this analysis below,

Temporal Reasoning: The event linker occasionally performs insufficient temporal reasoning in the context (see example 1 in Table 5). Since our dataset contains numerous event sequences, such temporal reasoning is often important.

Temporal and Spatial expressions: In cases where the anchor text is a temporal or spatial expression, we found the system sometimes struggle to link to the event even if the link can be infered given the context information (see example 2 in Table 5). We believe these examples will also serve as interesting challenge for future work on our dataset.

Event Descriptions: Crosslingual system occasionally struggles with the English description. In example 4 from Table 5, we notice the mention matches exactly with the language Wikipedia title but it struggles with English description. Therefore, depending on the event, we hypothesize that language-specific event descriptions can sometimes be more informative than the English description.

Dataset Errors: We found instances where the context doesn't provide sufficient information needed for grounding (see example 3 in Table 5). Albeit uncommon, we found a few cases where the human annotated hyperlinks in Wikipedia can sometimes be incorrect.[21]

5.3 Discussion

Retrieve+rank based methods have been effective for entity linking tasks (Wu et al., 2020; Botha et al., 2020). Our results indicate that the same retrieve+rank approach is useful for the task of event linking. However, our zero-shot results on Wikinews hint toward potential challenges in adapting to new domains. Additionally, as described above, event linking presents added challenges in dealing with temporal/spatial expressions and temporal reasoning. For further analysis, it would be interesting to contrast the performance differences between planned (e.g., sports competitions) and unplanned (e.g., wars) events.

6 Conclusion & Future Work

We present the task of multilingual event linking to Wikidata. To support this task, we first compile a dictionary of events from Wikidata using temporal and spatial properties. We prepare descriptions for these events from multilingual Wikipedia pages. We then identify a large collection of inlinks from various language Wikipedia. Depending on the language of event description, we present two variants of the task, multilingual (`lg⟶lg`) and crosslingual (`lg-->en`). Furthermore, to test cross-domain generalization we create a small evaluation set based on Wikinews articles. Our results using a retrieve+rank approach indicate that the crosslingual task is more challenging than the multilingual.

Event linking task has multiple interesting future directions. First, the Wikidata-based event dictionary can be expanded to include hierarchical event structures (Figure 2). Since events are inherently hierarchical, this will present a more realistic challenge for the linking systems. Second, mention coverage of our dataset can be expanded to include more verbal events. Third, event linking systems can be improved with better temporal reasoning and improved handling of temporal and spatial expressions. Fourth, the Wikidata-based event dictionary can be expanded to include events that do not contain any English Wikipedia descriptions.

References

N. Arivazhagan, Ankur Bapna, Orhan Firat, Dmitry Lepikhin, Melvin Johnson, Maxim Krikun, Mia Xu Chen, Yuan Cao, George F. Foster, Colin Cherry, Wolfgang Macherey, Z. Chen, and Yonghui Wu. 2019. Massively multilingual neural machine translation in the wild: Findings and challenges. *arXiv*, abs/1907.05019.

Akari Asai, Jungo Kasai, Jonathan Clark, Kenton Lee, Eunsol Choi, and Hannaneh Hajishirzi. 2021. XOR QA: Cross-lingual open-retrieval question answering. In *Proceedings of the 2021 Conference of the North American Chapter of the Association for Computational Linguistics: Human Language Technologies*, pages 547–564, Online. Association for Computational Linguistics.

Giuseppe Attardi. 2015. WikiExtractor.

Jan A. Botha, Zifei Shan, and Daniel Gillick. 2020. Entity Linking in 100 Languages. In *Proceedings of the 2020 Conference on Empirical Methods in Natural Language Processing (EMNLP)*, pages 7833–7845, Online. Association for Computational Linguistics.

Dorian Brown. 2020. Rank-BM25: A Collection of BM25 Algorithms in Python.

Razvan Bunescu and Marius Paşca. 2006. Using encyclopedic knowledge for named entity disambiguation. In *11th Conference of the European Chapter of*

[21] For more detailed examples, refer to Table 10, Table 12 and Table 13 in Appendix.

the Association for Computational Linguistics, pages 9–16, Trento, Italy. Association for Computational Linguistics.

Khyathi Raghavi Chandu, Yonatan Bisk, and Alan W Black. 2021. Grounding 'grounding' in NLP. In *Findings of the Association for Computational Linguistics: ACL-IJCNLP 2021*, pages 4283–4305, Online. Association for Computational Linguistics.

Jonathan H. Clark, Eunsol Choi, Michael Collins, Dan Garrette, Tom Kwiatkowski, Vitaly Nikolaev, and Jennimaria Palomaki. 2020. TyDi QA: A benchmark for information-seeking question answering in typologically diverse languages. *Transactions of the Association for Computational Linguistics*, 8:454–470.

Alexis Conneau, Kartikay Khandelwal, Naman Goyal, Vishrav Chaudhary, Guillaume Wenzek, Francisco Guzmán, Edouard Grave, Myle Ott, Luke Zettlemoyer, and Veselin Stoyanov. 2020. Unsupervised cross-lingual representation learning at scale. In *Proceedings of the 58th Annual Meeting of the Association for Computational Linguistics*, pages 8440–8451, Online. Association for Computational Linguistics.

Alexis Conneau, Ruty Rinott, Guillaume Lample, Adina Williams, Samuel Bowman, Holger Schwenk, and Veselin Stoyanov. 2018. XNLI: Evaluating cross-lingual sentence representations. In *Proceedings of the 2018 Conference on Empirical Methods in Natural Language Processing*, pages 2475–2485, Brussels, Belgium. Association for Computational Linguistics.

Jacob Devlin, Ming-Wei Chang, Kenton Lee, and Kristina Toutanova. 2019. BERT: Pre-training of deep bidirectional transformers for language understanding. In *Proceedings of the 2019 Conference of the North American Chapter of the Association for Computational Linguistics: Human Language Technologies, Volume 1 (Long and Short Papers)*, pages 4171–4186, Minneapolis, Minnesota. Association for Computational Linguistics.

Alon Eirew, Arie Cattan, and Ido Dagan. 2021. WEC: Deriving a large-scale cross-document event coreference dataset from Wikipedia. In *Proceedings of the 2021 Conference of the North American Chapter of the Association for Computational Linguistics: Human Language Technologies*, pages 2498–2510, Online. Association for Computational Linguistics.

Yotam Eshel, Noam Cohen, Kira Radinsky, Shaul Markovitch, Ikuya Yamada, and Omer Levy. 2017. Named entity disambiguation for noisy text. In *Proceedings of the 21st Conference on Computational Natural Language Learning (CoNLL 2017)*, pages 58–68, Vancouver, Canada. Association for Computational Linguistics.

Heng Ji and Ralph Grishman. 2011. Knowledge base population: Successful approaches and challenges. In *Proceedings of the 49th Annual Meeting of the Association for Computational Linguistics: Human Language Technologies*, pages 1148–1158, Portland, Oregon, USA. Association for Computational Linguistics.

Pratik Joshi, Sebastin Santy, Amar Budhiraja, Kalika Bali, and Monojit Choudhury. 2020. The state and fate of linguistic diversity and inclusion in the NLP world. In *Proceedings of the 58th Annual Meeting of the Association for Computational Linguistics*, pages 6282–6293, Online. Association for Computational Linguistics.

Adam Lerer, Ledell Wu, Jiajun Shen, Timothee Lacroix, Luca Wehrstedt, Abhijit Bose, and Alex Peysakhovich. 2019. Pytorch-biggraph: A large scale graph embedding system. In *Proceedings of Machine Learning and Systems*, volume 1, pages 120–131.

Robert Logan, Nelson F. Liu, Matthew E. Peters, Matt Gardner, and Sameer Singh. 2019. Barack's wife hillary: Using knowledge graphs for fact-aware language modeling. In *Proceedings of the 57th Annual Meeting of the Association for Computational Linguistics*, pages 5962–5971, Florence, Italy. Association for Computational Linguistics.

Lajanugen Logeswaran, Ming-Wei Chang, Kenton Lee, Kristina Toutanova, Jacob Devlin, and Honglak Lee. 2019. Zero-shot entity linking by reading entity descriptions. In *Proceedings of the 57th Annual Meeting of the Association for Computational Linguistics*, pages 3449–3460, Florence, Italy. Association for Computational Linguistics.

Ilya Loshchilov and Frank Hutter. 2019. Decoupled weight decay regularization. In *International Conference on Learning Representations*.

Yuanhua Lv and ChengXiang Zhai. 2011a. Lower-bounding term frequency normalization. In *Proceedings of the 20th ACM International Conference on Information and Knowledge Management*, CIKM '11, page 7–16, New York, NY, USA. Association for Computing Machinery.

Yuanhua Lv and ChengXiang Zhai. 2011b. When documents are very long, bm25 fails! In *Proceedings of the 34th International ACM SIGIR Conference on Research and Development in Information Retrieval*, SIGIR '11, page 1103–1104, New York, NY, USA. Association for Computing Machinery.

Rada Mihalcea and Andras Csomai. 2007. Wikify! linking documents to encyclopedic knowledge. In *Proceedings of the Sixteenth ACM Conference on Conference on Information and Knowledge Management*, CIKM '07, page 233–242, New York, NY, USA. Association for Computing Machinery.

Anne-Lyse Minard, Manuela Speranza, Ruben Urizar, Begoña Altuna, Marieke van Erp, Anneleen Schoen, and Chantal van Son. 2016. MEANTIME, the NewsReader multilingual event and time corpus. In

Proceedings of the Tenth International Conference on Language Resources and Evaluation (LREC'16), pages 4417–4422, Portorož, Slovenia. European Language Resources Association (ELRA).

Joel Nothman, James R. Curran, and Tara Murphy. 2008. Transforming Wikipedia into named entity training data. In *Proceedings of the Australasian Language Technology Association Workshop 2008*, pages 124–132, Hobart, Australia.

Joel Nothman, Matthew Honnibal, Ben Hachey, and James R. Curran. 2012. Event linking: Grounding event reference in a news archive. In *Proceedings of the 50th Annual Meeting of the Association for Computational Linguistics (Volume 2: Short Papers)*, pages 228–232, Jeju Island, Korea. Association for Computational Linguistics.

Adithya Pratapa, Zhengzhong Liu, Kimihiro Hasegawa, Linwei Li, Yukari Yamakawa, Shikun Zhang, and Teruko Mitamura. 2021. Cross-document event identity via dense annotation. In *Proceedings of the 25th Conference on Computational Natural Language Learning*, pages 496–517, Online. Association for Computational Linguistics.

Stephen E. Robertson, Steve Walker, Susan Jones, Micheline Hancock-Beaulieu, and Mike Gatford. 1994. Okapi at trec-3. In *TREC*.

Sebastian Ruder, Noah Constant, Jan Botha, Aditya Siddhant, Orhan Firat, Jinlan Fu, Pengfei Liu, Junjie Hu, Dan Garrette, Graham Neubig, and Melvin Johnson. 2021. XTREME-R: Towards more challenging and nuanced multilingual evaluation. In *Proceedings of the 2021 Conference on Empirical Methods in Natural Language Processing*, pages 10215–10245, Online and Punta Cana, Dominican Republic. Association for Computational Linguistics.

Avirup Sil, Ernest Cronin, Penghai Nie, Yinfei Yang, Ana-Maria Popescu, and Alexander Yates. 2012. Linking named entities to any database. In *Proceedings of the 2012 Joint Conference on Empirical Methods in Natural Language Processing and Computational Natural Language Learning*, pages 116–127, Jeju Island, Korea. Association for Computational Linguistics.

Sameer Singh, Amarnag Subramanya, Fernando Pereira, and Andrew McCallum. 2012. Wikilinks: A large-scale cross-document coreference corpus labeled via links to wikipedia. *Technical Report*.

Jannik Strötgen and Michael Gertz. 2015. A baseline temporal tagger for all languages. In *Proceedings of the 2015 Conference on Empirical Methods in Natural Language Processing*, pages 541–547, Lisbon, Portugal. Association for Computational Linguistics.

Ralph Weischedel, Martha Palmer, Mitchell Marcus, Eduard Hovy, Sameer Pradhan, Lance Ramshaw, Nianwen Xue, Ann Taylor, Jeff Kaufman, Michelle Franchini, Mohammed El-Bachouti, Robert Belvin, and Ann Houston. 2013. OntoNotes Release 5.0. *Linguistic Data Consortium, Philadelphia, PA*.

Thomas Wolf, Lysandre Debut, Victor Sanh, Julien Chaumond, Clement Delangue, Anthony Moi, Pierric Cistac, Tim Rault, Remi Louf, Morgan Funtowicz, Joe Davison, Sam Shleifer, Patrick von Platen, Clara Ma, Yacine Jernite, Julien Plu, Canwen Xu, Teven Le Scao, Sylvain Gugger, Mariama Drame, Quentin Lhoest, and Alexander Rush. 2020. Transformers: State-of-the-art natural language processing. In *Proceedings of the 2020 Conference on Empirical Methods in Natural Language Processing: System Demonstrations*, pages 38–45, Online. Association for Computational Linguistics.

Ledell Wu, Fabio Petroni, Martin Josifoski, Sebastian Riedel, and Luke Zettlemoyer. 2020. Scalable zero-shot entity linking with dense entity retrieval. In *Proceedings of the 2020 Conference on Empirical Methods in Natural Language Processing (EMNLP)*, pages 6397–6407, Online. Association for Computational Linguistics.

Xiaodong Yu, Wenpeng Yin, Nitish Gupta, and Dan Roth. 2021. Event Linking: Grounding Event Mentions to Wikipedia. *arXiv*.

A Appendix

A.1 Ethical Considerations

In this work, we presented a new dataset compiled automatically from Wikipedia, Wikinews and Wikidata. After the initial collection process, we perform rigorous post-processing steps to reduce potential errors in our dataset. Our dataset is multilingual with texts from 44 languages. In our main paper, we state these languages as well as their individual representation in our dataset. As we highlight in the paper, the proposed linking systems only work for specific class of events (eventive nouns) due to the nature of our dataset.

A.2 Dataset

After identifying potential events from Wikidata, we perform additional post-processing to remove any non-event items. Table 8 presents the list of all Wikidata properties used for removing non-event items from our corpus. Table 9 lists all languages from our dataset along with their language genealogy and distribution in the dataset.

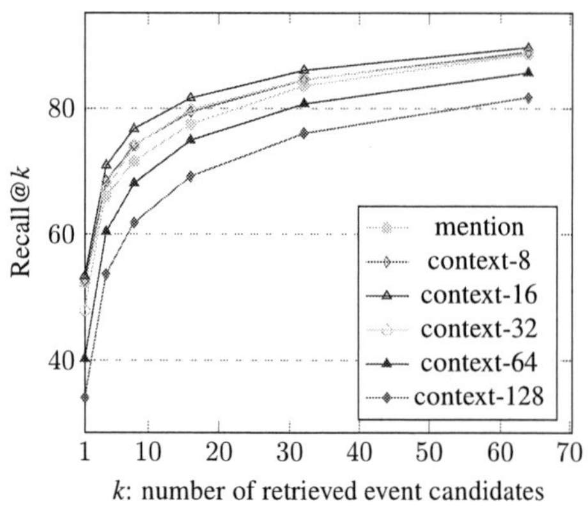

Figure 5: Effect of context window size on BM25+ retrieval performance.

Retriever	Multilingual		Crosslingual	
	Dev	Test	Dev	Test
BM25+	76.8	70.5	–	–
mBERT-bi	96.9	**97.1**	96.7	**97.2**
XLM-R-bi	96.3	96.7	94.2	95.3

Table 6: Event candidate retrieval results, Recall@8.

A.3 Modeling

Experiments: We use the base versions of mBERT and XLM-RoBERTa in all of our experiments. In the biencoder model, we use two multilingual encoders, one each for context and candidate encoding. In crossencoder, we use just one multilingual encoder and a classification layer. In all of our experiments, we optimize all the encoder layers. For biencoder training, we use AdamW optimizer (Loshchilov and Hutter, 2019) with a learning rate of 1e-05 and a linear warmup schedule. We restrict the context and candidate lengths to 128 sub-tokens and select the best epoch (of 5) on the development set. For crossencoder training, we also use AdamW optimizer with a learning rate of 2e-05 and a linear warmup schedule. We restrict the overall sequence length to 256 sub-tokens and select the best epoch (of 5) on the development set. We ran our experiments on a mix of GPUs, TITANX, v100, A6000 and a100. Each training and inference runs were run on a single GPU. Both biencoder and crossencoder were run for 5 epochs and we select the best set of hyperparameters based on the dev set performance. On a single a100 GPU, biencoder training takes about 1.5hrs per epoch and the crossencoder takes ~20hrs per epoch (with k=8).

Results: In Figure 5, we present results on the development set from all the explored configurations. In Table 6, we show the Recall@8 scores from all the retrieval models. Based on the performance on development set, we selected k=8 for our crossencoder training and inference. We also report the test scores for completeness. Figure 6 presents the retrieval recall scores. Figure 7 presents the retrieval recall scores for BM25+ (context length 16) method. Figure 9 presents a detailed comparison of per-language accuracies between multilingual and crosslingual tasks for each configuration.

Wikinews: Each Wikinews article contains meta information such as article title and publication date. Since this meta information provide additional context to the linker, we experimented by including this meta information along with the mention context. The meta information is encoded with the context as "`[CLS]` title `[SEP]` date `[SEP]` left context `[MENTION_START]` mention `[MENTION_END]` right context `[SEP]`". Table 7 presents the detailed results on the Wikinews evaluation set.

Examples: We also present full examples of system errors we identified through a qualitative analysis. Table 10 presents examples of system errors due to insufficient temporal reasoning in the con-

Model	Multilingual				Crosslingual			
	Ctxt	Ctxt+date	Ctxt+title	Ctxt+date+title	Ctxt	Ctxt+date	Ctxt+title	Ctxt+date+title
cross-domain								
mBERT-bi	81.2	87.4	83.4	87.7	85.4	90.0	87.4	90.6
XLM-R-bi	82.2	89.4	85.1	90.8	82.6	88.8	85.3	90.0
mBERT-cross	90.1	95.0	91.5	95.6	89.3	93.5	90.8	93.8
XLM-R-cross	89.7	94.0	91.6	94.7	88.9	93.6	90.6	93.7
zero-shot								
mBERT-bi	76.7	86.3	78.0	86.7	78.0	85.6	80.3	87.4
XLM-R-bi	76.7	86.0	80.1	89.0	76.4	85.8	78.7	87.2
mBERT-cross	84.4	92.2	86.5	93.8	76.2	81.7	77.6	81.5
XLM-R-cross	84.4	90.6	84.9	92.2	76.0	84.2	76.4	83.5

Table 7: Event linking accuracy on Wikinews test set. For each configuration, we report results using just the mention context (Ctxt), mention context + article publication date (Ctxt+date), mention context + article title (Ctxt+title) and mention context + article date & title (Ctxt+date+title). Most of the gain comes from including the date across all model configurations and tasks.

text. Table 11 presents examples of system errors on mentions that are temporal or spatial expressions. Table 12 presents examples of system errors on crosslingual task due to issues related with tackling non-English mentions. Table 13 presents examples of system errors that were caused due to dataset errors.

Property	Property_Label	URI	URI_Label
P31	instance_of	Q48349	empire
P31	instance_of	Q11514315	historical_period
P31	instance_of	Q3024240	historical_country
P31	instance_of	Q11042	culture
P31	instance_of	Q28171280	ancient_civilization
P31	instance_of	Q1620908	historical_region
P31	instance_of	Q3502482	cultural_region
P31	instance_of	Q465299	archaeological_culture
P31	instance_of	Q568683	age
P31	instance_of	Q763288	lander
P31	instance_of	Q4830453	business
P31	instance_of	Q24862	short_film
P31	instance_of	Q1496967	territorial_entity
P31	instance_of	Q68	computer
P31	instance_of	Q486972	human_settlement
P31	instance_of	Q26529	space_probe
P31	instance_of	Q82794	geographic_region
P31	instance_of	Q43229	organization
P31	instance_of	Q15401633	archaeological_period
P31	instance_of	Q5398426	television_series
P31	instance_of	Q24869	feature_film
P31	instance_of	Q11424	film
P31	instance_of	Q718893	theater
P31	instance_of	Q1555508	radio_program
P31	instance_of	Q17343829	unincorporated_community_in_the_United_States
P31	instance_of	Q254832	Internationale_Bauausstellung
P31	instance_of	Q214609	material
P31	instance_of	Q625298	peace_treaty
P31	instance_of	Q131569	treaty
P31	instance_of	Q93288	contract
P31	instance_of	Q15416	television_program
P31	instance_of	Q1201097	detachment
P31	instance_of	Q16887380	group
P31	instance_of	Q57821	fortification
P31	instance_of	Q15383322	cultural prize
P31	instance_of	Q515	city
P31	instance_of	Q537127	road_bridge
P31	instance_of	Q20097897	sea_fort
P31	instance_of	Q1785071	fort
P31	instance_of	Q23413	castle
P31	instance_of	Q1484988	project
P31	instance_of	Q149621	district
P31	instance_of	Q532	village
P31	instance_of	Q2630741	community
P31	instance_of	Q3957	town
P31	instance_of	Q111161	synod
P31	instance_of	Q1530022	religious_organization
P31	instance_of	Q51645	ecumenical_council
P31	instance_of	Q10551516	church_council
P31	instance_of	Q1076486	sports_venue
P31	instance_of	Q17350442	venue
P31	instance_of	Q13226383	facility
P31	instance_of	Q811979	architectural_structure
P31	instance_of	Q23764314	sports_location
P31	instance_of	Q15707521	fictional_battle
P36	capital	*	
P2067	mass	*	
P1082	population	*	
P1376	captial_of	*	
P137	operator	*	
P915	filming_location	*	
P162	producer	*	
P281	postal_code	*	
P176	manufacturer	*	
P2257	event_interval	*	
P527	has_part	*	
P279	subclass_of	*	

Table 8: List of properties used for postprocessing Wikidata events. If a candidate event has the property 'P31', we prune them depending on the corresponding. For example, we only prune items that are instances of empire, historical period etc., For other properties like P527, P36, we prune items if they contain this property.

Language	Code	Events	Mentions	Genus
Afrikaans	af	316	2036	Germanic
Arabic	ar	2691	28801	Semitic
Belarusian	be	737	7091	Slavic
Bulgarian	bg	1426	12570	Slavic
Bengali	bn	270	3136	Indic
Catalan	ca	2631	22296	Romance
Czech	cs	2839	36658	Slavic
Danish	da	1189	10267	Germanic
German	de	7371	209469	Germanic
Greek	el	997	13361	Greek
English	en	10747	328789	Germanic
Spanish	es	5064	91896	Romance
Persian	fa	1566	10449	Iranian
Finnish	fi	3253	47944	Finnic
French	fr	8183	136482	Romance
Hebrew	he	1871	34470	Semitic
Hindi	hi	216	1219	Indic
Hungarian	hu	3067	27333	Ugric
Indonesian	id	2274	14049	Malayo-Sumbawan
Italian	it	7116	108012	Romance
Japanese	ja	3832	49198	Japanese
Korean	ko	1732	13544	Korean
Malayalam	ml	136	730	Southern Dravidian
Marathi	mr	132	507	Indic
Malay	ms	824	4650	Malayo-Sumbawan
Dutch	nl	4151	41973	Germanic
Norwegian	no	2514	24092	Germanic
Polish	pl	6270	110381	Slavic
Portuguese	pt	4466	45125	Romance
Romanian	ro	1224	12117	Romance
Russian	ru	7929	180891	Slavic
Sinhala	si	31	65	Indic
Slovak	sk	726	5748	Slavic
Slovene	sl	1288	8577	Slavic
Serbian	sr	1611	24093	Slavic
Swedish	sv	2865	23152	Germanic
Swahili	sw	22	74	Bantoid
Tamil	ta	250	1682	Southern Dravidian
Telugu	te	39	243	South-Central Dravidian
Thai	th	800	4749	Kam-Tai
Turkish	tr	2342	19846	Turkic
Ukrainian	uk	3428	53098	Slavic
Vietnamese	vi	1439	13744	Viet-Muong
Chinese	zh	2759	21259	Chinese
Total		**10947**	**1805866**	

Table 9: Proposed dataset summary (by languages)

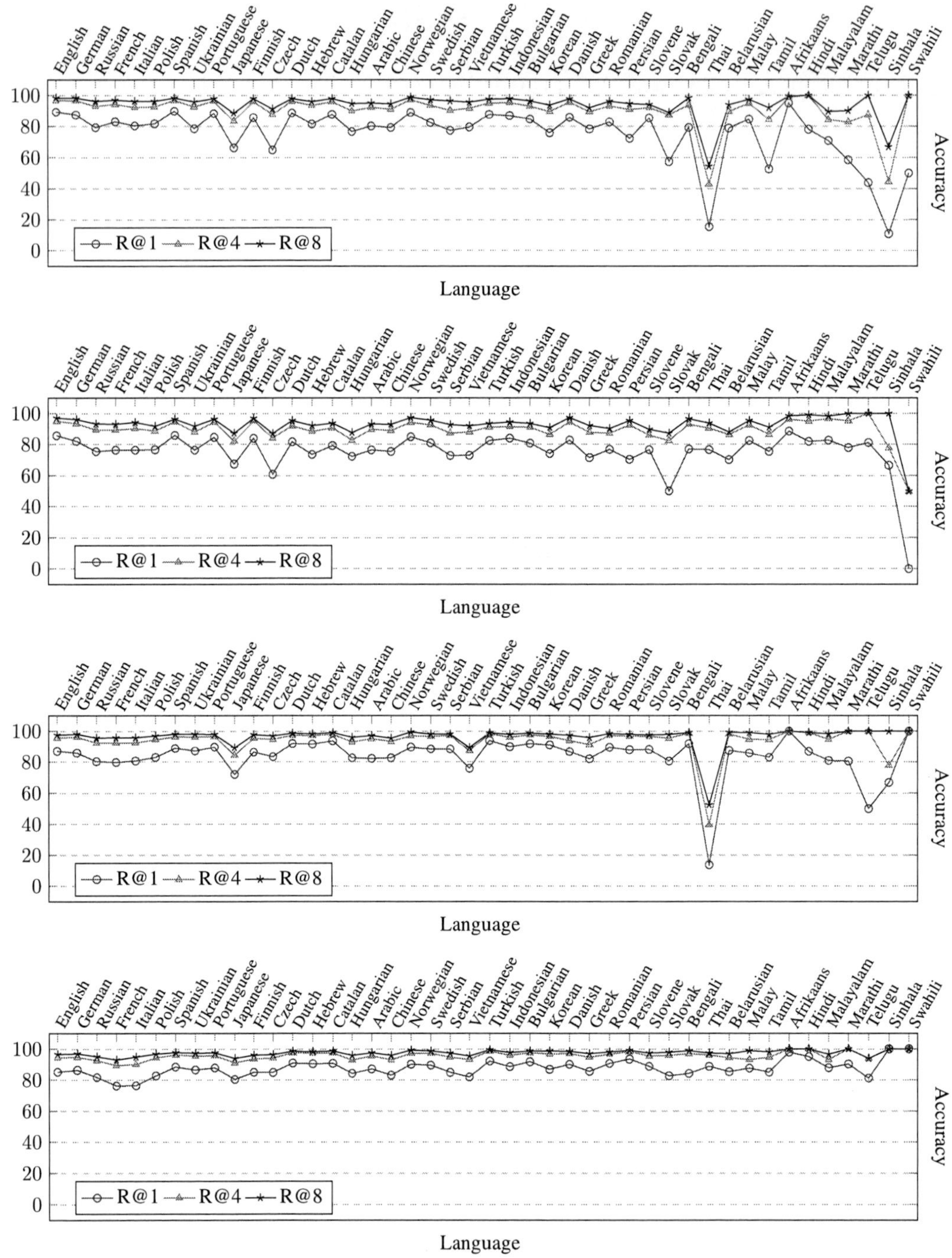

Figure 6: Retrieval recall scores on development set for mBERT and XLM-R in multilingual and crosslingual settings.

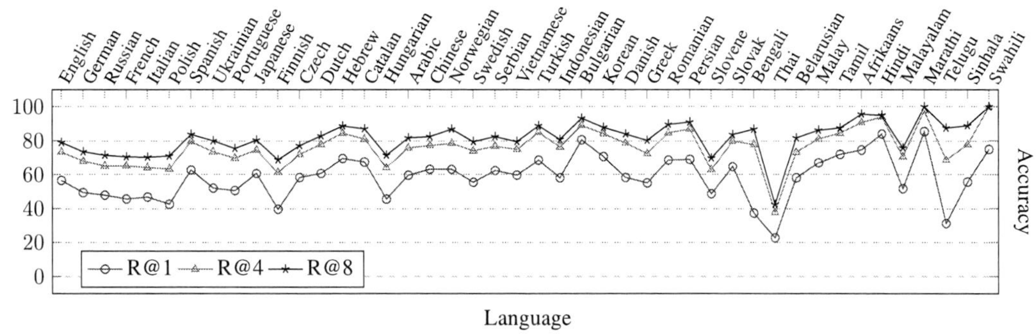

Figure 7: Retrieval recall scores on development set for BM25+ in multilingual setting.

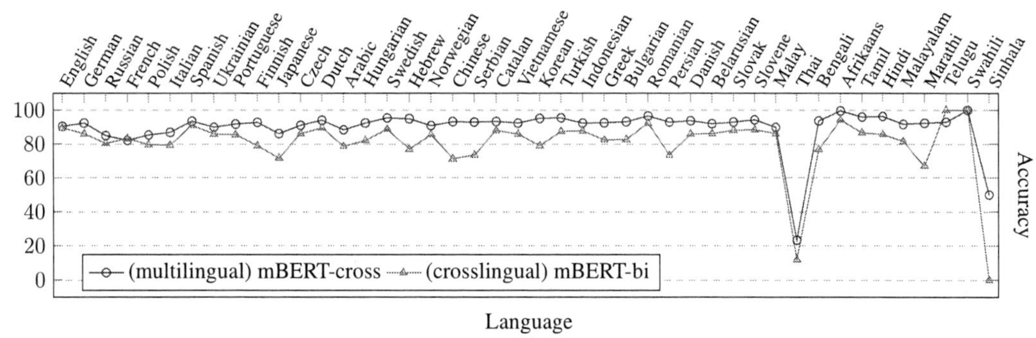

Figure 8: Test accuracy of mBERT-bi and mBERT-cross in multilingual and crosslingual tasks. The languages on the x-axis are sorted in the increasing order of mentions.

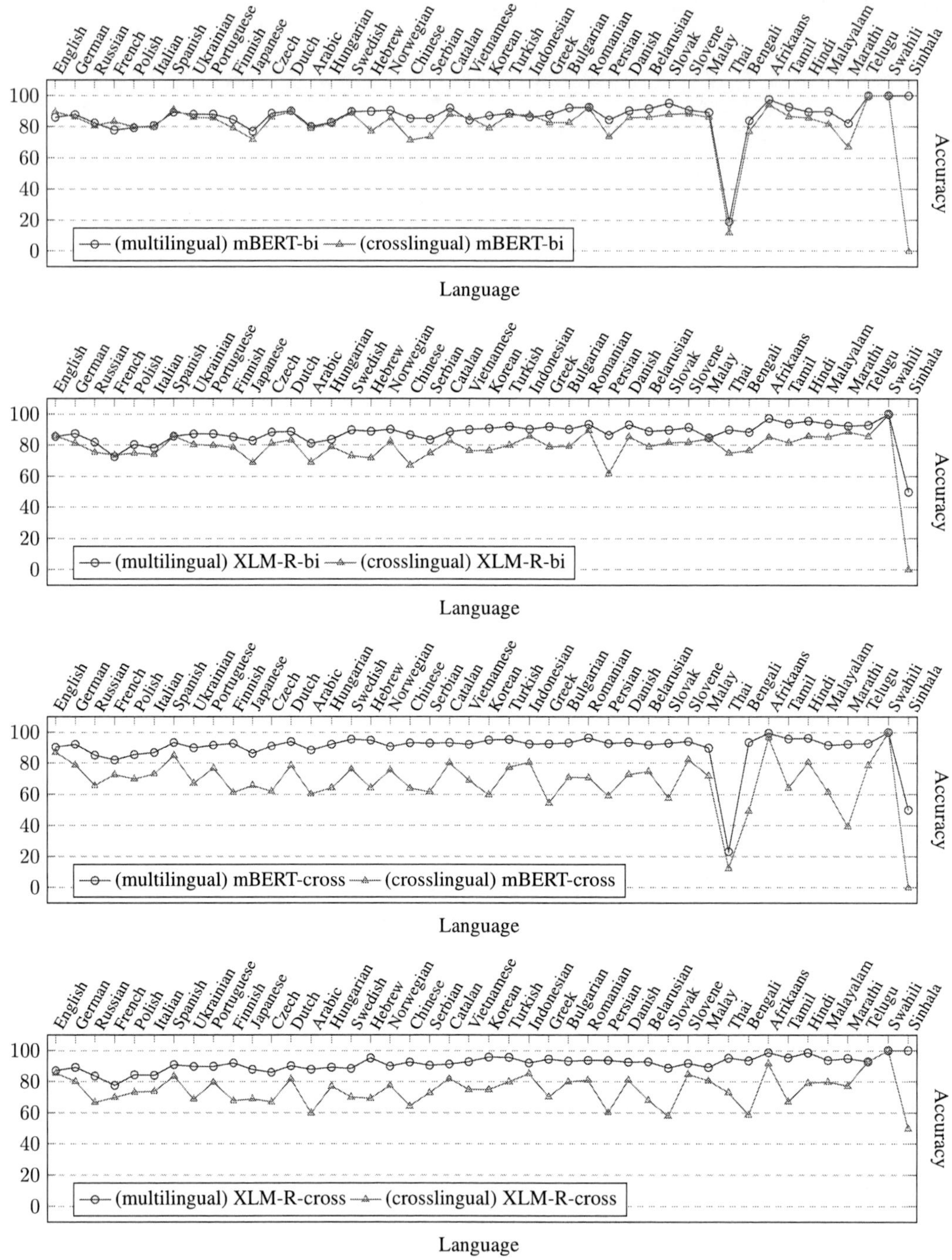

Figure 9: Test accuracy of mBERT-bi, XLM-R-bi, mBERT-cross, XLM-R-cross in multilingual and crosslingual tasks. The languages on the x-axis are sorted in the increasing order of mentions.

Mention Context: At the 2000 Summer Olympics in Sydney, Sitnikov competed only in two swimming events. He eclipsed a FINA B-cut of 51.69 (100 m freestyle) from the Kazakhstan Open Championships in Almaty. On the first day of the Games, Sitnikov placed twenty-first for the Kazakhstan team in the 4 × 100 m freestyle relay. Teaming with Sergey Borisenko, Pavel Sidorov, and Andrey Kvassov in heat three, Sitnikov swam a lead-off leg and recorded a split of 52.56, but the Kazakhs settled only for last place in a final time of 3:28.90. Three days later, in the **100 m freestyle**, Sitnikov placed fifty-third on the morning prelims. Swimming in heat five, he raced to a fifth seed by 0.15 seconds ahead of Chinese Taipei's Wu Nien-pin in 52.57. **Predicted Label:** *Swimming at the 2008 Summer Olympics – Men's 100 metre freestyle*: The men's 100 metre freestyle event at the 2008 Olympic Games took place on 12–14 August at the Beijing National Aquatics Center in Beijing, China. There were 64 competitors from 55 nations. **Gold Label:** *Swimming at the 2000 Summer Olympics – Men's 100 metre freestyle*: The men's 100 metre freestyle event at the 2000 Summer Olympics took place on 19–20 September at the Sydney International Aquatic Centre in Sydney, Australia. There were 73 competitors from 66 nations. Nations have been limited to two swimmers each since the 1984 Games.
Mention Context: In 2012, WWE reinstated their No Way Out pay-per-view (PPV), which had previously ran annually from 1999 to 2009. The following year, however, No Way Out was canceled and replaced by Payback, which in turn became an annual PPV for the promotion. The first Payback event was held on June 16, 2013 at the Allstate Arena in Rosemont, Illinois. The 2014 event was also held in June at the same arena and was also the first Payback to air on the WWE Network, which had launched earlier that year. In 2015 and 2016, the event was held in May. The 2016 event was also promoted as the first PPV of the New Era for WWE. In July 2016, WWE reintroduced the brand extension, dividing the roster between the Raw and SmackDown brands where wrestlers are exclusively assigned to perform. The **2017 event** was in turn held exclusively for wrestlers from the Raw brand, and was also moved up to late-April. **Predicted Label:** *Battleground (2017)*: Battleground was a professional wrestling pay-per-view (PPV) event and WWE Network event produced by WWE for their SmackDown brand division. It took place on July 23, 2017, at the Wells Fargo Center in Philadelphia, Pennsylvania. It was the fifth and final event under the Battleground chronology, as following WrestleMania 34 in April 2018, brand-exclusive PPVs were discontinued, resulting in WWE reducing the amount of yearly PPVs produced. **Gold Label:** *Payback (2017)*: Payback was a professional wrestling pay-per-view (PPV) and WWE Network event, produced by WWE for the Raw brand division. It took place on April 30, 2017 at the SAP Center in San Jose, California. It was the fifth event in the Payback chronology. Due to the Superstar Shake-up, the event included two interbrand matches with SmackDown wrestlers. It was the final Payback event until 2020, as following WrestleMania 34 in 2018, WWE discontinued brand-exclusive PPVs, which resulted in the reduction of yearly PPVs produced.

Table 10: Examples of errors by the event linking system. (temporal reasoning related)

Mention Context: Paul Wing (August 14, 1892 – May 29, 1957) was an assistant director at Paramount Pictures. He won the **1935** Best Assistant Director Academy Award for "The Lives of a Bengal Lancer" along with Clem Beauchamp. Wing was the assistant director on only two films owing to his service in the United States Army. During his service, Wing was in a prisoner camp that was portrayed in the film "The Great Raid" (2005).

Predicted Label: *8th Academy Awards*: The 8th Academy Awards were held on March 5, 1936, at the Biltmore Hotel in Los Angeles, California. They were hosted by Frank Capra. This was the first year in which the gold statuettes were called "Oscars".

Gold Label: *7th Academy Awards*: The 7th Academy Awards, honoring the best in film for 1934, was held on February 27, 1935, at the Biltmore Hotel in Los Angeles, California. They were hosted by Irvin S. Cobb.

Mention Context: Für "Holiday Land" (1934) war er bei der Oscarverleihung 1935 erstmals für einen Oscar für den besten animierten Kurzfilm nominiert. Eine weitere Nominierung in dieser Kategorie erhielt er **1938** für "The Little Match Girl" (1937).

Predicted Label: *9th Academy Awards*: The 9th Academy Awards were held on March 4, 1937, at the Biltmore Hotel in Los Angeles, California. They were hosted by George Jessel; music was provided by the Victor Young Orchestra, which at the time featured Spike Jones on drums. This ceremony marked the introduction of the Best Supporting Actor and Best Supporting Actress categories, and was the first year that the awards for directing and acting were fixed at five nominees per category.

Gold Label: *10th Academy Awards*: The 10th Academy Awards were originally scheduled for March 3, 1938, but due to the Los Angeles flood of 1938 were held on March 10, 1938, at the Biltmore Hotel in Los Angeles, California. It was hosted by Bob Burns.

Table 11: Examples of errors by the event linking system. (temporal or spatial expression related)

Mention Context: Nel 2018 ha preso parte alle Olimpiadi di Pyeongchang, venendo eliminata nel primo turno della finale e classificandosi diciannovesima nella gara di **gobbe**.

Predicted Label: *Snowboarding at the 2018 Winter Olympics – Women's parallel giant slalom*: The women's parallel giant slalom competition of the 2018 Winter Olympics was held on 24 February 2018 Bogwang Phoenix Park in Pyeongchang, South Korea.

Gold Label: *Freestyle skiing at the 2018 Winter Olympics – Women's moguls*: The Women's moguls event in freestyle skiing at the 2018 Winter Olympics took place at the Bogwang Phoenix Park, Pyeongchang, South Korea from 9 to 11 February 2018. It was won by Perrine Laffont, with Justine Dufour-Lapointe taking silver and Yuliya Galysheva taking bronze. For Laffont and Galysheva these were first Olympic medals. Galysheva also won the first ever medal in Kazakhstan in freestyle skiing.

Mention Context:
تقارب إسرائيل واليابان على أساس القيم الديموقراطيةوا لاشتراكية ا لمشتركة، واستطاعت من خ لال عضويتها في ا
لاشتراكية الدولية أن تنشئ صلات وثيقة مع الحزب ا لاشتراكي الياباني الذي تبنى مهمة التعريف بإسرائيل ومنجزاتها في
اليابان. وإ ّبان **حرب 1956** انضمت اليابان إلى الدول التي طالبت مصر باحترام ا لمعاهدات الدولية الخاصة با لملاحة
في قناة السويس. وأصدرت بيان مقتضب .أعلنت فيه أسفها لوصول ا لأمور إلى حد الصدام ا لمسلح

Predicted Label: *Hungarian Revolution of 1956*: The Hungarian Revolution of 1956 (), or the Hungarian Uprising, was a nationwide revolution against the Hungarian People's Republic and its Soviet-imposed policies, lasting from 23 October until 10 November 1956. Leaderless at the beginning, it was the first major threat to Soviet control since the Red Army drove Nazi Germany from its territory at the end of World War II in Europe.

Gold Label: *Suez Crisis*: The Suez Crisis, or the Second Arab–Israeli war, also called the Tripartite Aggression () in the Arab world and the Sinai War in Israel,

---

Mention Context: 攝津號戰艦於1909年4月1日在須賀海軍工廠鋪設龍骨，後於1909年1日18日舉行下水儀式，並於1912年7月1日竣工，總造價為11,010,000日圓。海軍大佐田中盛秀於1912年12月1日出任本艦艦長，並編入第一分遣艦隊。翌年的多數時候，攝津號均巡航於中國外海或是接受戰備操演。當第一次世界大戰於1914年8月間爆發時，本艦正停泊於廣島縣市軍港。攝津號與其姐妹艦河號於1914年10月至11月間參與了**青島戰役**的最後階段，並於外海以艦砲密集轟炸軍陣地。本艦於1916年12月1日離開第一分遣艦隊，並送往市進行升級作業。升級作業於1917年12月1日完成，該艦隨後編入第二分遣艦隊，直至1918年7月23日重新歸入第一分遣艦隊為止。自此時起，攝津號戰艦上所有的QF 12磅3英吋40倍徑艦砲均移除，並以QF 12磅3英吋40倍徑防空砲取代，另亦移除了兩具魚雷發射管。1918年10月28日，攝津號戰艦成為大正天皇於海上校時所搭乘的旗艦。

Predicted Label: *Battle of the Yellow Sea*: The Battle of the Yellow Sea (;) was a major naval battle of the Russo-Japanese War, fought on 10 August 1904. In the Russian Navy, it was referred to as the Battle of 10 August. The battle foiled an attempt by the Russian fleet at Port Arthur to break out and form up with the Vladivostok squadron, forcing them to return to port. Four days later, the Battle off Ulsan similarly ended the Vladivostok group's sortie, forcing both fleets to remain at anchor.

Gold Label: *Siege of Tsingtao*: The siege of Tsingtao (or Tsingtau) was the attack on the German port of Tsingtao (now Qingdao) in China during World War I by Japan and the United Kingdom. The siege was waged against Imperial Germany between 27 August and 7 November 1914. The siege was the first encounter between Japanese and German forces, the first Anglo-Japanese operation of the war, and the only major land battle in the Asian and Pacific theatre during World War I.

Table 12: Examples of errors by the event linking system. (language-related)

Mention Context: He established his own production company, Emirau Productions, named after the **battle in World War II** in which Warren was injured.

Predicted Label: *First Battle of El Alamein*: The First Battle of El Alamein (1–27 July 1942) was a battle of the Western Desert Campaign of the Second World War, fought in Egypt between Axis forces (Germany and Italy) of the Panzer Army Africa () (which included the under Field Marshal () Erwin Rommel) and Allied (British Imperial and Commonwealth) forces (Britain, British India, Australia, South Africa and New Zealand) of the Eighth Army (General Claude Auchinleck).

Gold Label: *Landing on Emirau*: The Landing on Emirau was the last of the series of operations that made up Operation Cartwheel, General Douglas MacArthur's strategy for the encirclement of the major Japanese base at Rabaul. A force of nearly 4,000 United States Marines landed on the island of Emirau on 20 March 1944. The island was not occupied by the Japanese and there was no fighting. It was developed into an airbase which formed the final link in the chain of bases surrounding Rabaul. The isolation of Rabaul permitted MacArthur to turn his attention westward and commence his drive along the north coast of New Guinea toward the Philippines.

Mention Context: Ivanova won the silver medal at the 1978 World Junior Championships. She made her senior World debut at the **1979 World Championships**, finishing 18th. Ivanova was 16th at the 1980 Winter Olympics.

Predicted Label: *FIBT World Championships 1979*: The FIBT World Championships 1979 took place in Königssee, West Germany. It was the first championships that took place on an artificially refrigerated track. The track also hosted the luge world championships that same year, the first time that had ever happened in both bobsleigh and luge in a non-Winter Olympic year (Igls hosted both events for the 1976 games in neighboring Innsbruck.).

Gold Label: *1979 World Figure Skating Championships*: The 1979 World Figure Skating Championships were held in Vienna, Austria from March 13 to 18. At the event, sanctioned by the International Skating Union, medals were awarded in men's singles, ladies' singles, pair skating, and ice dance.

Mention Context: Изначально открытие башни должно было состояться в декабре 2011 года, но после землетрясения строительство замедлилось из-за нехватки средств.

Predicted Label: *2011 Christchurch earthquake*: A major earthquake occurred in Christchurch, New Zealand, on Tuesday 22 February 2011 at 12:51 p.m. local time (23:51 UTC, 21 February). The () earthquake struck the Canterbury region in the South Island, centred south-east of the centre of Christchurch, the country's second-most populous city. It caused widespread damage across Christchurch, killing 185 people, in the nation's fifth-deadliest disaster.

Gold Label: *2011 Tōhoku earthquake and tsunami*: The occurred at 14:46 JST (05:46 UTC) on 11 March. The magnitude 9.0–9.1 (Mw) undersea megathrust earthquake had an epicenter in the Pacific Ocean, east of the Oshika Peninsula of the Tōhoku region, and lasted approximately six minutes, causing a tsunami. It is sometimes known in Japan as the , among other names. The disaster is often referred to in both Japanese and English as simply 3.11 (read šan ten ichi-ichiïn Japanese).

Mention Context: ポワント・デュ・オック (Pointe du Hoc) から向かったアメリカ軍のレンジャー部隊の8個中隊と共に、アメリカ第29歩兵師団は海岸の西側の側面を攻撃した。アメリカ第1歩兵師団は東側からのアプローチを行った。これは、この戦争において、北アフリカ、シチリア島に続く3回目の強襲上陸であった。オマハビーチの上陸部隊の主目標は、サン=ロー (Saint-Lô) の南に進出する前にポール=アン=ベッサン (Port-en-Bessin) とヴィル川 (Vire River) 間の橋頭堡を守ることであった。

Predicted Label: *Tunisian campaign*: The Tunisian campaign (also known as the Battle of Tunisia) was a series of battles that took place in Tunisia during the North African campaign of the Second World War, between Axis and Allied forces. The Allies consisted of British Imperial Forces, including a Greek contingent, with American and French corps. The battle opened with initial success by the German and Italian forces but the massive supply interdiction efforts led to the decisive defeat of the Axis. Over 250,000 German and Italian troops were taken as prisoners of war, including most of the Afrika Korps.

Gold Label: *Operation Torch*: Operation Torch (8 November 1942 – 16 November 1942) was an Allied invasion of French North Africa during the Second World War. While the French colonies formally aligned with Germany via Vichy France, the loyalties of the population were mixed. Reports indicated that they might support the Allies. American General Dwight D. Eisenhower, supreme commander of the Allied forces in Mediterranean Theater of Operations, planned a three-pronged attack on Casablanca (Western), Oran (Center) and Algiers (Eastern), then a rapid move on Tunis to catch Axis forces in North Africa from the west in conjunction with Allied advance from east.

Table 13: Examples of errors by the event linking system. (also errors in the dataset)

Complex Word Identification in Vietnamese: Towards Vietnamese Text Simplification

Phuong Nguyen
Computer Science Department
Pomona College
phuong.nguyen@pomona.edu

David Kauchak
Computer Science Department
Pomona College
david.kauchak@pomona.edu

Abstract

Text Simplification has been an extensively researched problem in English, but has not been investigated in Vietnamese. We focus on the Vietnamese-specific Complex Word Identification task, often the first step in Lexical Simplification (Shardlow, 2013). We examine three different Vietnamese datasets constructed for other natural language processing tasks and show that, like in other languages, frequency is a strong signal in determining whether a word is complex, with a mean accuracy of 86.87%. Across the datasets, we find that the 10% most frequent words in many corpus can be labeled as simple, and the rest as complex, though this is more variable for smaller corpora. We also examine how human annotators perform at this task. Given the subjective nature, there is a fair amount of variability in which words are seen as difficult, though majority results are more consistent.

1 Introduction

Text Simplification is a task that focuses on improving the readability and understandability of text while preserving the original content and meaning. Text Simplification applications have been shown to benefit a variety of target audiences, including readers with low-literacy levels (Mason, 1978), non-native speakers (Paetzold, 2016), language learners (Gardner et al., 2007; Crossley et al., 2007), deaf people (Marschark and Spencer, 2010), people with reading comprehension problems such as aphasia (Carroll et al., 1998) and dyslexia (Rello et al., 2013), and people with Autistic Spectrum Disorder (Evans et al., 2014). It is also a useful preprocessing step for other NLP tasks, including parsing (Chandrasekar et al., 1996), information extraction (Evans, 2011; Miwa et al., 2010), and question generation (Heilman and Smith, 2010).

Although significant progress has been made in text simplification in multiple languages, including English (Coster and Kauchak, 2011; Nisioi et al., 2017; Woodsend and Lapata, 2011), Spanish (Saggion et al., 2015; Bott et al., 2012), Portuguese (Aluísio et al., 2008), Japanese (Katsuta and Yamamoto, 2019; Maruyama and Yamamoto, 2017), Korean (Chung et al., 2013), and Italian (Barlacchi and Tonelli, 2013), the problem remains a relatively new area of research in Vietnamese, a language spoken by over 70 million people (Van Driem, 2001) in Vietnam, the South East Asia region, France, Australia, and the United States. Sentence splitting has been conducted for the Vietnamese – English machine translation task (Hung et al., 2012), which can be helpful as an initial step for Text Simplification, but no further work has been recorded.

Other tasks in Vietnamese have been explored, from core problems such as dependency parsing, word segmentation, and part-of-speech parsing to more recent ones such as sentiment analysis, automatic speech recognition, and question answering.[1] Text Summarization is the most closely related task to Text Simplification that has been attempted in Vietnamese.

Progress on the specific task of Complex Word Identification in Vietnamese has not been reported so far. Although the terms *complex words* and *simple words* have appeared in literature on the Word Segmentation task, such as in Nguyen et al. (2006b), Nguyen et al. (2006a), and Anh et al. (2015), they refer to the length of each word (whether they are monosyllabic or polysyllabic words such as compound and reduplicative words) rather than the understandability and readability of each word in the context of Text Simplification.

We implement two approaches to solve the Complex Word Identification task in Vietnamese: frequency-based and classification-based with Support Vector Machines. We conclude with an experiment involving human annotators to predict the

[1] https://github.com/undertheseanlp/NLP-Vietnamese-progress

Proceedings of the Workshop on Multilingual Information Access (MIA), pages 59 - 68
July 15, 2022 ©2022 Association for Computational Linguistics

suitability of our datasets for this task.

2 Characteristics of Vietnamese

The characteristics presented in this section are extracted from Hạo (2000) and Hữu et al. (1998).

2.1 Language Family

Vietnamese is classified to be in the VietMuong group of the Mon-Khmer branch in the Austro-Asiatic language family.

Due to past colonization periods, Vietnamese is also heavily influenced by Chinese, as exemplified by the significant number of Sino-Vietnamese words (words with Chinese origin or consists of morphemes of Chinese origin) in the vocabulary, French, as seen in the use of calque (or loan translation), and English.

2.2 Language Type

Vietnamese is an isolating and tonal language with the following characteristics:

- It uses a Latin alphabet in conjunction with diacritics and several other letters.
- There are six tones marked by accents: level ("ngang"), falling ("huyền"), broken ("ngã"), curve ("hỏi"), rising ("sắc"), and drop ("nặng"). The pronunciation of these tones differ across the Northern, Southern and Central regions of Vietnam (Alves, 1995).
- It is a monosyllabic language.
- It is neither inflected nor conjugated, i.e. all words in Vietnamese are immutable.
- All grammatical relations are established by word order and function words.

2.3 A Word Unit

Vietnamese has a unit denoted "tiếng" that can represent either (Nguyễn et al., 2006):

1. a syllable with regards to phonology
2. a morpheme with regards to morpho-syntax
3. a word with regards to sentence constituent creation

Based on current literature, this unit is commonly referred to as a syllable. Thus, the Vietnamese vocabulary includes monosyllabic words ("từ đơn", words with a single syllable) or compound words ("từ phức", words with more than one syllable). About 85% of Vietnamese words are compound words and more than 80% of syllables are standalone words (Phuong et al., 2008; Dinh et al., 2008). This means that unlike in English and other Occidental languages that also utilize Latin alphabets, white spaces are not reliable indicators of word boundaries in Vietnamese. For example, "học sinh" (student) is a compound word that includes two syllables separated by a white space.

3 Data

We conduct two experiments across three Vietnamese corpora of various sizes extracted from different domains. We obtain a simple word list, a stopword list, and use the two lists to extract three complex word lists from the three corpora for evaluation purposes. The simple and complex wordlists for the three corpora are available online.[2]

3.1 Word Lists

The following two word lists are used:

- **Simple Word List**: A list of 3,000 words obtained by Luong et al. (2018) to construct a Vietnamese text readability formula. The list was used to replace the list of 3,000 words that fourth grade students can understand used in the Dale-Chall formula for English readability (Dawkins et al., 1956) in the development of an equivalent readability formula in Vietnamese.
- **Stopword List**: A list of 1942 stop words.[3]

3.2 Corpora

The following three corpora are used to conduct experiments. They are named according to the purpose of their construction.

- **READABILITY** (Luong et al., 2020)

  This corpus, constructed for research in Vietnamese text readability, contains 1,825 documents of approximately 3 million words in the literature domain. The documents were sourced from college-level textbooks, stories and literature websites, and were preprocessed for the minimization of spelling errors and standardization of punctuation, encoding, and

[2] `https://github.com/phuongnguyen00/cwi-in-vietnamese`

[3] `https://github.com/stopwords/vietnamese-stopwords`

tone. The corpus was then divided by experts into four categories: Very Easy (intended for children or people with middle-school education), Easy (intended for middle-school children or people with middle-school education), Medium (intended for high-school students or people with high-school education), and Difficult (specialized text intended for people with college education). Based on the Vietnamese Dictionary by Hoang (2017), more difficult groups of texts are more likely to include Sino-Vietnamese words and other words borrowed from English and French.

For this work we only use the Difficult subcorpus.

- **CLUSTER** (Tran et al., 2020)

  This dataset was constructed for the task of abstractive multi-document summarization. The dataset includes 600 summaries of 300 clusters with 1,945 news articles on five topics: world news, domestic news, business, entertainment and sports extracted from various news outlets aggregated by Google News in Vietnamese. Every cluster contains 4 - 10 articles, and the average number of articles per cluster is 6. Each document contains the following information: the title, the text content, the news source, the date of publication, the author(s), the tag(s), and the headline summary. These pieces of information are labelled using English.

  For this work we only use the original documents.

- **CLASSIFICATION** (Hoang et al., 2007)

  This corpus was constructed to solve the Text Classification task (labeling documents with a predefined topic). The corpus was comprised of articles from four major online newspapers, including VnExpress, TuoiTre Online, Thanh Nien Online, and Nguoi Lao Dong online. The data preprocessing phase included the removal of HTML tags, normalization of spelling, and other heuristics. There are 27 predefined topics ranging from music, family, and eating and drinking, to international business, new computer products and fine arts.

  The authors constructed 2 corpora of 2 levels of topic specificity (the higher level one included more fine-grained topic categorization). Corpus level 2 is used in this project.

3.3 Data Preprocessing

Since whitespace cannot be used to identify words in Vietnamese, we use the VNCoreNLP toolkit (Vu et al., 2018) for the word segmentation process. The word segmentation tool in the toolkit relies on the use of the Single Classification Ripple Down Rules (SCRDR) tree and was reported to achieve the best F1 score out of notable segmenters including vnTokenizer, JVnSegmenter, and DongDu (Nguyen et al., 2017).

We extract three complex word lists from the three corpora by removing all of the simple words, stopwords, proper nouns (words whose syllables are all capitalized), invalid words (such as words that contain numbers, letters, hyperlinks, and English words that are used repeatedly). The syllables in each word are concatenated with "_" as white spaces are not reliable indicators of word boundaries in Vietnamese. The remaining words are then identified as *complex*.

Table 1 shows various statistics for the three corpora. The Readability corpus has the smallest number of documents, but the documents tend to be longer. The Cluster corpus is the smallest of the three corpus with just over half a millions words. The Classification corpus is the largest, both in the number of documents and the number of words. These sizes are paralleled in the number of unique words from each corpora, though the Cluster corpus is high given its size indicating a slightly more difficult corpus. All of the corpora are comprised of about 60% simple words, though, again the Cluster corpus is slightly smaller than this.

For the experiments, we rely on the simple word list, and the 3 complex word lists as extracted above. We concatenate the simple word list with each of the 3 complex word lists to create 3 three separate datasets. These word lists will be referred to by their corpus' name in the following sections.

4 Methods

For each dataset, we have the simple word list and the list of unique complex words. This creates three complex word identification tasks to identify whether a word is simple or complex. We examine two approaches for the this task: frequency threshold and feature-based using Support Vector Machines.

	REA	CLU	CLA
docs	321	1945	25,286
words	1.58M	563K	4.96M
simple words	1.01M (64%)	315K (56%)	2.95M (59%)
stopwords	666K (42%)	174K (31%)	1.77M (36%)
unique complex words	10,273*	7,548	27,764

Table 1: Preliminary quantitative information of the three corpora. [REA = READABILITY, CLU = CLUSTER, CLA = CLASSIFICATION]

* *involves manual processing to remove foreign words and invalid words*

4.1 Frequency Threshold

For the Complex Word Identification task in English, frequency is an overpowering signal in determining whether a word is complex (Paetzold and Specia, 2016). The frequency approach only uses the frequency of a word in a particular corpus to label it as *complex* or *simple*.

For each of the three datasets that include both simple and complex words, we split it into training (75%) and testing (25%) data. Within the training dataset, we sort all of the words by frequency, and consider each frequency f out of all frequencies recorded as a cutoff point. For each frequency f, a word will be labelled complex if its frequency is smaller than or equal to f, and it will be labelled simple otherwise. We consider all possible frequencies f as the cutoff point and and identify the frequency that has the highest classification accuracy as our threshold for applying to the testing data.

4.2 Support Vector Machines Classifier

The frequency approach only utilizes a single feature. Many features have been suggested for use in the complex word identification task (Paetzold and Specia, 2016). For our classifier we used four features: corpus-specific frequency, number of syllables, number of characters, and number of characters and diacritics. All of the features besides word length try and capture different notions of word length. Some of these have worked well in other languages and some of these are specifically available in Vietnamese (i.e., diacritics).

The number of syllables is calculated based on the number of underscores found in a word. Because white spaces are not reliable indicators of word boundaries in Vietnamese, we concatenate the syllables of one word together with underscores in the data preprocessing step.

The number of characters and diacritics are calculated as the length of the word after being normalized into NFD (Normal Form D, also known as canonical decomposition)[4] with the `unicodedata` Python module.[5]

We used the `scikit-learn` package (Pedregosa et al., 2011) with the default regularization parameter $C = 1$ and the radial basis function kernel.

5 Experiments

We evaluate the performance of the two approaches on the three corpora based on overall accuracy and precision, recall, and F1 (for identifying simple words).

5.1 Frequency Threshold

Frequency has been shown to be a strong signal in the CWI process. Figure 1 shows the frequency distribution of the three datasets. As expected, all three follow the standard Zipf's like distribution with a small number of words occurring very frequently and most of the words only occuring a small number of times.

Table 2 shows the accuracy, precision, recall and F1 scores. Overall, the approach does quite well with accuracies above 80% on all three corpora. The recall is high, highlighting that the approach is particularly good at identifying simple words. The results are significantly higher across all metrics on the Classification corpus. This is the corpus with the most data, and all documents represent news articles, which may have helped with consistency both because of source as well as writing practices.

Table 3 shows the cutoff frequencies and cutoff percentiles (if the words have frequencies below the percentile, then they are complex words). While cutoff itself varies significantly (mostly due to the size of the corpus), the percentage this frequency represents is much more consistent. For the two larger corpora, Readability and Classification, there is only a one percentage point difference: the top 10% most frequent words are the simple words. The Cluster dataset has a lower frequency cutoff.

[4]This method does not account for the diacritic found in the letter "đ", but accounts for all other diacritics.

[5]`https://docs.python.org/3/library/unicodedata.html`

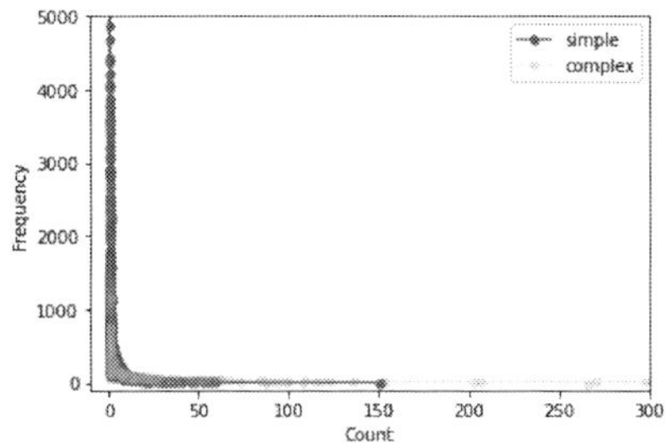

(a) READABILITY

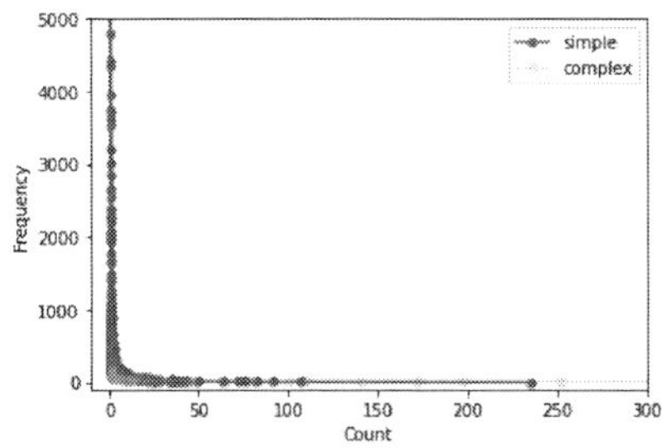

(b) CLUSTER

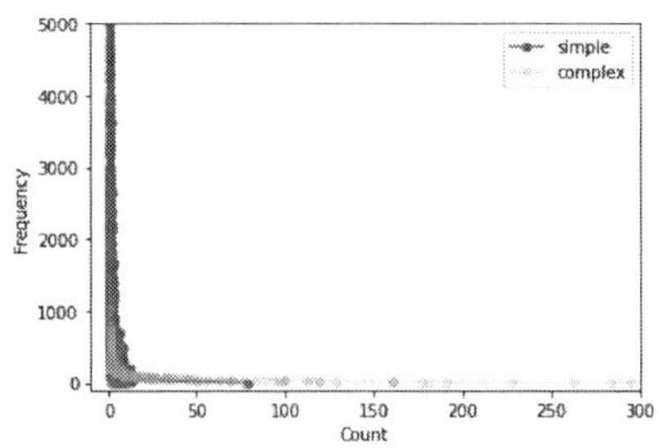

(c) CLASSIFICATION

Figure 1: The frequency distribution of the three full (unsplit) datasets.

	accuracy	precision	recall	F1
REA	0.817	0.924	0.972	0.947
CLU	0.836	0.810	0.937	0.869
CLA	0.953	0.935	0.986	0.960

Table 2: The accuracy, precision, recall, and F1 scores of the Frequency Threshold approach across the three testing datasets. [REA = READABILITY, CLU = CLUSTER, CLA = CLASSIFICATION]

	cutoff frequency	cutoff percentile
REA	154	91.5%
CLU	21	79.6%
CLA	168	92.6%

Table 3: The cutoff frequency and the cutoff percentile of the three testing datasets. [REA = READABILITY, CLU = CLUSTER, CLA = CLASSIFICATION]

We hypothesize this may have to do with its small size, though the source of the corpus might also play a role. More investigation is needed.

Figure 2 shows the accuracy distributions across possible cutoff frequencies for the three datasets. The pattern is consistent across the three datasets. The classification accuracy reaches a peak very quickly and then tends to taper off. The accuracy slightly drops and hits a plateau, except in the case of the Classification dataset in which the accuracy remains very high beyond the peak accuracy point.

5.2 Support Vector Machines Classifier

Table 4 shows the accuracy, precision, recall and F1 number for the feature-based SVM approach. The SVM approach tends to have slightly higher recall than the threshold approach, but the other met-

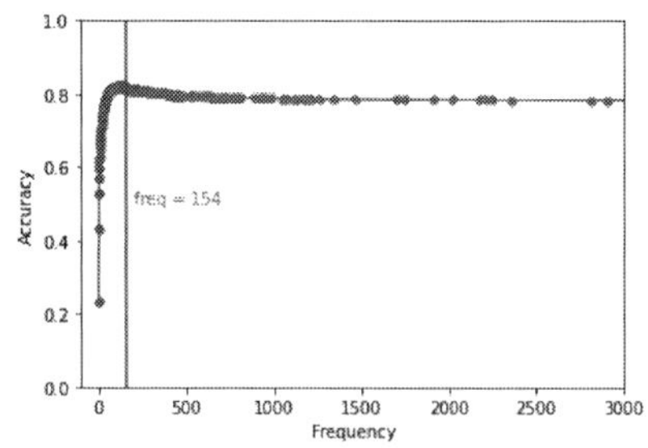

(a) READABILITY

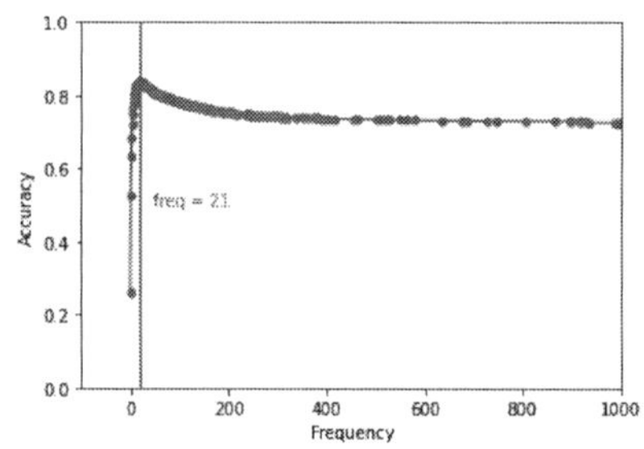

(b) CLUSTER

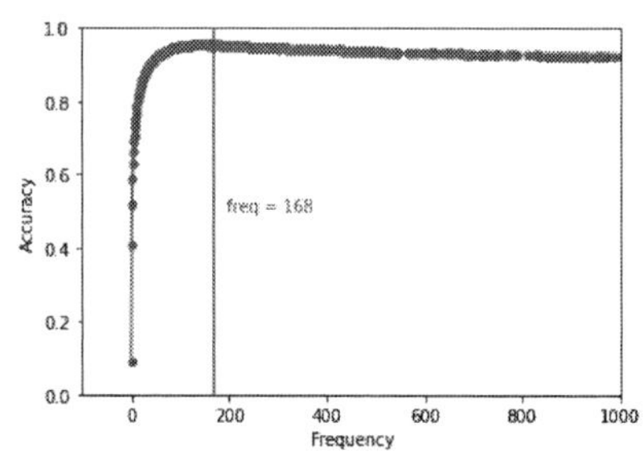

(c) CLASSIFICATION

Figure 2: The accuracy distributions across possible cutoff frequencies of the three testing datasets.

	accuracy	precision	recall	F1
REA	0.821	0.820	0.983	0.894
CLU	0.825	0.821	0.967	0.888
CLA	0.954	0.958	0.992	0.975

Table 4: The accuracy, precision, recall, and F1 scores of the SVM classifier of the three testing datasets. [REA = READABILITY, CLU = CLUSTER, CLA = CLASSIFICATION]

	accuracy	precision	recall	F1
All	0.437	0.727	0.459	0.563
M	0.824	1.0	0.739	0.850

Table 5: The accuracy, precision, recall, and F1 scores of the human annotation process. [M = Majority]

rics are not significantly different. The additional features may provide some small information, but the SVM is still heavily relying on the frequency feature to make its prediction.

6 Human Annotation

To quantify the quality of the datasets for the automated CWI task in Vietnamese, three participants were asked to manually classify 199 words as simple or complex, with 100 words randomly picked from the simple words list and 99 words from the Readability complex word list. The words were presented by themselves without any additional context. All participants were native Vietnamese speakers pursuing a college degree in the United States. The instructions were provided in Vietnamese, in which an example of one simple word and one complex word is demonstrated. The participants were reassured that there are no right or wrong answers, encouraged to use their intuition when making the decision, and to label a word as complex when in doubt. Results are reported under two circumstances: a word gets assigned a label during this collective classification process if (a) the label is chosen by all 3 of the participants and (b) the label is chosen by a majority (i.e., 2 out of 3) participants.

Table 5 shows the results for the humans annotators. There is a drastic increase across all of the metrics when we remove the restriction that all annotators need to agree on a label. Accuracy increases two-fold from around 43% to 82%, and precision rises to 100%, meaning no simple words are mislabelled. Recall nearly reaches 75%, which reflects a decent level of agreement between the annotators' idea of complexity and what is represented in the Readability dataset. However, both between annotators as well as between the task construction, there is still some contention about which words are simple and complex. This highlights the difficulty and the subjectivity of this task.

7 Discussion

Frequency is an overpowering signal in determining whether a word is complex or simple as shown by the accuracy, precision, recall and F1 scores of the **Frequency Threshold** experiment, which are all are greater than 0.8 (see Table 2). Recall scores are all greater than 0.9 across the three datasets, indicating that this approach can reliably identify complex words. This finding is consistent with the results obtained from the Complex Word Classification task in English (Paetzold and Specia, 2016).

We analyze three corpora to try understand how consistent frequency is. For the larger corpora, it is surprisingly consistent with words in the top 10% most frequent words as simple. For smaller corpora this is more varied.

There are some shortcomings in the datasets that may affect the performance. There exist words in the simple word list that are acronyms that may be obvious to a certain target audience but not for the majority of Vietnamese readers (such as "UBND", which stands for "Uỷ ban nhân dân" (people's committee)), and can mean different things in different contexts (such as TP, which can mean "thành phố" (city) or "thành phần" (ingredient)). The Cluster and Classification datasets also involve foreign words, especially English words, that can add noise to the data.

Support Vector Machines are also explored to incorporate additional information into the prediction task. Three more features are added in addition to frequency for the SVM model: number of syllables, number of characters, and number of characters and diacritics. We hypothesize that longer words and words with more diacritics will be harder to recognize and understand. For example, "cỏ cây" (trees and plants) can be perceived as a simpler word to understand than "đường sá" (streets). However, results show that using SVM with more features do not improve the performance of the classification task compared to using a frequency threshold. In fact, we observe a decline in precision (from 92.40% to 81.95%) and F1 score (from 94.73% to 89.39%) on the Readability dataset. This can be explained by the fact that surface-level word features do not necessarily make the word more complex in terms of readability and understandability. Coming back to our example, although the former word "cỏ cây" is shorter and has fewer diacritics, it can also be simpler because both words have clear meanings ("cỏ" - grass and "cây" - plant), while the second syllable of the latter word "đường sá" is a Sino-Vietnamese word that may not be clearly decipherable. Because of this reason, "trung kiên" (loyal), which is a Sino-Vietnamese word, can be viewed as more complex than "phương hướng" (direction), which is a more common word. Again, this particular example shows that frequency gives a very strong signal.

The **Human Annotation** experiment shows a great difference between labeling based on the agreement between all three annotators or between the majority of annotators (2 out of 3 annotators). The accuracy and recall scores nearly double, and the precision score is 1.0 for the majority vote. This means that the majority of annotators' labeling of complex words is consistent with the data we obtain, which can indicate the suitability of the Readability dataset for the CWI training purposes.

8 Conclusions and Future Work

Several next steps can be taken beyond this project:

More Salient Features: Features that describe a word's characteristics beyond its pronunciation can be helpful to obtain a better classification performance. Some examples include sense count (number of entries in a dictionary for example), synonym count, and word type (whether the word is loan word).

Context: The approach we explore predicts words as simple/complex regardless of their context. In some cases, the context information can help provide additional information and additional features to help the identification (Paetzold and Specia, 2016).

More Diverse Human Annotators: Developing a clear definition of "word simplicity" and "word complexity" that reflects the needs of specific audiences by creating a bigger and more diverse pool of annotators with regards to gender, education background, and income level can also be helpful in constructing models that personalize text simplification for readers from different groups.

Text Simplification is the process of reducing the syntactical and lexical complexity of original text to make it more readable and understandable. Although this task has been shown to benefit various groups of audience and has been researched and experimented with extensively in English and several other languages, there has not been considerable progress made in Vietnamese-specific Text Simplification. In this study, we focus on the Complex Word Identification step in the Lexical Simplification pipeline, one approach to solve the Text Simplification problem. We view the question as a binary classification task, and conduct three experiments Frequency Threshold, Support Vector Machines, and Human Annotation to identify important features in the classification process and investigate the quality of our datasets for this particular purpose.

We observe that frequency is a very strong signal in the Complex Word Identification process in Vietnamese, shown by the Frequency Threshold experiment where we achieve a mean accuracy of 86.87% across our three datasets. The consistency of results across the three datasets give us a general rule to identify complex words in any corpus: the 10-20% of most frequent words are likely to be simple words. The use of Support Vector Machines with surface-level word features such as number of syllables and number of characters only marginally improves the recall scores but makes no significant difference in terms of accuracy, precision, and F1 scores. The Human Annotation experiment demonstrates how with a small number of annotators and a small sample, we can quantify how one dataset aligns with the definition of word complexity of college-educated native Vietnamese speakers. Considering the absence of significant progress on the Vietnamese-specific Text Simplification task and specifically the Complex Word Identification question, these three experiments constitute a first step in the exploration of the Lexical Simplification pipeline for Vietnamese.

References

Sandra M Aluísio, Lucia Specia, Thiago AS Pardo, Erick G Maziero, and Renata PM Fortes. 2008. Towards brazilian portuguese automatic text simplification systems. In *Proceedings of the eighth ACM symposium on Document engineering*, pages 240–248.

Mark Alves. 1995. Tonal features and the development

of vietnamese tones. *Working Papers in Linguistics*, 27:1–13.

Tran Ngoc Anh, Nguyen Phuong Thai, Dao Thanh Tinh, and Nguyen Hong Quan. 2015. Identifying reduplicative words for vietnamese word segmentation. In *The 2015 IEEE RIVF International Conference on Computing & Communication Technologies-Research, Innovation, and Vision for Future (RIVF)*, pages 77–82. IEEE.

Gianni Barlacchi and Sara Tonelli. 2013. Ernesta: A sentence simplification tool for children's stories in italian. In *International Conference on Intelligent Text Processing and Computational Linguistics*, pages 476–487. Springer.

Stefan Bott, Horacio Saggion, and Simon Mille. 2012. Text simplification tools for spanish. In *Proceedings of the Eighth International Conference on Language Resources and Evaluation (LREC'12)*, pages 1665–1671.

John Carroll, Guido Minnen, Yvonne Canning, Siobhan Devlin, and John Tait. 1998. Practical simplification of english newspaper text to assist aphasic readers. In *Proceedings of the AAAI-98 Workshop on Integrating Artificial Intelligence and Assistive Technology*, pages 7–10. Citeseer.

Raman Chandrasekar, Christine Doran, and Srinivas Bangalore. 1996. Motivations and methods for text simplification. In *COLING 1996 Volume 2: The 16th International Conference on Computational Linguistics*.

Jin-Woo Chung, Hye-Jin Min, Joonyeob Kim, and Jong C Park. 2013. Enhancing readability of web documents by text augmentation for deaf people. In *Proceedings of the 3rd International Conference on Web Intelligence, Mining and Semantics*, pages 1–10.

William Coster and David Kauchak. 2011. Learning to simplify sentences using wikipedia. In *Proceedings of the workshop on monolingual text-to-text generation*, pages 1–9.

Scott A Crossley, Max M Louwerse, Philip M McCarthy, and Danielle S McNamara. 2007. A linguistic analysis of simplified and authentic texts. *The Modern Language Journal*, 91(1):15–30.

John Dawkins, Edgar Dale, and Jeanne S Chall. 1956. A reconsideration of the dale-chall formula [with reply]. *Elementary English*, 33(8):515–522.

Quang Thang Dinh, Hong Phuong Le, Thi Minh Huyen Nguyen, Cam Tu Nguyen, Mathias Rossignol, and Xuan Luong Vu. 2008. Word segmentation of vietnamese texts: a comparison of approaches. In *6th international conference on Language Resources and Evaluation-LREC 2008*.

Richard Evans, Constantin Orasan, and Iustin Dornescu. 2014. An evaluation of syntactic simplification rules for people with autism. Association for Computational Linguistics.

Richard J Evans. 2011. Comparing methods for the syntactic simplification of sentences in information extraction. *Literary and linguistic computing*, 26(4):371–388.

Elizabeth C Dee Gardner et al. 2007. Effects of lexical simplification during unaided reading of english informational texts. *TESL Reporter*, 40:33–33.

Eva Hasler, Adrià de Gispert, Felix Stahlberg, Aurelien Waite, and Bill Byrne. 2017. Source sentence simplification for statistical machine translation. *Computer Speech & Language*, 45:221–235.

Michael Heilman and Noah A Smith. 2010. Good question! statistical ranking for question generation. In *Human Language Technologies: The 2010 Annual Conference of the North American Chapter of the Association for Computational Linguistics*, pages 609–617.

Phe Hoang. 2017. *Từ điển Tiếng Việt (Vietnamese Dictionary)*. Da Nang Publising House.

Vu Cong Duy Hoang, Dien Dinh, Nguyen Le Nguyen, and Hung Quoc Ngo. 2007. A comparative study on vietnamese text classification methods. In *2007 IEEE international conference on research, innovation and vision for the future*, pages 267–273. IEEE.

Bui Thanh Hung, Nguyen Le Minh, and Akira Shimazu. 2012. Sentence splitting for vietnamese-english machine translation. In *2012 Fourth International Conference on Knowledge and Systems Engineering*, pages 156–160. IEEE.

Cao Xuân Hạo. 2000. Tiếng việt-mấy vấn đề ngữ âm, ngữ pháp, ngữ nghĩa (vietnamese-some questions on phonetics, syntax and semantics). *NXB Giáo dục, Hanoi*.

Đạt Hữu, TD Trần, and TL Đào. 1998. Cơ sở tiếng việt (basis of vietnamese).

Akihiro Katsuta and Kazuhide Yamamoto. 2019. Improving text simplification by corpus expansion with unsupervised learning. In *2019 International Conference on Asian Language Processing (IALP)*, pages 216–221. IEEE.

An-Vinh Luong, Diep Nguyen, and Dien Dinh. 2018. A new formula for vietnamese text readability assessment. In *2018 10th International Conference on Knowledge and Systems Engineering (KSE)*, pages 198–202. IEEE.

An-Vinh Luong, Diep Nguyen, and Dien Dinh. 2020. Building a corpus for vietnamese text readability assessment in the literature domain. *Universal Journal of Educational Research*, 8(10):4996–5004.

Marc Marschark and Patricia Elizabeth Spencer. 2010. *The Oxford handbook of deaf studies, language, and education, vol. 2*. Oxford University Press.

Takumi Maruyama and Kazuhide Yamamoto. 2017. Sentence simplification with core vocabulary. In *2017 International Conference on Asian Language Processing (IALP)*, pages 363–366. IEEE.

Jana M Mason. 1978. Facilitating reading comprehension through text structure manipulation. *Center for the Study of Reading Technical Report; no. 092*.

Makoto Miwa, Rune Saetre, Yusuke Miyao, and Jun'ichi Tsujii. 2010. Entity-focused sentence simplification for relation extraction. In *Proceedings of the 23rd International Conference on Computational Linguistics (Coling 2010)*, pages 788–796.

Cam-Tu Nguyen, Trung-Kien Nguyen, Xuan-Hieu Phan, Minh Le Nguyen, and Quang Thuy Ha. 2006a. Vietnamese word segmentation with crfs and svms: An investigation. In *Proceedings of the 20th Pacific Asia Conference on Language, Information and Computation*, pages 215–222.

Dat Quoc Nguyen, Dai Quoc Nguyen, Thanh Vu, Mark Dras, and Mark Johnson. 2017. A fast and accurate vietnamese word segmenter. *arXiv preprint arXiv:1709.06307*.

Thanh V Nguyen, Hoang K Tran, Thanh TT Nguyen, and Hung Nguyen. 2006b. Word segmentation for vietnamese text categorization: an online corpus approach. *RIVF06*.

Thị Minh Huyền Nguyễn, Laurent Romary, Mathias Rossignol, and Xuân Lương Vũ. 2006. A lexicon for vietnamese language processing. *Language Resources and Evaluation*, 40(3):291–309.

Sergiu Nisioi, Sanja Štajner, Simone Paolo Ponzetto, and Liviu P Dinu. 2017. Exploring neural text simplification models. In *Proceedings of the 55th annual meeting of the association for computational linguistics (volume 2: Short papers)*, pages 85–91.

Gustavo Paetzold and Lucia Specia. 2016. Semeval 2016 task 11: Complex word identification. In *Proceedings of the 10th International Workshop on Semantic Evaluation (SemEval-2016)*, pages 560–569.

Gustavo Henrique Paetzold. 2016. *Lexical Simplification for Non-Native English Speakers*. Ph.D. thesis, University of Sheffield.

F. Pedregosa, G. Varoquaux, A. Gramfort, V. Michel, B. Thirion, O. Grisel, M. Blondel, P. Prettenhofer, R. Weiss, V. Dubourg, J. Vanderplas, A. Passos, D. Cournapeau, M. Brucher, M. Perrot, and E. Duchesnay. 2011. Scikit-learn: Machine learning in Python. *Journal of Machine Learning Research*, 12:2825–2830.

Hông Phuong, Nguyên Thi Minh Huyên, Azim Roussanaly, Hô Tuòng Vinh, et al. 2008. A hybrid approach to word segmentation of vietnamese texts. In *International conference on language and automata theory and applications*, pages 240–249. Springer.

Luz Rello, Ricardo Baeza-Yates, Laura Dempere-Marco, and Horacio Saggion. 2013. Frequent words improve readability and short words improve understandability for people with dyslexia. In *IFIP Conference on Human-Computer Interaction*, pages 203–219. Springer.

Horacio Saggion, Sanja Štajner, Stefan Bott, Simon Mille, Luz Rello, and Biljana Drndarevic. 2015. Making it simplext: Implementation and evaluation of a text simplification system for spanish. *ACM Transactions on Accessible Computing (TACCESS)*, 6(4):1–36.

Matthew Shardlow. 2013. A comparison of techniques to automatically identify complex words. In *51st Annual Meeting of the Association for Computational Linguistics Proceedings of the Student Research Workshop*, pages 103–109.

Matthew Shardlow. 2014. A survey of automated text simplification. *International Journal of Advanced Computer Science and Applications*, 4(1):58–70.

Advaith Siddharthan. 2006. Syntactic simplification and text cohesion. *Research on Language and Computation*, 4(1):77–109.

Advaith Siddharthan. 2011. Text simplification using typed dependencies: A comparision of the robustness of different generation strategies. In *Proceedings of the 13th European Workshop on Natural Language Generation*, pages 2–11.

Advaith Siddharthan and Angrosh Mandya. 2014. Hybrid text simplification using synchronous dependency grammars with hand-written and automatically harvested rules. In *Proceedings of the 14th Conference of the European Chapter of the Association for Computational Linguistics*, pages 722–731.

Nhi-Thao Tran, Minh-Quoc Nghiem, Nhung TH Nguyen, Ngan Luu-Thuy Nguyen, Nam Van Chi, and Dien Dinh. 2020. Vims: a high-quality vietnamese dataset for abstractive multi-document summarization. *Language Resources and Evaluation*, 54(4):893–920.

George Van Driem. 2001. *Languages of the Himalayas: an ethnolinguistic handbook of the greater Himalayan region*, volume 2. Brill.

Thanh Vu, Dat Quoc Nguyen, Dai Quoc Nguyen, Mark Dras, and Mark Johnson. 2018. Vncorenlp: A vietnamese natural language processing toolkit. *arXiv preprint arXiv:1801.01331*.

Kristian Woodsend and Mirella Lapata. 2011. Learning to simplify sentences with quasi-synchronous grammar and integer programming. In *Proceedings of the 2011 Conference on Empirical Methods in Natural Language Processing*, pages 409–420.

Wei Xu, Courtney Napoles, Ellie Pavlick, Quanze Chen, and Chris Callison-Burch. 2016. Optimizing statistical machine translation for text simplification.

Transactions of the Association for Computational Linguistics, 4:401–415.

Benchmarking Language-agnostic Intent Classification for Virtual Assistant Platforms

Gengyu Wang*, **Cheng Qian***, **Lin Pan**, **Haode Qi**
Ladislav Kunc, **Saloni Potdar**
IBM Watson
{gengyu, cheng.qian, haode.qi, lada}@ibm.com
potdars@us.ibm.com

Abstract

Current virtual assistant (VA) platforms are beholden to the limited number of languages they support. Every component, such as the tokenizer and intent classifier, is engineered for specific languages in these intricate platforms. Thus, supporting a new language in such platforms is a resource-intensive operation requiring expensive re-training and re-designing. In this paper, we propose a benchmark for evaluating language-agnostic intent classification, the most critical component of VA platforms. To ensure the benchmarking is challenging and comprehensive, we include 29 public and internal datasets across 10 low-resource languages and evaluate various training and testing settings with consideration of both accuracy and training time. The benchmarking result shows that Watson Assistant, among 7 commercial VA platforms and pre-trained multilingual language models (LMs), demonstrates close-to-best accuracy with the best accuracy-training time trade-off.

1 Introduction

Virtual assistant (VA) platforms that enable customers to train and deploy their chatbots have seen growing demand in recent years. This has attracted significant interest from both industry and academia to develop new machine learning (ML) models and datasets for these task-oriented dialog systems. In a dialog system, intent classification as the core component identifies user intent of a user's utterance so that the system can respond appropriately by triggering dialog nodes in predefined dialog trees.

Although there has been a lot of exploration around implementing intent classification models for English, not much work has been extended to low-resource languages. Due to the vast number of world languages, it is not trivial for an enterprise VA platform to support its global customers.

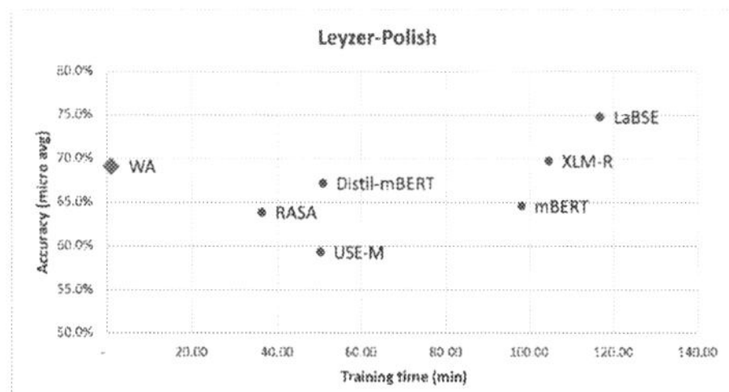

Figure 1: **Training time vs. accuracy on Leyzer (Polish) dataset for all models.** Full train set and test set are used. All methods, except WA and RASA, are trained using GPU. WA offers the best trade-off between training time and accuracy.

Currently, VA platforms usually take the following two methods to handle unsupported languages:

- Use without modification: VA platforms usually include language-specific components for each supported language, such as language models (LMs), tokenizers, part-of-speech taggers. Directly applying them to unsupported languages could dramatically hurt the performance. Several preprocessing steps, such as contraction handling, stemming, lemmatization, can produce unpredictable behavior when used with an unsupported language.
- Using translation: Translating unsupported language to the supported ones is an intuitive solution. However, low-quality translation can result in classification errors. Also, there is additional round-trip time and cost when including a translation component. In enterprise scenarios, this may lead to the deployed solution being more expensive.

While we see an increasing need to develop such a framework for non-English languages, developing a language-agnostic modeling paradigm that can serve a large number of languages carries important business applications as language-specific

*Equal contributions from the corresponding authors.

Proceedings of the Workshop on Multilingual Information Access (MIA), pages 69 - 76
July 15, 2022 ©2022 Association for Computational Linguistics

solutions are difficult and expensive to maintain.

In addition to the above challenge, there are two more considerations while developing such language-agnostic VAs. Firstly, due to the high cost of curating training data for multiple languages, real-world intent detection models usually must be able to train and perform well on few-shot training datasets. Secondly, the training time is also a critical factor to be considered. Given a commercial VA platform, authoring an assistant for a specific domain still takes dozens of hours, and the whole process involves hundreds to thousands of times of iteration. As model training is called in each iteration, keeping training time in the range of seconds is crucial.

In this paper, we conduct a comprehensive and robust evaluation of several modeling approaches across multiple low-resource languages in real-world settings and focus on their accuracy, training time, and computation requirements. We benchmark two commercial VA platforms, including IBM Watson Assistant (WA)[1], RASA[2], [3] and five representative multilingual LMs with different model sizes and architectures.

To benchmark the models on as many low-resource languages as possible, we include 9 public datasets from the research community across 5 languages and curate 20 real-world datasets from a commercial VA platform across 7 languages and 9 domains in the evaluation. We also create the few-shot version of these datasets to evaluate the models' performance on small datasets. Additionally, after observing the close accuracy results among the models, we follow Arora et al. (2020) and Qi et al. (2021) to create the TF*IDF and jaccard based difficult testing set to differentiate them better. [4]

Overall, our benchmark generates about 1000 data points, including accuracy and training time in default, few-shot training, and difficult testing settings. While LaBSE (Feng et al., 2020) produces the highest accuracy in almost all settings, along with all other LMs, their training time is too long to be used in commercial production. On the contrary, Watson Assistant achieves the best accuracy-training trade-off by achieving the competitive accuracy and consistent short training time of less than one minute. Figure1 demonstrates this comparison on one of the benchmarking datasets.

[1]https://www.ibm.com/products/watson-assistant

[2]https://rasa.com

[3]We do not include other commercial VA providers due to the benchmarking prohibition in their terms of use.

[4]The difficult test sets inherit the same licenses and terms of original datasets. https://github.com/posuer/benchmark-multilingual-intent-classification

2 Related Work

Multilingual Intent Classification A line of work has studied commercial conversational AI services (Braun et al., 2017; Arora et al., 2020; Liu et al., 2019) and pretrained LMs (Casanueva et al., 2020; Larson et al., 2019; Arora et al., 2020; Bunk et al., 2020; Qi et al., 2021) on intent classification task in English. Li et al. (2020) built a benchmark on their proposed multilingual dataset, but only evaluated two multilingual pretrained LMs. Comparing to previous work, we conduct a comprehensive benchmarking study by evaluating seven conversational AI services or LMs on 9 public datasets and 20 internal datasets covering 10 languages.

Resource Efficiency When applying a VA system in a production environment, the training cost of the model is an important consideration. Most of the prior work only focuses on the accuracy of models but does not evaluate the training time they require given the same training resources. Casanueva et al. (2020) only compare three models. In our work, we compared the training time of the 7 models in addition to their accuracy.

Few-shot Training Li et al. (2020) and Casanueva et al. (2020) conducted zero-shot or few-shot training to resemble the training process of a commercial VA system, but did not conduct a comprehensive evaluation.

3 Benchmarking

In this section, we firstly introduce the three benchmarking settings in our experiments, and then describe the VA platforms and models we evaluate. Lastly, we present and analyze the results.

3.1 Experimental Settings

Standard Training This corresponds to the standard benchmark setting where we train on the full train set and evaluate on the full test set.

Few-shot Training In a real production environment, the dialog system is usually fine-tuned for specific topics with scarce labeled data. Therefore, we propose a few-shot setting where we create five few-shot subsets by sampling 5, 15, and 30 examples per intent class from each of the datasets.

Testing with difficult examples In experiments with the standard train/test splits in the data, we observe that most models can achieve high accuracy. One of the possible reasons could be that the semantic and lexical distribution of test and train set are very similar. To better evaluate and compare the performance of the models, we create difficult test subsets with selected examples from the original test set.

We use a similar setup as described in Arora et al. (2020) and Qi et al. (2021) to create two difficult test subsets, ***TF*IDF*** and ***jaccard***, for each of the datasets. Specifically, we firstly concatenate all tokenized training examples and transform them into a vector space of TF*IDF scores (Salton and McGill, 1986) (count scores for jaccard), then use the initialized TF*IDF (or jaccard) vectorizer to transform each testing example and calculate the cosines distance (or jaccard score). For each intent class, 5 farthest testing examples are selected to build the difficult subset.

3.2 Models

In this work, we benchmark 7 different intent classification models or services. Among them, 5 are multilingual pre-trained LMs, and the remaining 2 are commercial VA platforms, IBM Watson Assistant and RASA.

Watson Assistant provides language-specific models for 13 popular languages, and a language-agnostic model that responds to all other languages. We focus on the latter for the experiments in the paper. We use public API to train and evaluate the model. For training time, we measure the round-trip latency from sending the training request until we receive the status that the model is trained and available for serving.

RASA is an automated dialogue framework that allows incorporating various text processing tools and pre-trained LMs. In our experiment, we follow the default setting that feeds count-based features to an intent classifier, DIET (Bunk et al., 2020). We fine-tune the model with each of the dataset for 100 epochs.

We also evaluate following multilingual pretrained LMs: multilingual BERT (**mBERT$_{\text{base-cased}}$**) (Devlin et al., 2018) , **Distil-mBERT$_{\text{base-cased}}$**[5] (Sanh et al., 2019), **XLM-R$_{\text{base}}$** (Conneau et al., 2019), USE-Multilingual (**USE-M$_{\text{large}}$**)[6] (Yang et al., 2019), and **LaBSE**[7] (Feng et al., 2020).

For mBERT, Distil-mBERT, XLM-R, and LaBSE model, we add a softmax classifier on top of the [CLS] token and fine-tune all layers. We use AdamW (Loshchilov and Hutter, 2018) with 0.01 weight decay and a linear learning rate scheduler. We choose a batch size of 32, epochs of 30 [8], max sequence length 128 and learning rate warmup for the first 50 iterations, peaking at 0.00005.

For USE-M, we train a softmax layer on top of the sentence representation and fine-tune all layers for 100 epochs. A learning rate of 0.01 and batch size of 32 are used for all train set variants. All models are trained or fine-tuned with a single CPU core or a single K80 GPU.

4 Benchmarking Datasets

Based on the availability and quality of public intent classification datasets, we propose our benchmark consisting of 9 public datasets across 5 languages, including *Hindi, Polish, Russian, Thai & Turkish*, and 20 internal datasets across 7 languages and 9 domains. A summary of dataset statistics and preprocessing details are provided in Table 1.

MTOP (Li et al., 2020) is an almost parallel multilingual dataset covering 6 languages and 11 domains (e.g., weather, calling, alarm, etc.). English utterances and annotations are generated by crowd-sourced workers and annotators and then human translated to other languages. We use the Hindi and Thai subset of MTOP in our experiments.

Multilingual ATIS (MultiATIS) (Upadhyay et al., 2018) contains airline travel inquiries in Hindi and Turkish, which are manually translated from the original English ATIS dataset. In our experiments, utterances with more than one intent label (concatenated by white space) are expanded into multiple records, one for each intent label.

Leyzer (Sowański and Janicki, 2020) is a multilingual chatbot dataset which contains a large number of intents and covers 20 domains such as email, contacts, etc. This corpus is generated with a grammar-based approach. We use the Polish subset of Leyzer in our experiments.

[5]https://huggingface.co/distilbert-base-multilingual-cased

[6]https://tfhub.dev/google/universal-sentence-encoder-multilingual-large/1

[7]https://huggingface.co/sentence-transformers/LaBSE

[8]We experimented with both 30 and 40 epochs settings and present the results of 30 epochs as it produced compatible results with shorter training time.

Public Datasets				
Language	Dataset	Train	Test	Intent Types
Hindi	MTOP	11,251	2,789	113
	MultiATIS	1,565	909	16
Polish	Leyzer	6,366	991	168
Russian	Chatbot-ru	5,517	1,380	79
	PSTU	1,082	271	7
Thai	MultiTOD	1,928	1,692	10
	MTOP	10,622	2,765	110
Turkish	Chatbot-tr	761	191	24
	MultiATIS	628	725	15

Internal Datasets				
Language	Domain	Train	Test	Intent Types
Finnish	COVID-19	1045	262	60
Greek	COVID-19	198	50	15
	Insurance	281	71	28
Norwegian Bokmål	banking	223	56	13
	customer service	304	76	18
	telco	317	80	19
	utilities	176	44	10
Norwegian Nynorsk	banking	224	57	13
	customer service	300	76	18
	teleco	350	88	21
	utilities	176	45	10
Polish	general	795	199	43
Russian	banking	1364	342	92
	COVID-19	1392	349	122
	general	623	158	46
Swedish	banking	211	54	13
	customer care	294	74	18
	teleco	345	87	21
	utilities	172	43	10
Turkish	customer care	184	46	9

Table 1: **Dataset Statistics.** Prepossessing has been done on all datasets (details in Datasets Section). Numbers reflect the actual size used in our experiment.

Multilingual Task Oriented Data (MultiTOD) (Schuster et al., 2018) contains annotated utterances in English, Spanish, and Thai across the topics like weather, alarm, etc. English utterances are first produced by native English speakers and labelled by annotators, then translated into Spanish and Thai by native speakers of the target languages.

Chatbot-ru (Russian)[9], **PSTU** (Russian)[10], and **Chatbot-tr** (Turkish)[11] are three intent classification datasets publicly released on Github. For each of the three datasets, we split them into train and test set in a stratified fashion, using intent type as the class labels. Intents with only one utterance are discarded.

Internal Datasets To enable benchmarking with real-world data and evaluate the models in more languages, we curate 20 internal datasets in 8 languages across 9 domains from users of a virtual assistant platform. Different from the public datasets, these internal datasets are used in enterprise production environment to train real-world virtual assistants and serve customers in domains including banking, COVID-19 and telecommunication. The detailed size, domain and language information of these datasets are listed in Table 1.

Dataset Preprocessing We conducted following preprocessing for above datasets. We firstly transform all utterances in the train sets into lower case and perform deduplication. After this process, we use the original data without duplication for experiments. Test sets of Leyzer and MultiATIS contain utterances with intents unseen in the training data. We keep such utterances in the test sets to ensure a fair comparison with others' work on these datasets.

5 Results and Analysis

Standard Training Setting Table 2 shows results of WA, RASA, and 5 pretrained LMs on 9 public datasets across 5 languages. We train on the full train sets and report results on the full test sets, measured by accuracy. In Table 3, we present the results for internal datasets in the same setting. Overall, LaBSE performs best among the 7 models on both public and internal datasets. However, considering that fine-tuning large LMs, such as LaBSE, requires significantly more computational resources, WA makes a great trade-off by achieving 84.8% average accuracy that is only 4.5% lower than LaBSE.

Few-shot Training Setting In table 4, we present the accuracy of models trained on the full set and three subsets consisting of 5/15/30 examples per intent type and evaluated on the full test set. We obtain the accuracy per language by averaging the accuracy of all datasets in that language.

Among the models, WA shows an advantage over RASA and mBERT in the few-shot setting of 5 examples per intent based on the average accuracy across the 5 languages in Table 4. For all models, we observe significant drop in accuracy in *5 examples per intent* train set compared to the *full* train set, decreasing from about 80% to about 60% on average. This shows that the limitation in

[9]https://github.com/Koziev/chatbot/blob/master/data/intents.txt

[10]https://github.com/Perevalov/pstu_assistant/blob/master/data/data.txt

[11]https://github.com/zerocodenlu/chatbot-tr/blob/master/data/nlu/intent_data.csv

Models	Hindi		Polish	Russian		Thai		Turkish		Average
	MTOP	MultiATIS	Leyzer	Chatbot-ru	PSTU	MultiTOD	MTOP	Chatbot-tr	MultiATIS	
WA	90.7	87.6	69.1	81.5	79.7	96.6	89.8	80.6	87.2	84.8
RASA	88.5	88.3	64.0	66.7	75.3	96.6	89.5	81.7	88.3	82.1
mBERT	92.9	90.0	64.6	81.9	79.7	97.1	92.5	77.5	85.7	84.6
XLM-R	94.3	89.9	69.7	86.1	81.5	96.9	94.2	84.8	89.1	87.4
USE-M	75.4	81.6	59.3	84.5	80.8	97.4	93.5	83.2	84.8	82.3
LaBSE	94.4	91.6	74.8	87.2	83.8	97.4	94.5	87.4	92.6	89.3
Distil-mBERT	92.5	89.1	67.2	79.4	80.1	97.2	92.0	78.5	87.2	84.8

Table 2: **Accuracy on 9 public datasets for WA, RASA, and 5 pretrained LMs.** Each model is trained on full train set and evaluated on full test set.

Models	Finnish	Greek	Norwegian Bokmål	Norwegian Nynorsk	Polish	Russian	Swedish	Turkish	Average
WA	66.9	70.2	74.8	73.9	68.3	77.6	75.0	80.6	73.4
RASA	64.6	66.1	75.7	73.8	62.3	70.0	68.5	77.8	69.9
mBERT	71.9	65.1	74.6	73.1	84.4	78.3	78.6	75.0	75.1
XLM-R	75.8	84.2	86.6	82.0	79.4	79.4	85.9	75.0	81.0
USE-M	65.8	56.1	66.6	64.6	78.9	78.3	70.2	72.2	69.1
LaBSE	78.1	85.9	89.9	86.6	87.4	81.9	88.8	86.1	85.6
Distil-mBERT	69.6	71.2	73.8	67.4	80.9	76.1	73.4	72.2	73.1

Table 3: **Macro accuracy over internal datasets for each language.** Models are trained on the full train set of each dataset and evaluated on the full test set. Averaged accuracy at the last row is the simple averaging.

	Hindi				**Polish**				**Russian**				**Thai**				**Turkish**				**Average**			
Models	5	15	30	full	5	15	30	full	5	15	30	full	5	15	30	full	5	15	30	full	5	15	30	full
WA	50.4	60.7	76.0	89.1	60.1	67.2	69.6	69.1	51.3	64.6	71.8	80.6	63.3	77.4	82.9	93.2	61.9	72.5	76.5	83.9	57.4	68.5	75.4	83.2
RASA	29.6	46.3	61.2	88.4	47.1	58.9	61.0	63.9	32.7	44.6	51.3	71.0	43.6	62.3	73.2	93.0	43.4	64.0	69.0	85.0	39.3	55.2	63.1	80.2
mBERT	62.3	75.6	80.4	91.5	61.4	66.9	68.2	64.6	48.3	58.4	67.8	80.8	56.7	81.0	85.8	94.8	48.6	69.3	75.6	81.6	55.4	70.2	75.6	82.6
XLM-R	64.8	78.8	82.4	92.1	66.7	73.6	73.8	69.7	52.8	67.2	73.9	83.8	72.0	46.4	47.3	95.6	55.7	73.3	82.0	87.0	62.4	67.8	71.9	85.6
USE-M	24.6	37.3	48.3	78.5	60.0	62.2	61.0	59.3	63.5	67.6	72.8	82.7	81.2	87.5	89.8	95.4	75.2	80.8	84.6	84.0	60.9	67.1	71.3	80.0
LaBSE	74.8	85.0	89.5	93.0	69.9	75.3	74.9	74.8	60.2	69.5	74.7	85.5	73.9	88.1	91.3	96.0	66.7	81.1	84.6	90.0	69.1	79.8	83.0	87.8
Distil-mBERT	54.9	69.4	78.4	90.8	57.6	65.1	65.5	67.2	32.9	57.4	68.8	79.7	54.3	78.8	84.7	94.6	46.3	63.8	74.8	82.9	49.2	66.9	74.4	83.0

Table 4: **Few-shot setting on public datasets with full test set.** Accuracy for each language is averaged over all datasets for that language. Second row corresponds to 5, 15, 30 & all examples per intent in the train set.

	Hindi			**Polish**			**Russian**			**Thai**			**Turkish**			**Average**		
Models	full	jaccard	tf*idf	full	jaccard	tf*idf	full	jaccard	tf*idf	full	jaccard	tf*idf	full	jaccard	tf*idf	full	jaccard	tf*idf
WA	89.1	55.6	49.5	69.1	68.0	68.8	80.6	67.5	64.0	93.2	70.4	60.9	83.9	61.9	57.9	83.2	64.7	60.2
RASA	88.4	56.7	50.0	63.9	59.5	60.2	71.0	64.5	58.2	93.0	70.2	67.5	85.0	62.3	60.9	80.2	62.7	59.4
mBERT	91.5	67.8	62.4	64.6	65.7	66.5	80.8	76.5	73.1	94.8	77.8	71.3	81.6	59.4	52.8	82.6	69.4	65.2
XLM-R	92.1	68.3	62.6	69.7	71.1	70.6	83.8	78.8	76.4	95.6	80.7	76.2	87.0	72.0	67.1	85.6	74.2	70.6
USE-M	78.5	40.1	34.2	59.3	59.2	58.5	82.7	76.0	76.0	95.4	78.9	73.1	84.0	61.2	58.4	80.0	63.1	60.0
LaBSE	93.0	72.2	68.7	74.8	76.8	76.8	85.5	79.0	78.3	96.0	82.2	75.2	90.0	79.1	75.6	87.8	77.8	74.9
Distil-mBERT	90.8	63.1	57.0	67.2	66.2	65.5	79.7	69.7	70.4	94.6	78.3	72.1	82.9	59.2	55.2	83.0	67.3	64.0

Table 5: **Difficult test accuracy comparison on public datasets.** Accuracy for each language is averaged over all datasets in the corresponding language. *full*, *jaccard*, and *tf*idf* refer to full, jaccard and tf*idf test sets accordingly.

		Hindi		Polish	Russian		Thai		Turkish	
Models	Resource	MTOP	MultiATIS	Leyzer	Chatbot-ru	PSTU	MultiTOD	MTOP	Chatbot-tr	MultiATIS
WA	CPU	**0.64**	**0.34**	**0.92**	**0.79**	**0.45**	**0.40**	**1.03**	**0.38**	**0.45**
RASA	CPU	66.49	8.32	36.34	35.99	15.48	7.11	73.61	2.12	3.08
mBERT	GPU	175.89	24.70	98.11	83.17	16.44	29.12	160.35	11.45	9.50
XLM-R	GPU	185.41	25.85	104.68	90.82	17.92	31.69	174.50	12.63	10.46
USE-M	GPU	103.46	19.94	50.06	40.44	14.70	14.73	72.84	6.95	7.39
LaBSE	GPU	207.02	28.77	116.80	101.58	19.98	35.48	195.59	14.01	11.62
Distil-mBERT	GPU	90.02	12.55	50.75	44.11	8.73	15.46	85.34	6.09	5.04

Table 6: **Training time.** Macro averaged training time in minutes and resource types while training on full train set and evaluating on full test set for each public dataset.

Models	5 ex/intent Time	5 ex/intent Acc.	30 ex/intent Time	30 ex/intent Acc.	full Time	full Acc.
HINDI						
MTOP						
WA	0.44	45.7%	0.56	75.1%	0.64	90.7%
RASA	2.15	21.0%	10.90	54.6%	66.49	88.5%
mBERT	8.02	51.0%	33.44	82.1%	175.89	92.9%
XLM-R	8.45	68.4%	35.21	88.4%	185.41	94.3%
USE-M	6.80	18.4%	21.32	44.1%	103.46	75.4%
LaBSE	9.40	73.6%	39.22	88.8%	207.02	94.4%
Distil-mBERT	4.10	46.2%	17.08	78.5%	90.02	92.5%
MultiATIS						
WA	0.37	55.1%	0.34	76.9%	0.34	87.6%
RASA	0.38	38.1%	1.35	67.4%	8.32	88.3%
mBERT	0.98	73.6%	3.85	78.8%	24.70	90.0%
XLM-R	1.03	61.1%	4.10	76.5%	25.85	89.9%
USE-M	2.91	30.8%	4.93	52.5%	19.94	81.6%
LaBSE	1.15	76.0%	4.55	90.2%	28.77	91.6%
Distil-mBERT	0.50	63.6%	1.98	78.4%	12.55	89.1%
POLISH						
Leyzer						
WA	0.44	60.1%	0.70	69.6%	0.92	69.1%
RASA	2.62	47.2%	12.83	60.8%	36.34	64.0%
mBERT	11.91	61.4%	43.71	68.2%	98.11	64.6%
XLM-R	13.08	66.7%	48.18	73.8%	104.68	69.7%
USE-M	7.62	60.0%	23.43	61.0%	50.06	59.3%
LaBSE	14.55	69.9%	53.32	74.9%	116.80	74.8%
Distil-mBERT	6.36	57.6%	23.18	65.5%	50.75	67.2%
RUSSIAN						
Chatbot-ru						
WA	0.34	52.4%	0.48	73.2%	0.79	81.5%
RASA	2.06	22.6%	10.57	42.8%	35.99	66.7%
mBERT	6.04	50.1%	28.53	70.2%	83.17	81.9%
XLM-R	6.64	52.9%	31.27	76.2%	90.82	86.1%
USE-M	4.82	67.6%	14.89	75.6%	40.44	84.5%
LaBSE	7.39	63.2%	34.91	79.6%	101.58	87.2%
Distil-mBERT	3.23	39.2%	15.16	68.9%	44.11	79.4%
PSTU						
WA	0.29	50.2%	0.35	70.5%	0.45	79.7%
RASA	0.56	42.8%	3.27	59.8%	15.48	75.3%
mBERT	0.62	46.5%	3.16	65.3%	16.44	79.7%
XLM-R	0.70	52.8%	3.47	71.6%	17.92	81.5%
USE-M	2.64	59.4%	4.48	70.1%	14.70	80.8%
LaBSE	0.81	57.2%	3.89	69.7%	19.98	83.8%
Distil-mBERT	0.34	26.6%	1.69	68.6%	8.73	80.1%

Models	5 ex/intent Time	5 ex/intent Acc.	30 ex/intent Time	30 ex/intent Acc.	full Time	full Acc.
THAI						
MultiTOD						
WA	0.40	77.3%	0.38	90.9%	0.40	96.6%
RASA	0.32	65.7%	1.18	90.1%	7.11	96.6%
mBERT	0.81	62.7%	4.18	92.1%	29.12	97.1%
XLM-R	0.90	82.2%	4.58	93.9%	31.69	96.9%
USE-M	2.66	90.0%	4.02	94.0%	14.73	97.4%
LaBSE	1.02	77.1%	5.12	94.3%	35.48	97.4%
Distil-mBERT	0.44	69.9%	2.23	91.2%	15.46	97.2%
MTOP						
WA	0.41	49.3%	0.47	75.0%	1.03	89.8%
RASA	2.43	21.5%	11.61	56.2%	73.61	89.5%
mBERT	7.57	50.6%	31.67	79.6%	160.35	92.5%
XLM-R	8.30	61.8%	34.76	0.8%	174.50	94.2%
USE-M	5.55	72.5%	15.99	85.5%	72.84	93.5%
LaBSE	9.26	70.6%	38.66	88.3%	195.59	94.5%
Distil-mBERT	4.04	38.8%	16.90	78.1%	85.34	92.0%
TURKISH						
Chatbot-tr						
WA	0.42	56.0%	0.36	74.9%	0.38	80.6%
RASA	0.44	39.3%	1.41	67.5%	2.12	81.7%
mBERT	1.85	51.3%	7.45	73.3%	11.45	77.5%
XLM-R	2.03	60.7%	8.19	83.2%	12.63	84.8%
USE-M	2.92	72.8%	5.37	83.2%	6.95	83.2%
LaBSE	2.26	68.1%	9.12	83.8%	14.01	87.4%
Distil-mBERT	0.98	48.7%	3.96	72.8%	6.09	78.5%
MultiATIS						
WA	0.35	67.7%	0.40	78.1%	0.45	87.2%
RASA	0.33	47.6%	0.78	70.5%	3.08	88.3%
mBERT	0.84	45.9%	2.77	77.9%	9.50	85.7%
XLM-R	0.93	50.8%	3.06	80.7%	10.46	89.1%
USE-M	2.68	77.7%	3.61	85.9%	7.39	84.8%
LaBSE	1.05	65.4%	3.40	85.5%	11.62	92.6%
Distil-mBERT	0.45	44.0%	1.47	76.8%	5.04	87.2%
MACRO AVERAGE						
WA	**0.38**	57.1%	**0.45**	76.0%	**0.60**	84.8%
RASA	1.26	38.4%	5.99	63.3%	27.62	82.1%
mBERT	4.29	54.8%	17.64	76.4%	67.64	84.6%
XLM-R	4.67	61.9%	19.20	71.7%	72.66	87.4%
USE-M	4.29	61.0%	10.89	72.5%	36.72	82.3%
LaBSE	5.21	**69.0%**	21.35	**83.9%**	81.21	**89.3%**
Distil-mBERT	2.27	48.3%	9.30	75.4%	35.34	84.8%

Table 7: **Training time (minutes) and accuracy on full test set for each public datasets.** *5 ex/intent*, *30 ex/intent*, and *full* refer to 5 examples per intent, 30 examples per intent, and full train set accordingly.

training data brings a huge challenge for all models, and the few-shot train sets provide a better testbed for the ability to handle such situations, which is crucial for real-world VA systems.

Difficult Test Setting In Table 2, we observe that most models can achieve about 90% accuracy. To better compare these models, we evaluate them on the difficult test sets, *jaccard* and *tf*idf*. Results are presented in Table 5. In this setting, we observe a significant gap between the original test set and difficult sets for all models. Among all the models, mBERT performs the best as it shows the least accuracy drop. However, WA still stands on top considering the trade-off between training time and accuracy, which will be further explained below.

5.1 Training Time vs. Accuracy Trade-off

We record the training time per dataset along with the resource requirement and accuracy in Table 6. Pretrained LMs require significantly longer training time compared to WA. The detailed result of each public dataset is in Table 7.

In Figure 1, we present a visualization of accuracy and training time for each model on the Leyzer dataset. WA achieves comparable performance to XLM-R but only requires less than 1 minute training time, compared to 104 minutes for XLM-R on the Leyzer dataset. WA offers the best trade-off in terms of accuracy vs. training time.

6 Conclusion

In this paper, we propose a robust evaluation framework to benchmark 7 intent classification models in multiple languages. On 9 public datasets and 20 internal datasets covering 10 languages. The benchmark results show that while LaBSE produces the highest accuracy in almost all evaluation settings, Watson Assistant achieves competitive performance with much less cost of training time and resource. The large LMs does not always outperform the models that only need CPUs. Through our work, we hope to encourage more research and development on language-agnostic chatbot solutions.

References

Gaurav Arora, Chirag Jain, Manas Chaturvedi, and Krupal Modi. 2020. Hint3: Raising the bar for intent detection in the wild. *arXiv preprint arXiv:2009.13833*.

Daniel Braun, Adrian Hernandez Mendez, Florian Matthes, and Manfred Langen. 2017. Evaluating natural language understanding services for conversational question answering systems. In *Proceedings of the 18th Annual SIGdial Meeting on Discourse and Dialogue*, pages 174–185.

Tanja Bunk, Daksh Varshneya, Vladimir Vlasov, and Alan Nichol. 2020. Diet: Lightweight language understanding for dialogue systems. *arXiv preprint arXiv:2004.09936*.

Inigo Casanueva, Tadas Temčinas, Daniela Gerz, Matthew Henderson, and Ivan Vulić. 2020. Efficient intent detection with dual sentence encoders. *arXiv preprint arXiv:2003.04807*.

Alexis Conneau, Kartikay Khandelwal, Naman Goyal, Vishrav Chaudhary, Guillaume Wenzek, Francisco Guzmán, Edouard Grave, Myle Ott, Luke Zettlemoyer, and Veselin Stoyanov. 2019. Unsupervised cross-lingual representation learning at scale. *arXiv preprint arXiv:1911.02116*.

Jacob Devlin, Ming-Wei Chang, Kenton Lee, and Kristina Toutanova. 2018. Bert: Pre-training of deep bidirectional transformers for language understanding. *arXiv preprint arXiv:1810.04805*.

Fangxiaoyu Feng, Yinfei Yang, Daniel Cer, Naveen Arivazhagan, and Wei Wang. 2020. Language-agnostic bert sentence embedding. *arXiv preprint arXiv:2007.01852*.

Stefan Larson, Anish Mahendran, Joseph J Peper, Christopher Clarke, Andrew Lee, Parker Hill, Jonathan K Kummerfeld, Kevin Leach, Michael A Laurenzano, Lingjia Tang, et al. 2019. An evaluation dataset for intent classification and out-of-scope prediction. *arXiv preprint arXiv:1909.02027*.

Haoran Li, Abhinav Arora, Shuohui Chen, Anchit Gupta, Sonal Gupta, and Yashar Mehdad. 2020. Mtop: A comprehensive multilingual task-oriented semantic parsing benchmark. *arXiv preprint arXiv:2008.09335*.

Xingkun Liu, Arash Eshghi, Pawel Swietojanski, and Verena Rieser. 2019. Benchmarking natural language understanding services for building conversational agents.

Ilya Loshchilov and Frank Hutter. 2018. Fixing weight decay regularization in adam.

Haode Qi, Lin Pan, Atin Sood, Abhishek Shah, Ladislav Kunc, Mo Yu, and Saloni Potdar. 2021. Benchmarking commercial intent detection services with practice-driven evaluations. In *Proceedings of the 2021 Conference of the North American Chapter of the Association for Computational Linguistics: Human Language Technologies: Industry Papers*, pages 304–310.

Gerard Salton and Michael J McGill. 1986. Introduction to modern information retrieval.

Victor Sanh, Lysandre Debut, Julien Chaumond, and Thomas Wolf. 2019. Distilbert, a distilled version of bert: smaller, faster, cheaper and lighter. *arXiv preprint arXiv:1910.01108*.

Sebastian Schuster, Sonal Gupta, Rushin Shah, and Mike Lewis. 2018. Cross-lingual transfer learning for multilingual task oriented dialog. *CoRR*, abs/1810.13327.

Marcin Sowański and Artur Janicki. 2020. Leyzer: A dataset for multilingual virtual assistants. In *International Conference on Text, Speech, and Dialogue*, pages 477–486. Springer.

Shyam Upadhyay, Manaal Faruqui, Gokhan Tür, Hakkani-Tür Dilek, and Larry Heck. 2018. (almost) zero-shot cross-lingual spoken language understanding. In *2018 IEEE International Conference on Acoustics, Speech and Signal Processing (ICASSP)*, pages 6034–6038. IEEE.

Yinfei Yang, Daniel Cer, Amin Ahmad, Mandy Guo, Jax Law, Noah Constant, Gustavo Hernandez Abrego, Steve Yuan, Chris Tar, Yun-Hsuan Sung, et al. 2019. Multilingual universal sentence encoder for semantic retrieval. *arXiv preprint arXiv:1907.04307*.

ZusammenQA: Data Augmentation with Specialized Models for Cross-lingual Open-retrieval Question Answering System

Chia-Chien Hung[1], **Tommaso Green**[1], **Robert Litschko**[1],
Tornike Tsereteli[1], **Sotaro Takeshita**[1], **Marco Bombieri**[2],
Goran Glavaš[3] and **Simone Paolo Ponzetto**[1]
[1] Data and Web Science Group, University of Mannheim, Germany
[2] ALTAIR Robotics Lab, University of Verona, Italy
[3] CAIDAS, University of Würzburg, Germany
{chia-chien.hung, tommaso.green, robert.litschko,
tornike.tsereteli, sotaro.takeshita, ponzetto}@uni-mannheim.de
marco.bombieri_01@univr.it, goran.glavas@uni-wuerzburg.de

Abstract

This paper introduces our proposed system for the MIA Shared Task on Cross-lingual Open-retrieval Question Answering (COQA). In this challenging scenario, given an input question the system has to gather evidence documents from a multilingual pool and generate from them an answer in the language of the question. We devised several approaches combining different model variants for three main components: *Data Augmentation*, *Passage Retrieval*, and *Answer Generation*. For passage retrieval, we evaluated the monolingual BM25 ranker against the ensemble of *re-rankers based on multilingual pretrained language models* (PLMs) and also variants of the shared task baseline, re-training it from scratch using a recently introduced contrastive loss that maintains a strong gradient signal throughout training by means of mixed negative samples. For answer generation, we focused on language- and domain-specialization by means of continued language model (LM) pretraining of existing multilingual encoders. Additionally, for both passage retrieval and answer generation, we augmented the training data provided by the task organizers with automatically generated question-answer pairs created from Wikipedia passages to mitigate the issue of data scarcity, particularly for the low-resource languages for which no training data were provided. Our results show that language- and domain-specialization as well as data augmentation help, especially for low-resource languages.

1 Introduction

Open-retrieval Question Answering (OQA), where the agent helps users to retrieve answers from large-scale document collections with given *open* questions, has arguably been one of the most challenging natural language processing (NLP) applications in recent years (e.g., Lewis et al., 2020; Karpukhin et al., 2020; Izacard and Grave, 2021). As is the case with the vast majority of NLP tasks, much of the OQA focused on English, relying on a pipeline that crucially depends on a neural passage retriever, i.e., a (re-)ranking model – trained on large-scale English QA datasets – to find evidence passages in English (Lewis et al., 2020) for answer generation. Unlike in many other retrieval-based tasks, such as ad-hoc document retrieval (Craswell et al., 2021), parallel sentence mining (Zweigenbaum et al., 2018), or Entity Linking (Wu et al., 2020), the progress toward *Cross-lingual Open-retrieval Question Answering (COQA)* has been hindered by the lack of efficient integration and consolidation of knowledge expressed in different languages (Loginova et al., 2021). COQA is especially relevant for opinionated information, such as news, blogs, and social media. In the era of fake news and deliberate misinformation, training on only (or predominantly) English texts is more likely to lead to more biased and less reliable NLP models. Further, an Anglo- and Indo-European-centric NLP (Joshi et al., 2020) is unrepresentative of the needs of the majority of the world's population (e.g., Mandarin and Spanish have more native speakers than English, and Hindi and Arabic come close) and contributes to the widening of the digital language divide.[1] Developing solutions for cross-lingual open QA (COQA) thus contributes towards the goal of global equity of information access.

COQA is the task of automatic question answering, where the answer is to be found in a large

[1] http://labs.theguardian.com/digital-language-divide/

Proceedings of the Workshop on Multilingual Information Access (MIA), pages 77 - 90
July 15, 2022 ©2022 Association for Computational Linguistics

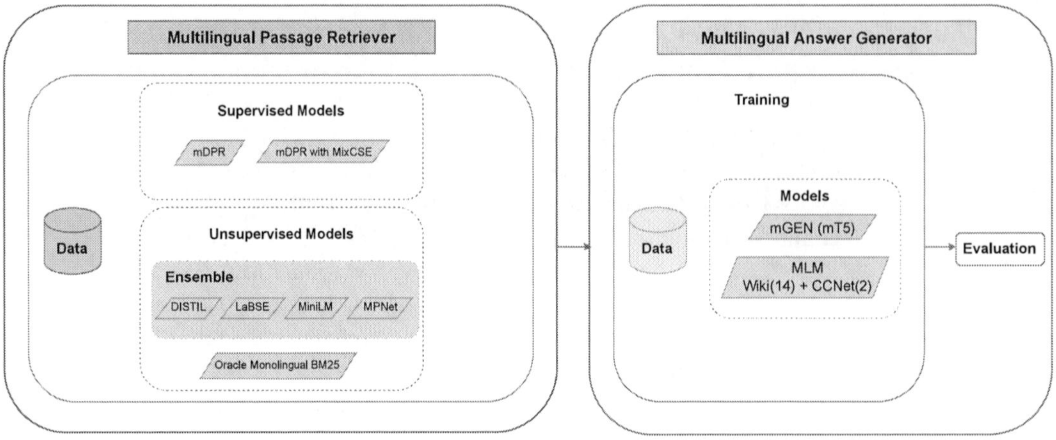

Figure 1: The proposed pipeline for the cross-lingual QA problem. The pipeline is composed of two stages: (i) the retrieval of documents containing a possible answer (red box) and the generation of an answer (blue box). For the retrieval part, we exploited different methods, based both on training mDPR variants and on the ensembling of *blackbox* models. For training the mDPR variants, we enlarge the original training dataset with samples from our data augmentation pipeline. For the generation part, we enrich the existing baseline method with data augmentation and masked language modeling.

multilingual document collection. It is a challenging NLP task, with questions written in a user's preferred language, where the system needs to find evidence in a large-scale document collection written in different languages; the answer then needs to be returned to the user in their preferred language (i.e., the language of the question).

More formally, the goal of a COQA system is to find an answer a to the query q in the collection of documents $\{D\}_i^N$. In the cross-lingual setting, q and $\{D\}_i^N$ are, in general, in different languages. For example, the users can ask a question in Japanese, and the system can search an English document for an answer that then needs to be returned to the user in Japanese.

In this work, we propose data augmentation for specialized models that correspond to the two main components of a standard COQA system – *passage retrieval* and *answer generation*: (1) we first extract the passages from all documents of all languages, exploiting both *unsupervised* and *supervised* (e.g., mDPR variants) passage retrieval methods; (2) we then use the retrieved passages from the previous step and further conduct intermediate training of a pretrained language model (e.g., mT5 (Xue et al., 2021)) on the extracted augmented data in order to inject language-specific knowledge into the model, and then generate the answers for each question from different language portions. As a result, we obtain a specialized model trained on the augmented data for the COQA system. The overall process is illustrated in Figure 1.

2 Data Augmentation

We use a language model to generate question-answer (QA) pairs from English texts, which we then filter according to a number of heuristics and translate into the other 15 languages.[2] An example can be seen in Figure 2 in the Appendix.

2.1 Question-Answer Generation

For generating the question-answer pairs, we use the provided Wikipedia passages as the input to a language model, which then generates questions and answers based on the input text. We based our choice of the model on the findings by Dong et al. (2019) and Bao et al. (2020), who showed that language models that are fine-tuned jointly on Question Answering and Question Generation, outperform individual models fine-tuned independently on those tasks. More specifically, we use the model by Dugan et al. (2022) and make slight modifications. Dugan et al. (2022) used a T5 model fine-tuned on SQuAD and further fine-tuned it on three tasks simultaneously: Question Generation (GQ), Question Answering (QA), and Answer Extraction (AE). They also included a summarization

[2] Arabic(AR), Bengali(BN), Finish(FI), Japanese(JA), Korean(KO), Russian(RU), Telugu(TE), Spanish(ES), Khmer(KM), Malay(MS), Swedish(SV), Turkish(TR), Chinese(ZH-CN), Tagalog(TL) and Tamil(TA).

module to create lexically diverse question-answer pairs. We found that using this module sometimes leads to factually incorrect passages, and leave this to future work. Similar to Dugan et al. (2022), we split the original passages into whole sentences that are shorter than 512 tokens.[3] We then generate the pairs using the first three sub-passages.

2.2 Filtering

Before translating question-answer pairs, to ensure better translations, we enforce each pair to satisfy at least one of a number of heuristics, which we determined through manual evaluation of the generated pairs. Each pair is evaluated on whether one of the following is true (in the respective order): the answer is a number, the question starts with the word *who*, the question starts with the words *how many*, or the answer contains a number or a date. After filtering, we are left with roughly 339,000 question-answer pairs.

2.3 Translation

We use the Google Translate API provided by *translatepy*[4] to translate the filtered question-answer pairs from English into the relevant 15 languages. Each language has an equal number of question-answer pairs. In total, we generate about 5.4 million pairs for all languages combined.

3 Methodology

Following the approach described in Asai et al. (2021b), we consider the COQA problem as two sub-components: the *retrieval* of documents containing a possible answer and the *generation* of an answer. Figure 1 summarizes the proposed methods. This section is organized as follows: we present the proposed retrieval methods in §3.1 and demonstrate the language-specialized methods for answer generation in §3.2.

3.1 Passage Retrieval

For the passage retrieval phase, we explored the approaches described in the following sections, which fall into three main categories: the enhancement of the training procedure of the mDPR baseline, the ensembling of *blackbox* models (i.e. retrieval using multilingual sentence encoders trained for semantic similarity) and lexical retrieval using BM25. While the first category is a *supervised* approach, which uses QA datasets to inject task knowledge into pre-trained models, the others use general linguistic knowledge for retrieving (i.e., *unsupervised*).

Baseline: mDPR We take as a baseline the method proposed in Asai et al. (2021b). They propose mDPR (Multilingual Dense Passage Retriever), a model that extends the Dense Passage Retriever (DPR) (Qu et al., 2021) to a multilingual setting. It is made of two mBERT-based encoders (Devlin et al., 2019), one for the question and one for the passages. The training approach proceeds over two subsequent stages: (i) *parameter updates* and (ii) *cross-lingual data mining*.

In the first phase, both mDPR and mGEN (§3.2) are trained one after the other. For mDPR, the model processes a dataset $\mathcal{D} = \{(q_i, p_i^+, p_{i,1}^-, p_{i,2}^-, \ldots, p_{i,n}^-)\}_{i=1}^m$ made of tuples containing a question q_i, the passage p_i^+ containing an answer (called positive or gold), and a set $\{p_{i,j}^-\}_{j=1}^n$ of negative passages. For every question, negatives are made up of the positive passages from the other questions or passages either extracted at random or produced by the subsequent data mining phase. To do this, they use a contrastive loss ($\mathcal{L}_{\text{mdpr}}$) that moves the embedding of the question close to its positive passage, while at the same time repelling the representations of negative passages:

$$\mathcal{L}_{\text{mdpr}} = -\log \frac{\langle \mathbf{e}_{q_i}, \mathbf{e}_{p_i^+} \rangle}{\langle \mathbf{e}_{q_i}, \mathbf{e}_{p_i^+} \rangle + \sum_{j=1}^{n} \langle \mathbf{e}_{q_i}, \mathbf{e}_{p_{i,j}^-} \rangle}$$

In the second stage, the training set is expanded by finding new positive and negative passages using Wikipedia language links and mGEN (§3.2) to automatically label passages. This two-staged training pipeline is repeated T times.

mDPR variants One of our approaches is to simply substitute the loss function presented above with a contrastive loss described in Zhang et al. (2022), named MixCSE. In this work, the authors tackle a common problem of out-of-the-box BERT sentence embeddings, called anisotropy (Li et al., 2020), which makes all the sentence representations to be distributed in a narrow cone. Contrastive learning has already proven effective in alleviating this issue by distributing embeddings in a larger space (Gao et al., 2021). Zhang et al. (2022) prove that hard negatives, i.e. data points hard to distinguish from the selected anchor, are key for keeping

[3]We use a different sentence splitting method, namely pySBD.

[4]https://github.com/Animenosekai/translate

a strong gradient signal; however, as learning proceeds, they become orthogonal to the anchor and make the gradient signal close to zero. For this reason, the key idea of MixCSE is to continually generate hard negatives via mixing positive and negative examples, which maintains a strong gradient signal throughout training. Adapting this concept to our retrieval scenario, we construct mixed negative passages as follows:

$$\tilde{e_i} = \frac{\lambda\, \mathbf{e}_{p_i^+} + (1-\lambda)\, \mathbf{e}_{p_{i,j}^-}}{\|\lambda\, \mathbf{e}_{p_i^+} + (1-\lambda)\, \mathbf{e}_{p_{i,j}^-}\|_2},$$

where $p_{i,j}^-$ is a negative passage chosen at random. We provide the equation of the loss in Appendix B. The main difference with $\mathcal{L}_{\text{mdpr}}$ is the addition of a mixed negative in the denominator and the similarity used (exponential of cosine similarity instead of dot product).

We train mDPR with the original loss and with the MixCSE loss on the concatenation of the provided training set for mDPR and the augmented data obtained via the methods described in §2. We refer to these two variants as *mDPR(AUG)* and *mDPR(AUG) with MixCSE*, respectively.

Ensembling "blackbox" models Following the approaches presented in Litschko et al. (2022), we also ensemble the ranking of some *blackbox* models that directly produce a semantic embedding of the input text. We provide a brief overview of the models included in our ensemble below.

- **DISTIL** (Reimers and Gurevych, 2020) is a teacher-student framework for injecting the knowledge obtained through specialization for semantic similarity from a specialized monolingual transformer (e.g., BERT) into a non-specialized multilingual transformer (e.g., mBERT). For semantic similarity, it first specializes a monolingual (English) teacher encoder using the available semantic sentence-matching datasets for supervision. In the second knowledge distillation step, a pretrained multilingual student encoder is trained to mimic the output of the teacher model. We benchmark different DISTIL models:
  - $\text{DISTIL}_{\text{use}}$: instantiates the student as the pretrained m-USE (Yang et al., 2020) instance;
  - $\text{DISTIL}_{\text{xlmr}}$: initializes the student model with the pretrained XLM-R (Conneau et al., 2020) transformer;
  - $\text{DISTIL}_{\text{dmbert}}$: distills the knowledge from the Sentence-BERT (Reimers and Gurevych, 2019) teacher into a multilingual version of DistilBERT (Sanh et al., 2019), a 6-layer transformer pre-distilled from mBERT.
- **LaBSE** (Language-agnostic BERT Sentence Embeddings Feng et al. (2022)) is a neural dual-encoder framework, trained with parallel data. LaBSE training starts from a pretrained mBERT instance. LaBSE additionally uses standard self-supervised objectives used in the pretraining of mBERT and XLM (Conneau and Lample, 2019): masked and translation language modelling (MLM and TLM).
- **MiniLM** (Wang et al., 2020) is a student model trained by deeply mimicking the self-attention behavior of the last Transformer layer of the teacher, which allows a flexible number of layers for the students and alleviates the effort of finding the best layer mapping.
- **MPNet** (Song et al., 2020) is based on a pre-training method that leverages the dependency among the predicted tokens through permuted language modeling and makes the model see auxiliary position information to reduce the discrepancy between pre-training and fine-tuning.

We produce an ensembling of the *blackbox* models by simply taking an average of the ranks for each of the documents retrieved, which is denoted as *EnsembleRank*.

Oracle Monolingual BM25 (Sparck Jones et al., 2000; Jonesa et al., 2000) This approach is made of two phases: first, we automatically detect the language of the question, then we query the index in the detected language. As a weighting scheme in the vector space model, we choose BM25. It is based on a probabilistic interpretation of how terms contribute to the document's relevance. It uses exact term matching and the score is derived from a sum of contributions from each query term that appears in the document. We use an *oracle BM25* approach: this naming derives from the fact that we query the index with the answer rather than the question. This was done at training time to increase the probability of the answer to be in the passages consumed by mGEN, so that the generation model would hopefully learn to extract the answer from its input, rather than generating it from the question only. At inference time, we query the index using the question.

3.2 Answer Generation

Our answer generation modules take a concatenation of the question and the related documents retrieved by the retrieval module as an input and generate an answer. In this section, we first explain the baseline system which is the basis of our proposed approaches and then present our specialization method.

Baseline: mGEN We use mGEN (Multilingual Answer Generator; Asai et al. (2021b)) as the baseline for the answer generation phase. They propose to take mT5 (Xue et al., 2021), a multilingual version of a pretrained transformer-based encoder-decoder model (Raffel et al., 2020), and fine-tune it for multilingual answer generation. The pre-training process of mT5 is based on a variant of masked language modeling named span-corruption, in which the objective is to reconstruct continuously masked tokens in an input sentence (Xue et al., 2021). For fine-tuning, the model is trained on a sequence-to-sequence (seq2seq) task as follows:

$$P(a^L \mid q^L, P^N) = \prod_{i}^{T} p(a_i^L | a_{<i}^L, q^L, P^N)$$

The model predicts a probability distribution over its vocabulary at each time step (i). It is conditioned on the previously generated answer tokens ($a_{<i}^L$), the input question (q^L) and N retrieved passages (P^N). Because of a possible language mismatch between the answer and the passages, it is not possible to extract answers as in existing work in monolingual QA tasks (Karpukhin et al., 2020): for this reason, mGEN opts for directly generating answers instead.

Masked Language Modeling (MLM) Following successful work on language-specialized pretraining via language modeling (Glavaš et al., 2020; Hung et al., 2022), we investigate the effect of running MLM on the language-specific portions of Wikipedia passages (Asai et al., 2021b) and CC-Net (Wenzek et al., 2020) with mT5 (Xue et al., 2021). For the extracted texts of all 16 languages, 14 languages are from the released Wikipedia passages and the missing two *surprise* languages (Tamil, Tagalog) are from CCNet. We additionally clean all language portions by removing email addresses, URLs, extra emojis and punctuations, and selected 7K for training and 0.7K for validation for each language. In this way, we inject both the domain-specific (i.e., Wikipedia knowledge) and language-specific (i.e., 16 languages) knowledge into the multilingual pretrained language model via MLMing as an intermediate specialization step.

Augmentation Data Variants To further investigate model capability on (1) extracting answers from English passages or (2) extracting answers from translated passages, while keeping the Question-Answer pairs in other non-English languages, we conduct experiments on two augmentation data variants: **AUG-QA** and **AUG-QAP**. **AUG-QA** keeps the English passage with the translated Question-Answer pairs, while **AUG-QAP** translates the English passage to the same language as the translated Question-Answer pairs. Detailed examples are shown in Table 1.

4 Experimental Setup

We demonstrate the effectiveness of our proposed COQA systems by comparing them to the baseline models and thoroughly comparing different specialization methods from §1.

Evaluation Task and Measures Our proposed approaches are evaluated in 16 languages, 8 of which are not covered in the training data.[5] The training and evaluation data are originally from Natural Questions (Kwiatkowski et al., 2019), XOR-TyDi QA (Asai et al., 2021a), and MKQA (Longpre et al., 2020). Data size statistics for each resource and language are shown in Table 2 and 3.

The evaluation results are measured on the competition platform hosted at eval.ai.[6] The systems are evaluated on two COQA datasets: XOR-TyDi QA (Asai et al., 2021a), and MKQA (Longpre et al., 2020), using token-level F1 (**F1**), as common evaluation practice of open QA systems (Lee et al., 2019). For *non-spacing* languages, we follow the token-level tokenizers [7] for both predictions and

[5] Languages with training data: English(EN), Arabic(AR), Bengali(BN), Finish(FI), Japanese(JA), Korean(KO), Russian(RU), Telugu(TE). Without training data: Spanish(ES), Khmer(KM), Malay(MS), Swedish(SV), Turkish(TR), Chinese(ZH-CN). Tagalog(TL) and Tamil(TA) are considered as *surprise* languages.

[6] `https://eval.ai/`

[7] Tokenizers for non-spacing languages: Mecab (JA); khmernltk (KM); jieba (ZH-CN).

	AUG-QA	AUG-QAP
QA pair	**Q**: レゴグループを設立したのは誰ですか？ **A**: オレ・カーク・クリスチャンセン	
Passage	The Lego Group began manufacturing the interlocking toy bricks in 1949. Movies, games, competitions, and six Legoland amusement parks have been developed under the brand. As of July 2015, 600 billion Lego parts had been produced. In February 2015, Lego replaced Ferrari as Brand Finance's "world's most powerful brand". History. The Lego Group began in the workshop of Ole Kirk Christiansen	レゴグループは1949年に連動おもちゃのレンガの製造を開始しました。映画、ゲーム、競技会、および6つのレゴランド遊園地がこのブランドで開発されました。2015年7月現在、6,000 億個のレゴパーツが生産されています。2015年2月、レゴはブランドファイナンスの「世界で最も強力なブランド」としてフェラーリに取って代わりました。歴史。レゴグループは、OleKirkChristiansenのワークショップで始まりました

Table 1: Examples of augmented training instances for **AUG-QA** and **AUG-QAP**. Top row: translated question-answer pair in Japanese. Below are different training examples: (1) **AUG-QA**: the English Wikipedia passage is kept with the translated question-answer pair. (2) **AUG-QAP**: the English Wikipedia passage is translated to the same language as the question-answer pair.

Dataset	Lang	Train size
Natural Questions	en	76635
XOR-TyDi QA	ar	18402
	bn	5007
	fi	9768
	ja	7815
	ko	4319
	ru	9290
	te	6759

Table 2: The training data size for 8 languages.

Dataset	Lang	Dev size	Test size
MKQA (parallel)	12	1758	5000
XOR-TyDi QA	ar	590	1387
	bn	203	490
	fi	1368	974
	ja	1056	693
	ko	1048	473
	ru	910	1018
	te	873	564
Surprise	ta	-	350
	tl	-	350

Table 3: The development and test data size for each language. The data size for MKQA is equal for all 12 languages. Two *surprise* languages are provided without development data.

ground-truth answers. The overall score is calculated by using macro-average scores on XOR-TyDi QA and MKQA datasets, and then taking the average F1 scores of both datasets.

Data We explicitly state that we did not train on the development data or the subsets of the Natural Questions and TyDi QA, which are used to create MKQA or XOR-TyDi QA datasets. This makes all of our proposed approaches fall into the *constrained* setup proposed by the organizers.

For training the mDPR variants, we exploit the organizer's dataset that was obtained from DPR Natural Questions (Qu et al., 2021) and XOR-TyDiQA gold paragraph data. More specifically, for training and validation, we always use the version of the dataset containing augmented positive and negative passages obtained from the top 50 retrieval results of the organizer's mDPR. We merge this dataset with the augmented data, filtering the latter to get 100k samples for each of the 16 languages.

We base our training data for answer generation models on the organizer's datasets with the top 15 retrieved documents from the coupled retriever. To use automatically generated question-answer pairs for each language from §4 for fine-tuning, we align the format with retrieved results by randomly sampling passages from English Wikipedia as negative contexts,[8] while we keep the seed documents as positive ones. We explore two ways of merging the positive and negative passages: in the "shuffle" style, the positive passage appears in one of the top 3 documents; in the "non-shuffle" method, the positive passage always appears on the top. However, since these two configurations did not show large differences, we only report the former one in this paper. We also investigated if translating passages into the different 16 languages [9] may be beneficial with respect to keeping all the passages in English (**AUG-QA**). Due to computational limitations, in our data augmented setting for generation model fine-tuning, we use 2K question-answer pairs with positive/negative passages for each language for our final results.

Hyperparameters and Optimization For multilingual dense passage retrieval, we mostly follow the setup provided by the organizers: learning rate $1e-5$ with AdamW (Loshchilov and Hutter, 2019), linear scheduling with warm-up for 300 steps and

[8]For the negative contexts, we use the passages that were used for generating the question-answer pairs (i.e., the first three sub-passages). These were then trimmed down to 100 tokens. We ensure that the answer is not contained in the negative contexts through lowercase string-matching.

[9]Using the same Google Translate API adopted for the QA translation in §4.

dropout rate 0.1. For **mDPR(AUG) *with* MixCSE** (Zhang et al., 2022), we use $\lambda = 0.2$ and $\tau = 0.05$ for the loss (see Appendix B). We train with a batch size of 16 on 1 GPU for at most 40 epochs, using average rank on the validation data to pick the checkpoints. The training is done independently of mGEN, in a non-iterative fashion.

For retrieving the passages, we use cosine similarity between question and passage across all proposed retrieval models, returning the top 100 passages for each of the questions.

For language-specialized pretraining via MLM, we use AdaFactor (Shazeer and Stern, 2018) with the learning rate $1e-5$ and linear scheduling with warm-up for 2000 steps up to 20 epochs. For multilingual answer generation fine-tuning, we also mostly keep the setup from the organizers: learning rate $3e-5$ with AdamW (Loshchilov and Hutter, 2019), linear scheduling with warm-up for 500 steps, and dropout rate as 0.1. We take the top 15 documents from the retrieved results as our input and truncate the input sequence after $16,000$ tokens to fit the model into the memory constraints of our available infrastructure.

5 Results and Discussion

Results Overview Results in Table 4 show the comparison between the baseline and our proposed methods on XOR-TyDi QA while Table 5 shows the results on MKQA. While we can see that the additional pretraining on the answer generation model (*mDPR+MLM-14*) helps to outperform the baseline in XOR-TyDi QA, the same approach leads to a degradation in MKQA. None of the proposed methods for the retrieval module improved over the baseline mDPR in both datasets, as shown in Table 6.

Unsupervised vs Supervised Retrieval In all evaluation settings, unsupervised retrieval methods underperform supervised methods by a large margin (see Table 4 and 5). This might be due to the nature of the task, which is to find a document containing an answer, rather than simply finding a document similar to the input question. For this reason, such an objective might not align well with models specialized in semantic similarity (Litschko et al., 2022). Fine-tuning mBERT, however, makes the model learn to focus on retrieving an answer-containing document and not simply retrieving documents similar to the question.

Language Specialization We compare the evaluation results for the fine-tuned answer generation model with and without language specialization (i.e., MLMing): for *XORQA-ar* and *XORQA-te* we have +2.0 and +1.1 percentage points improvement compared to the baseline model (with mT5 trained on 100+ languages). We further distinguish MLM-14 and MLM-16, where the former is trained on the released Wikipedia passages for 14 languages and the latter is trained on the concatenation of Wikipedia passages and CCNet (Wenzek et al., 2020), to which we resort for the two *surprise* languages (Tamil and Tagalog), which were missing in the Wikipedia data. Overall, MLM-14 performs better than MLM-16: we hypothesize that this might be due to the domain difference between text coming from Wikipedia and CCNet: the latter is not strictly aligned with the structured text (i.e., clean) version of Wikipedia passages, and causes a slight drop in performance as we train for 2 additional languages.

Data Augmentation Data augmentation is considered a way to mitigate the performance of low-resource languages while reaching performance on par with high-resource languages (Kumar et al., 2019; Riabi et al., 2021; Shakeri et al., 2021). Two variations are considered: AUG-QA and AUG-QAP, while the former concatenates the XOR-Tydi QA training set with the additional augmented data with translated Question-Answer pairs, and the latter is made from the concatenation of both XOR-Tydi QA training set and the translated Question-Answer-Passage.[10] We assume that by also translating passages, the setting should be closer to test time when the retrieval module can retrieve passages in any of 14 languages (without the two surprise languages). In contrast, in AUG-QA setting, the input passages to the answer generation are always in English. Models trained with additional AUG-QA data could increase the capacity of *seeing* more data for unseen languages, while AUG-QAP may further enhance the ability of the model to generate answers from the translated passages. As expected, models trained with additional augmented data have better performance compared to the ones without. The encouraging finding states that, especially for two *surprise* languages, the language specialized models fine-tuned with both XOR-Tydi

[10]XORQA-Tydi QA training set is with 8 languages (see Table 2) and augmented data are with *all* 16 languages included in the test set.

Models	XOR-TyDi QA ar	bn	fi	ja	ko	ru	te	Avg.
mDPR + mGEN (baseline 1)	49.66	33.99	**39.54**	39.72	**25.59**	**40.98**	36.16	37.949
Unsupervised Retrieval								
OracleBM25 + MLM-14	0.34	0.49	0.52	2.56	0.19	0.57	5.16	1.404
EnsembleRank + MLM-14	0.34	0.49	1.33	2.56	0.38	6.27	16.21	3.161
Supervised Retrieval								
mDPR(AUG) *with* MixCSE + MLM-14	20.94	7.18	15.27	23.16	10.25	19.23	10.53	15.223
mDPR(AUG) + MLM-14	24.99	15.19	20.33	22.31	10.68	18.82	11.97	17.754
mDPR + MLM-14	**51.66**	31.96	38.68	40.89	25.35	39.87	**37.26**	**37.951**
mDPR + MLM-14(XORQA & AUG-QA)	49.41	32.90	37.95	**40.97**	24.22	39.29	35.76	37.213
mDPR + MLM-14(XORQA & AUG-QAP)	48.79	33.73	38.33	39.87	25.26	39.11	37.94	37.577
mDPR + MLM-16	49.92	31.16	37.20	39.92	24.63	38.78	34.30	36.558
mDPR + MLM-16(XORQA & AUG-QA)	49.45	31.59	38.33	40.44	23.83	38.67	35.92	36.889
mDPR + MLM-16(XORQA & AUG-QAP)	48.21	**34.20**	38.78	40.76	24.81	39.49	34.37	37.231

Table 4: Evaluation results on XOR-TyDi QA test data with F1 and macro-average F1 scores.

Models	MKQA ar	en	es	fi	ja	km	ko	ms	ru	sv	tr	zh-cn	Surprise ta	tl	Avg.
mDPR + mGEN (baseline1)	**9.52**	**36.34**	**27.23**	**22.70**	**15.89**	6.00	**7.68**	**25.11**	**14.60**	**26.69**	**21.66**	13.78	0.00	12.78	**17.141**
Unsupervised Retrieval															
OracleBM25 + MLM-14	2.80	10.81	3.70	3.29	5.89	1.53	1.51	5.49	1.85	7.42	2.94	1.81	0.00	8.23	4.090
EnsembleRank + MLM-14	6.43	31.66	20.02	17.38	10.68	**6.24**	4.38	21.03	6.27	21.09	17.13	7.22	0.00	8.39	12.709
Supervised Retrieval															
mDPR(AUG) *with* MixCSE + MLM-14	4.71	28.06	12.78	8.22	7.92	5.44	2.74	12.90	4.65	13.86	8.38	3.99	0.00	6.72	8.599
mDPR(AUG) + MLM-14	5.64	29.23	17.27	15.51	7.81	5.83	3.38	16.57	6.80	17.21	13.10	4.53	0.00	8.09	10.785
mDPR + MLM-14	8.73	35.32	25.54	20.42	14.27	6.06	6.78	24.10	12.01	25.97	20.27	13.95	0.00	11.14	16.040
mDPR + MLM-14(XORQA & AUG-QA)	8.46	35.12	24.74	19.50	14.38	5.62	7.22	23.24	11.46	24.49	19.67	**15.79**	**0.86**	12.18	15.909
mDPR + MLM-14(XORQA & AUG-QAP)	8.48	34.73	25.46	20.09	14.61	5.00	7.42	24.16	12.04	25.61	19.62	15.60	0.00	12.41	16.089
mDPR + MLM-16	8.15	34.14	24.85	19.38	13.73	5.93	6.51	22.21	11.46	24.91	18.82	13.62	0.00	12.59	15.451
mDPR + MLM-16(XORQA & AUG-QA)	8.21	34.06	25.65	20.14	14.22	5.80	6.70	24.40	11.82	25.71	19.92	15.42	0.40	12.36	16.057
mDPR + MLM-16(XORQA & AUG-QAP)	8.08	33.89	24.94	20.50	14.11	5.15	7.15	22.95	12.95	24.93	19.68	15.27	0.14	**13.07**	15.915

Table 5: Evaluation results on MKQA test dataset and two *surprise* languages with F1 and macro-average F1 scores.

Models	Avg.
mDPR + mGEN (baseline1)	**27.55**
Unsupervised Retrieval	
OracleBM25 + MLM-14	2.75
EnsembleRank + MLM-wiki14	7.94
Supervised Retrieval	
mDPR(AUG) *with* MixCSE + MLM-14	11.91
mDPR(AUG) + MLM-14	14.27
mDPR + MLM-14	27.00
mDPR + MLM-14(XORQA & AUG-QA)	26.56
mDPR + MLM-14(XORQA & AUG-QAP)	26.83
mDPR + MLM-16	26.00
mDPR + MLM-16(XORQA & AUG-QA)	26.47
mDPR + MLM-16(XORQA & AUG-QAP)	26.57

Table 6: Results of macro-average F1 for two QA datasets: XOR-TyDi QA, MKQA, and two *surprise* languages.

QA and AUG-QAP drastically improve the performance of these *unseen, low-resource* languages.

mDPR variants results As shown in Table 4 and 5, we can see that the mDPR variants we trained are considerably worse than the baseline. We think this is mainly caused by the limited batch size used (16) which is a constraint due to our infrastructure. The number of samples in a batch is critical for contrastive training, as larger batches provide a stronger signal due to a higher number of negatives. For this reason, we think that the mDPR variants have not been thoroughly investigated and might still prove beneficial when trained with larger batches.

6 Related Work

Passage Retrieval and Answer Generation To improve the information accessibility, open-retrieval question answering systems are attracting much attention in NLP applications (Chen et al., 2017; Karpukhin et al., 2020). Rajpurkar et al. (2016) were one of the early works to present a benchmark that requires systems to understand a passage to produce an answer to a given question. (Kwiatkowski et al., 2019) presented a more challenging and realistic dataset with questions collected from a search engine. To tackle these complex and knowledge-demanding QA tasks, Lewis et al. (2020) proposed to first retrieve related documents from a given question and use them as additional aids to predict an answer. In particular, they explored a general-purpose fine-tuning recipe for retrieval-augmented generation models, which combine pretrained parametric and non-parametric memory for language generation. Izacard and Grave (2021), they solved the problem in two steps, first retrieving support passages before processing them with a seq2seq model, and Sun et al. (2021) further extended to the cross-lingual conversational domain. Some works are explored with *translate-then-answer* approach, in which texts are translated into English, making the task monolingual (Ture and Boschee, 2016; Asai et al., 2021a). While this approach is conceptually simple, it is known to cause the *error propagation* problem in which errors of the translation get amplified in the answer generation stage (Zhu et al., 2019). To mitigate this problem, Asai et al. (2021b) proposed to extend Lewis et al. (2020) by using multilingual models for both the passage retrieval (Devlin et al., 2019) and answer generation (Xue et al., 2021).

Data Augmentation Data augmentation is a common approach to reduce the data sparsity for deep learning models in NLP (Feng et al., 2021). For Question Answering (QA), data augmentation has been used to generate paraphrases via *back-translation* (Longpre et al., 2019), to replace parts of the input text with translations (Singh et al., 2019), and to generate novel questions or answers (Riabi et al., 2021; Shakeri et al., 2021; Dugan et al., 2022). In the cross-lingual setting, available data have been translated into different languages (Singh et al., 2019; Kumar et al., 2019; Riabi et al., 2021; Shakeri et al., 2021) and language models have been used to train question and answer generation models (Kumar et al., 2019; Chi et al., 2020; Riabi et al., 2021; Shakeri et al., 2021).

Our approach is different from previous work in Cross-lingual Question Answering task in that it only requires English passages to augment the training data, as answers are generated automatically from the trained model by Dugan et al. (2022). In addition, our filtering heuristics remove incorrectly generated question-answer pairs, which allows us to keep only question-answer pairs with answers that are more likely to be translated correctly, thus limiting the problem of error propagation.

7 Reproducibility

To ensure full reproducibility of our results and further fuel research on COQA systems, we release the model within the Huggingface repository as the publicly available multilingual pretrained language model specialized in 14 and 16 languages.[11] We also release our code and data, which make our approach completely transparent and fully reproducible. All resources developed as part of this work are publicly available at: `https://github.com/umanlp/ZusammenQA`.

8 Conclusion

We introduced a framework for a cross-lingual open-retrieval question-answering system, using data augmentation with specialized models in a *constrained* setup. Given a question, we first retrieved top relevant documents and further generated the answer with the specialized models (i.e., MLM-ing on Wikipedia passages) along with the augmented data variants. We demonstrated the effectiveness of data augmentation techniques with language- and domain-specialized additional training, especially for resource-lean languages. However, there are still remaining challenges, especially in the retrieval model training with limited computational resources. Our future efforts will be to focus on more efficient approaches of both multilingual passage retrieval and multilingual answer generation (Abdaoui et al., 2020) with the investigation of different data augmentation techniques (Zhu et al., 2019). We hope that our generated QA language resources with the released models can catalyze the research focus on resource-lean languages for COQA systems.

References

Amine Abdaoui, Camille Pradel, and Grégoire Sigel. 2020. Load what you need: Smaller versions of mutililingual BERT. In *Proceedings of SustaiNLP: Workshop on Simple and Efficient Natural Language Processing*, pages 119–123, Online. Association for Computational Linguistics.

Akari Asai, Jungo Kasai, Jonathan H. Clark, Kenton Lee, Eunsol Choi, and Hannaneh Hajishirzi. 2021a. XOR QA: cross-lingual open-retrieval question answering. In *Proceedings of the 2021 Conference of the North American Chapter of the Association for Computational Linguistics: Human Language Technologies, NAACL-HLT 2021, Online, June 6-11, 2021*, pages 547–564. Association for Computational Linguistics.

Akari Asai, Xinyan Yu, Jungo Kasai, and Hanna Hajishirzi. 2021b. One question answering model for many languages with cross-lingual dense passage

[11]MLM-14: `https://huggingface.co/umanlp/mt5-mlm-wiki14`; MLM-16: `https://huggingface.co/umanlp/mt5-mlm-16`

retrieval. In *Advances in Neural Information Processing Systems 34: Annual Conference on Neural Information Processing Systems 2021, NeurIPS 2021, December 6-14, 2021, virtual*, pages 7547–7560.

Hangbo Bao, Li Dong, Furu Wei, Wenhui Wang, Nan Yang, Xiaodong Liu, Yu Wang, Jianfeng Gao, Songhao Piao, Ming Zhou, et al. 2020. Unilmv2: Pseudo-masked language models for unified language model pre-training. In *International Conference on Machine Learning*, pages 642–652. PMLR.

Danqi Chen, Adam Fisch, Jason Weston, and Antoine Bordes. 2017. Reading Wikipedia to answer open-domain questions. In *Proceedings of the 55th Annual Meeting of the Association for Computational Linguistics (Volume 1: Long Papers)*, pages 1870–1879, Vancouver, Canada. Association for Computational Linguistics.

Zewen Chi, Li Dong, Furu Wei, Wenhui Wang, Xian-Ling Mao, and Heyan Huang. 2020. Cross-lingual natural language generation via pre-training. *Proceedings of the AAAI Conference on Artificial Intelligence*, 34(05):7570–7577.

Alexis Conneau, Kartikay Khandelwal, Naman Goyal, Vishrav Chaudhary, Guillaume Wenzek, Francisco Guzmán, Edouard Grave, Myle Ott, Luke Zettlemoyer, and Veselin Stoyanov. 2020. Unsupervised cross-lingual representation learning at scale. In *Proceedings of the 58th Annual Meeting of the Association for Computational Linguistics*, pages 8440–8451, Online. Association for Computational Linguistics.

Alexis Conneau and Guillaume Lample. 2019. Cross-lingual language model pretraining. In *Advances in Neural Information Processing Systems*, volume 32. Curran Associates, Inc.

Nick Craswell, Bhaskar Mitra, Emine Yilmaz, Daniel Campos, and Jimmy Lin. 2021. Ms marco: Benchmarking ranking models in the large-data regime. In *Proceedings of the 44th International ACM SIGIR Conference on Research and Development in Information Retrieval*, pages 1566–1576.

Jacob Devlin, Ming-Wei Chang, Kenton Lee, and Kristina Toutanova. 2019. BERT: Pre-training of deep bidirectional transformers for language understanding. In *Proceedings of the 2019 Conference of the North American Chapter of the Association for Computational Linguistics: Human Language Technologies, Volume 1 (Long and Short Papers)*, pages 4171–4186, Minneapolis, Minnesota. Association for Computational Linguistics.

Li Dong, Nan Yang, Wenhui Wang, Furu Wei, Xiaodong Liu, Yu Wang, Jianfeng Gao, Ming Zhou, and Hsiao-Wuen Hon. 2019. Unified language model pre-training for natural language understanding and generation. In *Advances in Neural Information Processing Systems*, volume 32. Curran Associates, Inc.

Liam Dugan, Eleni Miltsakaki, Shriyash Upadhyay, Etan Ginsberg, Hannah Gonzalez, Dayheon Choi, Chuning Yuan, and Chris Callison-Burch. 2022. A feasibility study of answer-agnostic question generation for education. *arXiv preprint arXiv:2203.08685*.

Fangxiaoyu Feng, Yinfei Yang, Daniel Cer, Naveen Arivazhagan, and Wei Wang. 2022. Language-agnostic BERT sentence embedding. In *Proceedings of the 60th Annual Meeting of the Association for Computational Linguistics (Volume 1: Long Papers)*, pages 878–891, Dublin, Ireland. Association for Computational Linguistics.

Steven Y. Feng, Varun Gangal, Jason Wei, Sarath Chandar, Soroush Vosoughi, Teruko Mitamura, and Eduard Hovy. 2021. A survey of data augmentation approaches for NLP. In *Findings of the Association for Computational Linguistics: ACL-IJCNLP 2021*, pages 968–988, Online. Association for Computational Linguistics.

Tianyu Gao, Xingcheng Yao, and Danqi Chen. 2021. SimCSE: Simple contrastive learning of sentence embeddings. In *Proceedings of the 2021 Conference on Empirical Methods in Natural Language Processing*, pages 6894–6910, Online and Punta Cana, Dominican Republic. Association for Computational Linguistics.

Goran Glavaš, Mladen Karan, and Ivan Vulić. 2020. XHate-999: Analyzing and detecting abusive language across domains and languages. In *Proceedings of the 28th International Conference on Computational Linguistics*, pages 6350–6365, Barcelona, Spain (Online). International Committee on Computational Linguistics.

Chia-Chien Hung, Anne Lauscher, Ivan Vulić, Simone Paolo Ponzetto, and Goran Glavaš. 2022. Multi^{2}WOZ: A robust multilingual dataset and conversational pretraining for task-oriented dialog. Accepted for publication in *the North American Chapter of the Association for Computational Linguistics*: NAACL 2022.

Gautier Izacard and Edouard Grave. 2021. Leveraging passage retrieval with generative models for open domain question answering. In *Proceedings of the 16th Conference of the European Chapter of the Association for Computational Linguistics: Main Volume*, pages 874–880, Online. Association for Computational Linguistics.

K Sparck Jonesa, S Walkerb, and SE Robertsonb. 2000. A probabilistic model of information retrieval: development and comparative experiments part 2. *Information Processing and Management*, 36(809):840.

Pratik Joshi, Sebastin Santy, Amar Budhiraja, Kalika Bali, and Monojit Choudhury. 2020. The state and fate of linguistic diversity and inclusion in the NLP world. In *Proceedings of the 58th Annual Meeting of the Association for Computational Linguistics*, pages 6282–6293, Online. Association for Computational Linguistics.

Vladimir Karpukhin, Barlas Oguz, Sewon Min, Patrick Lewis, Ledell Wu, Sergey Edunov, Danqi Chen, and Wen-tau Yih. 2020. Dense passage retrieval for open-domain question answering. In *Proceedings of the 2020 Conference on Empirical Methods in Natural Language Processing (EMNLP)*, pages 6769–6781, Online. Association for Computational Linguistics.

Vishwajeet Kumar, Nitish Joshi, Arijit Mukherjee, Ganesh Ramakrishnan, and Preethi Jyothi. 2019. Cross-lingual training for automatic question generation. In *Proceedings of the 57th Annual Meeting of the Association for Computational Linguistics*, pages 4863–4872, Florence, Italy. Association for Computational Linguistics.

Tom Kwiatkowski, Jennimaria Palomaki, Olivia Redfield, Michael Collins, Ankur Parikh, Chris Alberti, Danielle Epstein, Illia Polosukhin, Jacob Devlin, Kenton Lee, Kristina Toutanova, Llion Jones, Matthew Kelcey, Ming-Wei Chang, Andrew M. Dai, Jakob Uszkoreit, Quoc Le, and Slav Petrov. 2019. Natural questions: A benchmark for question answering research. *Transactions of the Association for Computational Linguistics*, 7:452–466.

Kenton Lee, Ming-Wei Chang, and Kristina Toutanova. 2019. Latent retrieval for weakly supervised open domain question answering. In *Proceedings of the 57th Annual Meeting of the Association for Computational Linguistics*, pages 6086–6096, Florence, Italy. Association for Computational Linguistics.

Patrick S. H. Lewis, Ethan Perez, Aleksandra Piktus, Fabio Petroni, Vladimir Karpukhin, Naman Goyal, Heinrich Küttler, Mike Lewis, Wen-tau Yih, Tim Rocktäschel, Sebastian Riedel, and Douwe Kiela. 2020. Retrieval-augmented generation for knowledge-intensive NLP tasks. In *Advances in Neural Information Processing Systems 33: Annual Conference on Neural Information Processing Systems 2020, NeurIPS 2020, December 6-12, 2020, virtual.*

Bohan Li, Hao Zhou, Junxian He, Mingxuan Wang, Yiming Yang, and Lei Li. 2020. On the sentence embeddings from pre-trained language models. In *Proceedings of the 2020 Conference on Empirical Methods in Natural Language Processing (EMNLP)*, pages 9119–9130, Online. Association for Computational Linguistics.

Robert Litschko, Ivan Vulić, Simone Paolo Ponzetto, and Goran Glavaš. 2022. On cross-lingual retrieval with multilingual text encoders. *Information Retrieval Journal*, 25(2):149–183.

Ekaterina Loginova, Stalin Varanasi, and Günter Neumann. 2021. Towards end-to-end multilingual question answering. *Inf. Syst. Frontiers*, 23(1):227–241.

Shayne Longpre, Yi Lu, and Joachim Daiber. 2020. MKQA: A linguistically diverse benchmark for multilingual open domain question answering. *CoRR*, abs/2007.15207.

Shayne Longpre, Yi Lu, Zhucheng Tu, and Chris DuBois. 2019. An exploration of data augmentation and sampling techniques for domain-agnostic question answering. In *Proceedings of the 2nd Workshop on Machine Reading for Question Answering*, pages 220–227, Hong Kong, China. Association for Computational Linguistics.

Ilya Loshchilov and Frank Hutter. 2019. Decoupled weight decay regularization. In *International Conference on Learning Representations*.

Yingqi Qu, Yuchen Ding, Jing Liu, Kai Liu, Ruiyang Ren, Wayne Xin Zhao, Daxiang Dong, Hua Wu, and Haifeng Wang. 2021. Rocketqa: An optimized training approach to dense passage retrieval for open-domain question answering. In *Proceedings of the 2021 Conference of the North American Chapter of the Association for Computational Linguistics: Human Language Technologies, NAACL-HLT 2021, Online, June 6-11, 2021*, pages 5835–5847. Association for Computational Linguistics.

Colin Raffel, Noam Shazeer, Adam Roberts, Katherine Lee, Sharan Narang, Michael Matena, Yanqi Zhou, Wei Li, and Peter J. Liu. 2020. Exploring the limits of transfer learning with a unified text-to-text transformer. *Journal of Machine Learning Research*, 21(140):1–67.

Pranav Rajpurkar, Jian Zhang, Konstantin Lopyrev, and Percy Liang. 2016. SQuAD: 100,000+ questions for machine comprehension of text. In *Proceedings of the 2016 Conference on Empirical Methods in Natural Language Processing*, pages 2383–2392, Austin, Texas. Association for Computational Linguistics.

Nils Reimers and Iryna Gurevych. 2019. Sentence-BERT: Sentence embeddings using Siamese BERT-networks. In *Proceedings of the 2019 Conference on Empirical Methods in Natural Language Processing and the 9th International Joint Conference on Natural Language Processing (EMNLP-IJCNLP)*, pages 3982–3992, Hong Kong, China. Association for Computational Linguistics.

Nils Reimers and Iryna Gurevych. 2020. Making monolingual sentence embeddings multilingual using knowledge distillation. In *Proceedings of the 2020 Conference on Empirical Methods in Natural Language Processing (EMNLP)*, pages 4512–4525, Online. Association for Computational Linguistics.

Arij Riabi, Thomas Scialom, Rachel Keraron, Benoît Sagot, Djamé Seddah, and Jacopo Staiano. 2021. Synthetic data augmentation for zero-shot cross-lingual question answering. In *Proceedings of the 2021 Conference on Empirical Methods in Natural Language Processing*, pages 7016–7030, Online and Punta Cana, Dominican Republic. Association for Computational Linguistics.

Victor Sanh, Lysandre Debut, Julien Chaumond, and Thomas Wolf. 2019. Distilbert, a distilled version of BERT: smaller, faster, cheaper and lighter. *CoRR*, abs/1910.01108.

Siamak Shakeri, Noah Constant, Mihir Kale, and Linting Xue. 2021. Towards zero-shot multilingual synthetic question and answer generation for cross-lingual reading comprehension. In *Proceedings of the 14th International Conference on Natural Language Generation*, pages 35–45, Aberdeen, Scotland, UK. Association for Computational Linguistics.

Noam Shazeer and Mitchell Stern. 2018. Adafactor: Adaptive learning rates with sublinear memory cost. In *International Conference on Machine Learning*, pages 4596–4604. PMLR.

Jasdeep Singh, Bryan McCann, Nitish Shirish Keskar, Caiming Xiong, and Richard Socher. 2019. XLDA: cross-lingual data augmentation for natural language inference and question answering. *CoRR*, abs/1905.11471.

Kaitao Song, Xu Tan, Tao Qin, Jianfeng Lu, and Tie-Yan Liu. 2020. Mpnet: Masked and permuted pre-training for language understanding. In *Advances in Neural Information Processing Systems 33: Annual Conference on Neural Information Processing Systems 2020, NeurIPS 2020, December 6-12, 2020, virtual*.

K. Sparck Jones, S. Walker, and S.E. Robertson. 2000. A probabilistic model of information retrieval: development and comparative experiments: Part 1. *Information Processing & Management*, 36(6):779–808.

Weiwei Sun, Chuan Meng, Qi Meng, Zhaochun Ren, Pengjie Ren, Zhumin Chen, and Maarten de Rijke. 2021. Conversations powered by cross-lingual knowledge. In *Proceedings of the 44th International ACM SIGIR Conference on Research and Development in Information Retrieval*, pages 1442–1451.

Ferhan Ture and Elizabeth Boschee. 2016. Learning to translate for multilingual question answering. In *Proceedings of the 2016 Conference on Empirical Methods in Natural Language Processing*, pages 573–584, Austin, Texas. Association for Computational Linguistics.

Wenhui Wang, Furu Wei, Li Dong, Hangbo Bao, Nan Yang, and Ming Zhou. 2020. Minilm: Deep self-attention distillation for task-agnostic compression of pre-trained transformers. In *Advances in Neural Information Processing Systems 33: Annual Conference on Neural Information Processing Systems 2020, NeurIPS 2020, December 6-12, 2020, virtual*.

Guillaume Wenzek, Marie-Anne Lachaux, Alexis Conneau, Vishrav Chaudhary, Francisco Guzmán, Armand Joulin, and Edouard Grave. 2020. CCNet: Extracting high quality monolingual datasets from web crawl data. In *Proceedings of the 12th Language Resources and Evaluation Conference*, pages 4003–4012, Marseille, France. European Language Resources Association.

Ledell Wu, Fabio Petroni, Martin Josifoski, Sebastian Riedel, and Luke Zettlemoyer. 2020. Scalable zero-shot entity linking with dense entity retrieval. In *Proceedings of the 2020 Conference on Empirical Methods in Natural Language Processing (EMNLP)*, pages 6397–6407, Online. Association for Computational Linguistics.

Linting Xue, Noah Constant, Adam Roberts, Mihir Kale, Rami Al-Rfou, Aditya Siddhant, Aditya Barua, and Colin Raffel. 2021. mT5: A massively multilingual pre-trained text-to-text transformer. In *Proceedings of the 2021 Conference of the North American Chapter of the Association for Computational Linguistics: Human Language Technologies*, pages 483–498, Online. Association for Computational Linguistics.

Yinfei Yang, Daniel Cer, Amin Ahmad, Mandy Guo, Jax Law, Noah Constant, Gustavo Hernandez Abrego, Steve Yuan, Chris Tar, Yun-hsuan Sung, Brian Strope, and Ray Kurzweil. 2020. Multilingual universal sentence encoder for semantic retrieval. In *Proceedings of the 58th Annual Meeting of the Association for Computational Linguistics: System Demonstrations*, pages 87–94, Online. Association for Computational Linguistics.

Yanzhao Zhang, Richong Zhang, Samuel Mensah, Xudong Liu, and Yongyi Mao. 2022. Unsupervised sentence representation via contrastive learning with mixing negatives.

Junnan Zhu, Qian Wang, Yining Wang, Yu Zhou, Jiajun Zhang, Shaonan Wang, and Chengqing Zong. 2019. NCLS: Neural cross-lingual summarization. In *Proceedings of the 2019 Conference on Empirical Methods in Natural Language Processing and the 9th International Joint Conference on Natural Language Processing (EMNLP-IJCNLP)*, pages 3054–3064, Hong Kong, China. Association for Computational Linguistics.

Pierre Zweigenbaum, Serge Sharoff, and Reinhard Rapp. 2018. Overview of the third bucc shared task: Spotting parallel sentences in comparable corpora. In *Proceedings of 11th Workshop on Building and Using Comparable Corpora*, pages 39–42.

A Data Augmentation Example

Figure 2 shows an example of a Wikipedia passage about *An American in Paris*. The passage in orange is the set of sentences whose length does not exceed 512 tokens, which is the first of three sub-passages used for generating question-answer pairs. The generated pairs can be seen at the bottom of the figure. Questions and answers highlighted in red are those that satisfy the filtering heuristics detailed in §2.2. These are then translated into other languages.

Title: An American in Paris

URL: `https://en.wikipedia.org/wiki?curid=309`

Text: An American in Paris is a jazz-influenced orchestral piece by American composer George Gershwin written in 1928. It was inspired by the time that Gershwin had spent in Paris and evokes the sights and energy of the French capital in the 1920s. Gershwin composed "An American in Paris" on commission from conductor Walter Damrosch. He scored the piece for the standard instruments of the symphony orchestra plus celesta, saxophones, and automobile horns. He brought back some Parisian taxi horns for the New York premiere of the composition, which took place on December 13, 1928 in Carnegie Hall, with Damrosch conducting the New York Philharmonic. He completed the orchestration on November 18, less than four weeks before the work's premiere. He collaborated on the original program notes with critic and composer Deems Taylor. Gershwin was attracted by Maurice Ravel's unusual chords, and Gershwin went on his first trip to Paris in 1926 ready to study with Ravel. After his initial student audition with Ravel turned into a sharing of musical theories, Ravel said he could not teach him, saying, "Why be a second-rate Ravel when you can be a first-rate Gershwin?" While the studies were cut short, that 1926 trip resulted in a piece entitled "Very Parisienne", the initial version of "An American in Paris", written as a 'thank you note' to Gershwin's hosts, Robert and Mabel Shirmer. Gershwin called it "a rhapsodic ballet"; it is written freely and in a much more modern idiom than his prior works. Gershwin strongly encouraged Ravel to come to the United States for a tour. To this end, upon his return to New York, Gershwin joined the efforts of Ravel's friend Robert Schmitz, a pianist Ravel had met during the war, to urge Ravel to tour the U.S. Schmitz was the head of Pro Musica, promoting Franco-American musical relations, and was able to offer Ravel a $10,000 fee for the tour, an enticement Gershwin knew would be important to Ravel. ...

Question: When was an American in Paris written?
Answer: 1928
Type: Number

Question: When did George Gershwin write an American in Paris?
Answer: the 1920s
Type: Contains number

Question: Who was the conductor of "An American in Paris"?
Answer: Walter Damrosch
Type: Who

Question: What was the name of the instrument that Gershwin scored for?
Answer: automobile horns

Question: What was the name of the orchestral piece Gershwin composed in 1928?
Answer: New York Philharmonic

Question: When did Gershwin complete the orchestration of "An American in Paris"?
Answer: November 18
Type: Date

Question: Who did Gershwin collaborate on the original program notes with?
Answer: Deems Taylor
Type: Who

Figure 2: Example English question-answer pairs (on the bottom) generated from the highlighted text (in yellow) in the passage. The highlighted question-answer pairs (in red) are those that were kept after filtering.

B MixCSE Loss

The MixCSE loss described in 3.1 is given by:

$$\mathcal{L}_{\text{mixcse}} = -\log \frac{\exp(\cos(\mathbf{e}_{q_i}, \mathbf{e}_{p_i^+})/\tau)}{\exp(\cos(\mathbf{e}_{q_i}, \mathbf{e}_{p_i^+})/\tau) + \sum_{j=1}^{n} \exp(\cos(\mathbf{e}_{q_i}, \mathbf{e}_{p_{i,j}^-})/\tau) + \exp(\cos(\mathbf{e}_{q_i}, \text{SG}(\tilde{\mathbf{e}}_i))/\tau)}$$

where τ is a fixed temperature and SG is the stop-gradient operator, which prevents backpropagation from flowing into the mixed negative ($\tilde{\mathbf{e}}_i$).

Zero-shot cross-lingual open domain question answering

Sumit Agarwal, Suraj Tripathi, Teruko Mitamura, Carolyn Penstein Rose
{sumita, surajt, teruko, cprose}@cs.cmu.edu
Language Technologies Institute, Carnegie Mellon University

Abstract

People speaking different kinds of languages search for information in a cross-lingual manner. They tend to ask questions in their language and expect the answer to be in the same language, despite the evidence lying in another language. In this paper, we present our approach for this task of cross-lingual open-domain question-answering. Our proposed method employs a passage reranker, the fusion-in-decoder technique for generation, and a wiki data entity-based post-processing system to tackle the inability to generate entities across all languages. Our end-2-end pipeline shows an improvement of 3 and 4.6 points on F1 and EM metrics respectively, when compared with the baseline CORA model on the XOR-TyDi dataset. We also evaluate the effectiveness of our proposed techniques in the zero-shot setting using the MKQA dataset and show an improvement of 5 points in F1 for high-resource and 3 points improvement for low-resource zero-shot languages. Our team, CMUmQA's submission in the MIA-Shared task ranked 1st in the constrained setup for the dev and 2nd in the test setting.

1 Introduction

Question Answering (QA), especially in English, is a popular research area in NLP with abundance of datasets like SQuAD (Rajpurkar et al., 2018), Natural Questions (Kwiatkowski et al., 2019) and different types of tasks including machine reading comprehension or extractive QA, cloze-completion and open-domain QA (Richardson et al., 2013; Chen et al., 2017). Open-domain QA is the task of answering natural language questions without any specified predefined context. It usually requires the system to first search for the relevant documents as the context w.r.t. a given question from either a local document repository or Wikipedia-like document collection, and then generate the answer.

Cross-lingual Open-Domain Question Answering is a challenging NLP task, where questions are given in a user's preferred language, and the system needs to find evidence in cross-lingual large-scale document collections, like Wikipedia, and return an answer in the user's preferred language, as indicated by their question. We work on this cross-lingual open-domain QA challenge as a part of the MIA Shared task. [1]

Recent advancements in Open-Domain QA, usually for English are made by following a Retriever-Reader architecture, where the retriever is aimed at retrieving relevant documents w.r.t. a given question, which can be modeled as a dense passage retriever trained on large-scale English QA datasets to fetch evidence passages (Karpukhin et al., 2020), while Reader aims at inferring the final answer from the retrieved documents, which is usually a neural MRC model (Chen et al., 2017) or a generative model (Izacard and Grave, 2021). Extending such approaches to a multilingual setting usually suffers from two major problems - 1) Answering questions from different language sources because the answer for low resource languages might lie in documents from high resource languages (Asai et al., 2021a), and Wikipedia which might fail in cases of same language retrieval. (Clark et al., 2020a). 2) Large-scale cross-lingual datasets are not available that supply passages in a diverse number of languages which can enable better training of cross-lingual retrievers.

One specific approach that has been followed for bringing multilingual QA close to English QA is that the non-English question is translated into English and the answer from the English QA system is translated back to the query language. These systems suffer from the problem of machine translation error propagating itself in the downstream question answering. And also, these systems aren't able to exploit the fact that for high resource languages like Spanish, and Chinese the evidence might lie in the target language itself which is eas-

[1] https://mia-workshop.github.io/shared_task.html

Proceedings of the Workshop on Multilingual Information Access (MIA), pages 91 - 99
July 15, 2022 ©2022 Association for Computational Linguistics

ier than two-way translation.

In this paper, we aim to extend the task of cross-lingual question answering to tackle the following research questions - a) How can we adapt the retrieve-then-generate approaches for English open QA to cross-lingual QA that do not rely on machine translation? - b) How do multilingual QA models trained on a small set of languages perform in zero-shot settings?

We follow CORA (Asai et al., 2021b) which is a many-to-many multilingual QA model by following a four-stage pipeline for addressing cross-lingual QA. The DPR based on mBERT (mDPR) is a bi-encoder retriever that retrieves documents cross-lingually without relying on machine translation. XLM-RoBERTA which serves as a passage reranker is trained as a cross-encoder to capture the interactions between the question and the passage on the top k documents fetched by the mDPR retriever. The reranked documents are passed through a Fusion-in-Decoder based mT5 reader module which can effectively learn to collect evidence from multiple passages to arrive at the final answer. In some cases, the predicted answer is not in the target language as desired by the user because the generator is either not able to convert entities into the target language or evidence is directly extracted from a different language passage. Further, we use a postprocessing step to map entities from Wikidata to convert the answer into the target language.

We conduct our experiments on two multilingual open-domain QA datasets, XOR-TyDi QA (Asai et al., 2021a) and MKQA (Longpre et al., 2021) across 14 typologically diverse languages with CORA as the baseline. We also use English questions from NQ (Kwiatkowski et al., 2019) for training. Reranking the outputs from the retriever leads to consistent improvements across all languages in both XOR-TyDi and MKQA, even in zero-shot settings. We show that using a fusion-in-decoder based reader leads to 2.7 points improvement in EM and 0.6 points improvement in F1 for the XOR-TyDi dataset. Moreover, on applying Wikidata based postprocessing techniques we see a straight 4.6 points improvement in EM and 3 points in F1. We see that our proposed pipeline also helps in zero-shot settings for both high resource and low resource languages.

2 Datasets

In this work, we use the data corpus provided by the MIA Shared Task on Cross-lingual Open-Retrieval QA which consists of XOR-TyDi and MKQA corpus. The shared task also provides questions from the NQ corpus.

XOR-TyDi is the first corpus to combine information-seeking questions, and open-retrieval QA in the multilingual domain to enable cross-lingual answer retrieval. This dataset is an extension of the TyDi QA (Clark et al., 2020b) dataset and involves retrieving evidence passages from multilingual and English resources. This dataset consists of questions written by native speakers in 7 typologically diverse languages: Arabic, Bengali, Finnish, Japanese, Korean, Russian, and Telugu.

Language	#Train	#Dev	#Passages
En (English)	76.6k (n)	1.7k (m)	18M
Ar (Arabic)	18.4k (x)	3k (x,m)	1.3M
Bn (Bengali)	5k (x)	0.5k (x)	0.1M
Fi (Finnish)	9.7k (x)	2.7k (x,m)	0.9M
Ja (Japanese)	7.8k (x)	2.4k (x,m)	5.1M
Ko (Korean)	4.3k (x)	2.2k (x,m)	0.7M
Ru (Russian)	9.2k (x)	2.7k (x,m)	4.5M
Te (Telegu)	6.7k (x)	0.6k (x)	0.3M
Es (Spanish)	-	1.7k (m)	5.7M
Km (Khmer)	-	1.7k (m)	0.06M
Ms (Malay)	-	1.7k (m)	0.4M
Sv (Swedish)	-	1.7k (m)	4.6M
Tr (Turkish)	-	1.7k (m)	0.8M
Zh (Simplified Chinese)	-	1.7k (m)	3.4M
Total	137k	9115	45.86M

Table 1: Dataset Statistics showing the 14 diverse languages used in this task with the top 7 being seen and the bottom unseen. n, x and m denote the source of the dataset NQ, XOR-TyDi and MKQA respectively from which the examples are collected.

MKQA corpus was originally proposed in (Longpre et al., 2021) and consists of 10K question-answer pairs aligned across 26 typologically diverse languages (260K question-answer pairs in total). Answers for this corpus are heavily curated and obtained from language-independent data representation which makes this corpus ideal for evaluating across diverse languages and being independent of language-specific passages. MKQA corpus provided by the shared task is a filtered version that only includes questions with answer annotations and removes the "no answers" questions. For this task, 12 languages were collected from MKQA, six seen: Arabic, Finnish, Japanese, Korean, Russian, and six unseen(zero-shot): Spanish, Khmer, Malay, Swedish, Turkish, Simplified Chinese, each with

1.7k examples in the dev set.

NQ (Natural questions) is a factoid-based English question answering dataset with both short and long answers for each question from English Wikipedia. We focus on the subset which is given as a part of the training dataset in the shared task.

Table 1 shows the dataset statistics for the train and the dev across 7 different languages. We also experiment with MKQA corpus in the zero-shot setting with 6 languages.

3 Related Work

Open-domain question answering requires a model to answer questions without any pre-trained domain (Kwiatkowski et al., 2019). There have been some recent works to create a non-English QA corpus to analyze the model's effectiveness to transfer knowledge from the English language or other high-resource languages. Further, some works focus on generating loosely aligned data using translation or similar multilingual sources.

As mentioned some of the recent works in Question Answering (QA) aim to build systems that can work well with languages other than English. (Lewis et al., 2019) proposed MLQA which is a multi-way aligned extractive QA corpus. It consists of instances in 7 languages with each instance parallel between 4 languages on average. This work defines two tasks: the first one focuses on analyzing the model's ability to transfer by training and testing in different languages and the other task requires the model to retrieve passages in a different language than the question. One of the shortcomings of this corpus is that it contains context in the same language and therefore doesn't explicitly captures the cross-lingual aspect. This leads to a problem for a low-resource language question set as in real scenarios most of these questions have answers in a high resource language. (Liu et al., 2019) presents the XQA dataset to investigate cross-lingual OpenQA research. This corpus consists of the training set in English along with the development and test set in eight other languages. Their analysis of several baseline models indicates that the performance in a cross-lingual setting not only depends on the similarity of English and the target language but also on the complexity of the target language question set. Another work in the cross-lingual domain, XQuAD is proposed by (Artetxe et al., 2019) which is created by using a subset of SQuad v1.1 (Rajpurkar et al., 2018) corpus and translating them into ten other languages by professional translators. This paper also evaluates the hypothesis that multilingual models perform well due to the shared subword vocabulary and joint training across multiple languages and shows that monolingual representations can be adapted to produce similar performance without relying on a shared vocabulary or joint training.

Most previous works modeled cross-lingual QA as an extractive task which is mostly inspired by the datasets like XQuAD (Artetxe et al., 2019) which is a subset of SQuAD (Rajpurkar et al., 2018). The SQuAD dataset contains answer spans in the evidence passage to answer a given question. These answer spans were further used in the generation of the cross-lingual QA dataset, XQuAD, and therefore are more suitable to be modeled as an extractive task. More recently, there have been studies that work on generating answers from raw text. Works such as (Chi et al., 2019) (Kumar et al., 2019) study cross-lingual question generation. (Shakeri et al., 2020) proposed a method to generate multilingual question-answer pairs through the use of a single fine-tuned multilingual T5 generative model. Their work shows that these synthetic examples could be used to improve the performance of multilingual QA in the zero-shot setting on target languages. Previous works have also explored other variants of generative modeling but it was mostly limited to the domains where the model is expected to generate long answers. Recent work on FiD (Izacard and Grave, 2021) shows that generative approaches could achieve competitive results even in the cases where answers consist of a short text span. One of the widely used approaches for open-domain question answering named RAG (Lewis et al., 2020) makes use of the generative model approach. RAG model's reader module takes several retrieved passages from the retriever encoder simultaneously to generate the answer. Passage representations and their similarity score with the query are used to generate the final response in the reader module. Further, the RAG approach works efficiently at scale due to the independent processing of passages in the encoder module.

Bi-encoder retrievers are effective in bringing out relevant passages from a large index but sometimes reranking those passages is essential as the downstream reader can only see a limited number of them. (Fajcik et al., 2021) uses reranker

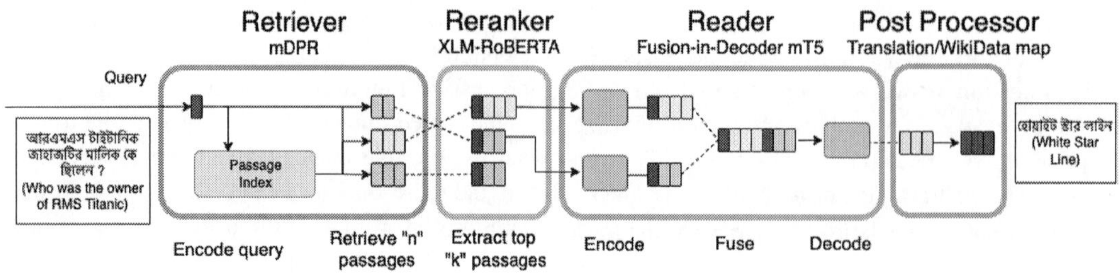

Figure 1: The proposed system architecture uses a mDPR based bi-encoder retriever which fetches the top 200 relevant passages from the passage index, followed by a XLM-R based cross-encoder for reranking. The top 50 passages are passed to FiD with mT5 to output the final response. The final response which is not in the target language is mapped using a Wikidata map to the target language.

after their retriever as a cross-encoder to improve the recall which proves effective in the end-to-end question answering pipeline. Incorporating Wikidata (Hu et al., 2021) in translation for sentences including named entities is common in literature because the pretrained multilingual reader is unable to translate these entities as it has not seen them during training.

4 Baseline

We use CORA (Asai et al., 2021b) as our baseline model which is a unified multilingual open QA model for many languages. CORA model is a combination of two models: Multilingual Dense Passage Retriever (mDPR) and Multilingual Answer Generation (mGEN).

mDPR extends Dense Passage Retriever (DPR) to a multilingual setting and uses an iterative training approach to fine-tune a pre-trained multilingual model (mBERT) to encode passages and questions separately. mGEN uses a multilingual sequence-to-sequence model (mT5) to generate answers in the target language token-by-token given the retrieved multi-lingual passages. The generation approach is used as it can generate an answer in the target language from passages across different languages.

5 Methodology

We employ the widely used Retrieve-then-generate, figure 1, architecture for open domain question answering. To tackle the challenge of passing a limited number of passages to the generator, we use a reranker. We also use a postprocessor to convert named entities into the query language.

5.1 Bi-encoder Retriever

Following the baseline (Asai et al., 2021b), we used the mDPR model trained on hard negatives mined using BM-25 and adversarial examples mined using hard negatives from 1st iteration of the mDPR model.

5.2 Cross-encoder Reranker

The multilingual retriever is trained as a bi-encoder where the questions and passages are encoded separately and compared during the inference time. Therefore, there is no cross-attention captured between the question and passage which is essential for cross-language retrieval. Cross-encoder can't be used for the retrieval because it isn't computationally feasible to compare the query with all the passages (which are in millions). Further, we can only pass a limited number of k passages (less than 50) to the reader model. Therefore, reranking is very essential in this scenario. Hence, we take the top k (here 200) passages fetched by the retriever and train a XLM-RoBERTA (Conneau et al., 2020) model as a cross-encoder by scoring the positive passages higher. We followed (Qu et al., 2020) to train the reranker by using a cross-entropy loss on the [CLS] token output. The negative passages for the reranker are mined using the finetuned baseline mDPR model.

5.3 Fusion-in-Decoder Reader

Given the recent popularity of generative reader models in English Open-domain QA (Izacard and Grave, 2021) (Lewis et al., 2020), we used a FiD model as a reader model with mT5 (Xue et al., 2021) which encodes the top-50 reranked/retrieved passages one-by-one and concatenates them before passing it to the decoder. FiD is useful because

Model	Target Language L_i Ar	Bn	Fi	Ja	Ko	Ru	Te	F1	EM
Baseline (CORA)	51.3	28.7	44.3	43.2	29.8	41.3	44.1	39.8	30.3
mDPR + mFiD	53.5	26.3	46.4	42.4	28.3	42.6	43.0	40.4	33.0
mDPR + mFiD + P	54.4	**31.7**	**46.7**	42.9	33.3	43.1	45.2	42.5	34.6
mDPR + mFiD + RR	55.1	28.0	46.2	43.2	30.6	42.8	44.5	41.5	34.0
mDPR + mFiD + RR + P	**55.6**	30.4	46.3	**43.7**	**34.7**	**43.2**	**45.8**	**42.8**	**34.9**
Baseline (Test)	49.7	**34.0**	39.5	39.7	25.6	41.0	36.2	37.9	-
mDPR + mFiD + RR + P (Test)	**55.1**	30.6	**41.3**	**42.4**	**28.8**	**42.6**	**40.8**	**40.2**	-

Table 2: XOR-TyDi dev and test set performance across 7 different languages for different ablations of our components. We tried settings where we removed the RR(reranker) and P(Postprocessing).

	Seen Target Language L_i						Zero Shot Target Language L_i							
Model	**Ar**	**En**	**Fi**	**Ja**	**Ko**	**Ru**	**Es**	**Km**	**Ms**	**Sv**	**Tr**	**Zh**	**F1**	**EM**
Baseline (CORA)	8.77	27.9	23.3	15.2	8.3	14.0	24.9	5.7	22.6	24.1	20.6	13.1	17.4	13.5
mDPR + mFiD	8.8	39.7	25.2	14.3	6.3	13.3	29.7	7.7	**30.1**	28.6	25.7	9.8	19.9	16.0
mDPR + mFiD + P	**14.5**	39.7	25.1	20.6	13.6	22.6	**30.2**	7.8	29.4	28.2	25.4	15.1	22.7	17.2
mDPR + mFiD + RR	9.3	40.6	26.2	14.9	6.5	14.6	29.5	8.3	29.9	**29.9**	**26.7**	10.6	20.6	16.5
mDPR + mFiD + RR + P	14.2	**40.6**	**26.1**	**21.5**	**14.8**	**22.7**	29.8	**8.3**	29.3	29.6	26.5	**16.2**	**23.3**	**17.8**
Basline (Test)	9.5	36.3	22.7	7.7	15.9	14.6	27.2	6.0	25.1	26.7	21.7	13.8	17.1	-
mDPR + mFiD + RR + P (Test)	**13.9**	**42.6**	**26.8**	**14.6**	**22.7**	**22.4**	**32.1**	**8.7**	**31.1**	**31.5**	**26.6**	**18.0**	**22.9**	-

Table 3: MKQA dev and test set performance across 12 different languages for different ablations of our components. There were 6 languages which were in a zero-shot setting. We note from the dataset statistics presented in 1, Es, Sv, Zh are high-resource whereas others are low resource languages.

it also learns to rerank the documents to collect the evidence from the documents. We followed the baseline to use mT5 as the underlying cross-lingual language model. This mT5 with FiD model, which we call mFID, is trained on the training data that is given, which is a mixture of Natural Questions and XOR-TyDi. This mFiD acts as a cross-lingual fusion reader without the necessity to translate the passages/free-text answers from which the evidence is collected. To add extra supervision during training, we always pass the gold passage which has the answer along with the other passages.

5.4 Answer Post Processing with Wikidata

Figure 2 shows the discrepancy between the language of the predicted output and the language of the question. This is because if the evidence is collected from a different language passage, the answer is not translated by the model in cases where there are entities in the answer. After all, the model hasn't seen those entities while training. In such cases, we require post-processing to convert entities in other languages to the answer language. We have only tackled the English case because we have seen that most of the time the model is not able to translate the English entity. We collected en-xx Wikidata [2] maps for the languages in our dev set to convert those English predicted answers.

Question	Predicted Answer	Gold Answer
ఆక్సిజన్ చిత్ర కథానాయకుడు ఎవరు? (Who is the protagonist of the film 'Oxygen'?)	Anu Emmanuel	అను ఇమ్మాన్యుయేల్
ভুটানের সবচেয়ে জনবহুল শহর কোনটি ? (Which is the most populous city of Bhutan?)	Thimpu	থিম্ফু
세상에서 가장 넓은 산은 무엇인가? (Which is the widest mountain in the world?)	Mount Everest	에베레스트산

Figure 2: The figure shows the predicted answer by the model which is in English (usually entities) which the model can't translate and hence requires post processing to convert to the final language.

6 Results & Discussion

Table 2 shows the performance of various components of our pipeline and compares it with the baseline on the XOR-TyDi dev and test set and Table 3 shows the overall performance on the MKQA dev set. MKQA dev set has 6 languages that have no training data. We do not add any training data using data augmentation for these languages as we want to evaluate improvement in models in a

[2] https://www.Wikidata.org/wiki/Wikidata:Main_Page

Model	R@50							
	Ar	Bn	Fi	Ja	Ko	Ru	Te	Avg
Baseline (mDPR)	67.8	52.9	**60.6**	16.6	40.2	60.9	50.4	53.5
XLM-R Reranker	**68.9**	**56.5**	60.3	**19**	**44.6**	**61.2**	**53.2**	**55.1**

Table 4: Reranking performance for R@50 across 7 different languages in the XOR-TyDI dev set.

Model	Seen R@50						Zero Shot R@50						
	Ar	En	Fi	Ja	Ko	Ru	Es	Km	Ms	Sv	Tr	Zh	Avg
Baseline (mDPR)	25.5	70.5	55.5	13.6	20.7	35.9	62.2	16.1	59.6	63.0	56.4	12.5	41.0
XLM-R Reranker	**27.7**	**73.5**	**58.5**	**15.9**	**23.3**	**38.9**	**64.7**	**18.6**	**62.3**	**65.2**	**59.0**	**15.4**	**43.6**

Table 5: Reranking performance for R@50 across 12 different languages in the MKQA dev set. 6 languages were zero shot (not seen in the training corpus).

zero-shot setting that is comparable to real-world scenarios.

For XOR-TyDi, we see that overall we achieve 3 and 4.6 points improvement in F1 and EM respectively, whereas for MKQA we achieve a 5.9 points F1 improvement. We see that adding FiD to the baseline mDPR leads to a significant increase in F1 for languages like Ar, Fi, and Ru. Further, adding postprocessing to the FiD output leads to a significant increase in both F1 and EM and the model outperforms the baseline for all the languages. Reranking is crucial for FiD because it sees only 50 documents as compared to the 100 that the baseline uses. Reranking the top 200 documents retrieved helps the resulting FiD which shows a consistent improvement over the baseline except for Bn and Ko for which the model usually outputs lots of entities in English that require post-processing. We get the best results for applying postprocessing (P) on the outputs by the reranker(RR) + FiD model. For zero-shot settings in the MKQA dataset, we also see consistent 5 points of F1 improvement over the baseline due to the combined effect of the FiD, reranker, and the postprocessor. For high-resource zero-shot languages Es, Sv, Zh we observe around 5 points improvement over baseline whereas for Km which is an extremely low-resource language we still show around 3 points improvement. We now provide detailed results and analysis for each component of our pipeline.

6.1 Reranker

Table 4 captures the reranker performance over the baseline mDPR model. Applying the reranker to the baseline mDPR gives a consistent improvement in R@50 for all the languages leading to about 1.6 points improvement. This essentially is because of two reasons - cross interactions between question and passage and the fact that XLM-RoBERTA is a better language model than mBERT. These reranked passages also help in the downstream FiD model (See Table 2) and lead to a 1 point F1 and EM improvement over the model which didn't receive the reranked passages (mDPR + mFiD). We also think that this model lacks in performance over the baseline for Bn because the number of training examples for Bn is very low as compared to other languages. For the MKQA dataset, in table 5, we see a significant increase over the mDPR model across all the languages for R@50. We see a 2.6 improvement in R@50 over the baseline. For zero-shot languages, we also see a significant increase in recall showing the effectiveness of the XLM-R model for unseen languages. This increased recall further helps in the downstream reader improvements as well.

6.2 Reader

The FiD with mT5 (mFiD) reader performs better than the normal mT5 as can be seen by the 3 points EM improvement over the baseline in Table 2, although FiD just uses 50 documents as compared to the 100 documents used by the baseline. The fusion-in-decoder approach also is an effective reranker by itself in searching for evidence to arrive at the final answer. Table 3 shows the final performance of the model on the MKQA dataset as well. We see that mFiD with reranking has 3 points improvement over the baseline and also shows great improvements for unseen languages like Es, Ms, and Tr. This further corroborates the effectiveness of the reranker and the mT5 based FiD for unseen

Question	Lang	Baseline Prediction	Our Model Answer	Gold Answer	Category
Как называется национальный костюм австрийских женщин? (What is the national costume of Australian women called?)	Ru	Баварский национальный костюм (Bavarian National Costume)	Дирндль (Drindl)	Дирндль (Drindl)	Rerank
من كان أول خليفة للدولة الأموية؟ (What is the oldest university in Netherlands?)	Ar	جامعة أوتريخت (Utrecht University)	جامعة لايدن (Leiden University)	جامعة لايدن (Leiden University)	FiD
스웨덴에서 가장 인구밀도가 높은 도시는 어디인가? (Which is the most densely populated city in Sweden?)	Ko	런던 (London)	스톡홀름 (Stockholm)	스톡홀름 (Stockholm)	Post Process
সমুদ্রপৃষ্ঠ থেকে মিরিকের গড় উচ্চতা কত ? (What is the average height of Mirik from sea level?)	Bn	১৪৯৫ মিটার (1495 m)	১৪৯৫ মিটার (1495 m)	1495 মি (1495 m)	Dataset Flaw

Figure 3: The figure shows 1 example each for our component improvement and also points to a flaw in the dataset. Here category indicates the model component which led to the correct prediction compared to the baseline model.

languages. Also, it is worth noting that for En language in MKQA, simply adding FiD improves the performance by 12 points, showing the advantage of the fusion-in-decoder technique.

6.3 Postprocessor

Converting entities using Wikidata maps in English to target languages is useful, especially for the high-resource languages, in both XOR-TyDI and MKQA datasets because the answers are expected in the question language and the reader models (mFiD) can't translate named entities. Table 2 shows that for languages Bn, and Ko the improvement of post-processing is the maximum because the predicted answers of these languages are usually in English, which when converted to their entities boost's the F1 and EM. In the zero-shot setting, there is a huge improvement of 6 points in Zh because of the same reason.

7 Error and Qualitative Analysis

7.1 Qualitative analysis

We present a qualitative analysis, in figure 3, of our model that highlights the component-wise improvement. For the first example with the category "Rerank", it implies that the original mDPR retrieval top-50 docs didn't have the ground truth passage but due to the reranker module, we were able to move ground truth passage into the top-50 passages and finally generate the correct answer. The second example indicates the improvement of the reader module due to the use of the FiD technique. In this example, both baseline and reranker retrieval output had the ground truth passage but only our reader module (FiD) can generate the correct response. For the 3rd example, our reader module generates an answer in the English language but our post-processing module can identify this English entity from the Wikidata mapping and convert it to the source language as expected by this task. For the last example, we try to highlight that both the models can generate the correct response but F1 comes 0 for both of them due to the limitation of the dataset (could have provided multiple answers) and the evaluation metric used for this task.

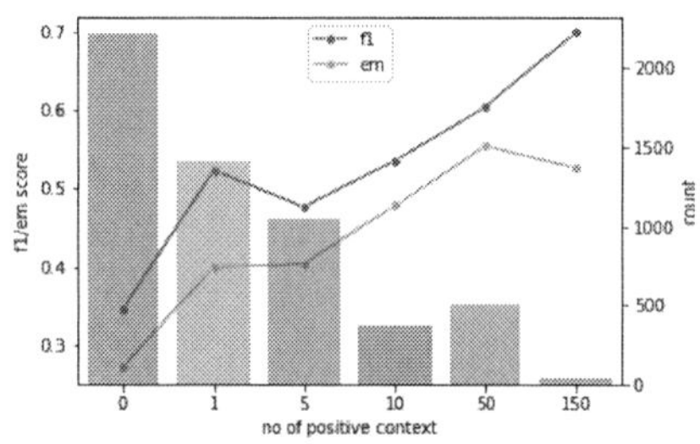

Figure 4: The graph shows the performance of our best model with respect to number of positive contexts.

7.2 # Positive context analysis

We look at the reranked results which are used by our best model to see the effect of the number of positive passages (passages containing the right answer) on the F1 and EM metrics. Figure 4 shows that with an increased number of positive contexts (greater than 10), it's easier for the FiD model to collect evidence and arrive at the final answer, which indicates that the retriever is the bottleneck. If the retriever is good enough to pull up multiple positive contexts having the correct answer, the FiD model will perform better in those cases.

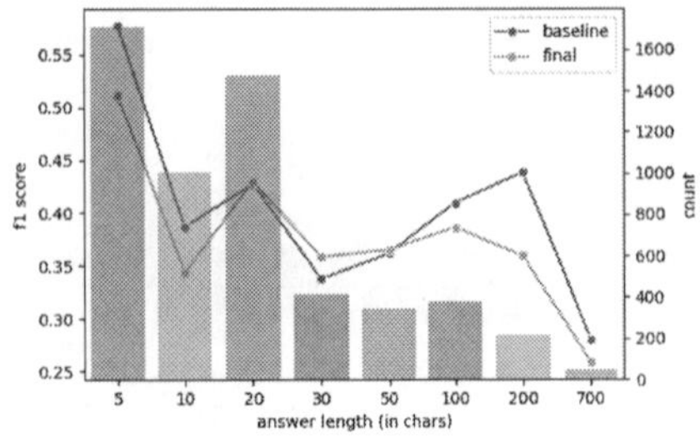

Figure 5: The graph shows a comparison of our model with the baseline model across correct answer length (in chars).

7.3 Answer length analysis

Figure 5 shows that our best model performs better than the baseline model for questions that have short answers whereas for long answers the baseline model outperforms our model. The FiD mT5 model might have learned some bias to truncate at short answers and it fails to emit long answers, which the normal mT5 does better.

8 Conclusion & Future Work

We introduced a modular end-to-end system with a retriever, reranker, reader, and postprocessor for cross-lingual question answering and showed improvements in both normal and zero-shot settings. These cross-lingual models consist of a large number of parameters and are very resource-intensive. The retriever model takes around 1 hr/epoch whereas the fusion-in-decoder model takes 8 hr/epoch on A6000 GPUs. For future work, we think it would be interesting to try sparse retrieval methods (Formal et al., 2021) in cross-lingual settings and also try incorporating more knowledge from Wikidata based entities in the pipeline.

References

Mikel Artetxe, Sebastian Ruder, and Dani Yogatama. 2019. On the cross-lingual transferability of monolingual representations. *CoRR*, abs/1910.11856.

Akari Asai, Jungo Kasai, Jonathan H. Clark, Kenton Lee, Eunsol Choi, and Hannaneh Hajishirzi. 2021a. XOR QA: Cross-lingual open-retrieval question answering. In *NAACL-HLT*.

Akari Asai, Xinyan Yu, Jungo Kasai, and Hannaneh Hajishirzi. 2021b. One question answering model for many languages with cross-lingual dense passage retrieval. In *NeurIPS*.

Danqi Chen, Adam Fisch, Jason Weston, and Antoine Bordes. 2017. Reading Wikipedia to answer open-domain questions. In *Proceedings of the 55th Annual Meeting of the Association for Computational Linguistics (Volume 1: Long Papers)*, pages 1870–1879, Vancouver, Canada. Association for Computational Linguistics.

Zewen Chi, Li Dong, Furu Wei, Wenhui Wang, Xian-ling Mao, and Heyan Huang. 2019. Cross-lingual natural language generation via pre-training. *CoRR*, abs/1909.10481.

Jonathan H. Clark, Eunsol Choi, Michael Collins, Dan Garrette, Tom Kwiatkowski, Vitaly Nikolaev, and Jennimaria Palomaki. 2020a. Tydi qa: A benchmark for information-seeking question answering in typologically diverse languages. *TACL*.

Jonathan H. Clark, Eunsol Choi, Michael Collins, Dan Garrette, Tom Kwiatkowski, Vitaly Nikolaev, and Jennimaria Palomaki. 2020b. Tydi QA: A benchmark for information-seeking question answering in typologically diverse languages. *CoRR*, abs/2003.05002.

Alexis Conneau, Kartikay Khandelwal, Naman Goyal, Vishrav Chaudhary, Guillaume Wenzek, Francisco Guzmán, Edouard Grave, Myle Ott, Luke Zettlemoyer, and Veselin Stoyanov. 2020. Unsupervised cross-lingual representation learning at scale. In *ACL*.

Martin Fajcik, Martin Docekal, Karel Ondrej, and Pavel Smrz. 2021. R2-d2: A modular baseline for open-domain question answering. In *Findings of the Association for Computational Linguistics: EMNLP 2021*, pages 854–870.

Thibault Formal, Carlos Lassance, Benjamin Piwowarski, and Stéphane Clinchant. 2021. Splade v2: Sparse lexical and expansion model for information retrieval. *arXiv preprint arXiv:2109.10086*.

Junjie Hu, Hiroaki Hayashi, Kyunghyun Cho, and Graham Neubig. 2021. Deep: Denoising entity pre-training for neural machine translation.

Gautier Izacard and Edouard Grave. 2021. Leveraging passage retrieval with generative models for open domain question answering. In *EACL 2021-16th Conference of the European Chapter of the Association for Computational Linguistics*, pages 874–880. Association for Computational Linguistics.

Vladimir Karpukhin, Barlas Oguz, Sewon Min, Patrick Lewis, Ledell Wu, Sergey Edunov, Danqi Chen, and Wen-tau Yih. 2020. Dense passage retrieval for open-domain question answering. In *Proceedings of the 2020 Conference on Empirical Methods in Natural Language Processing (EMNLP)*, pages 6769–6781.

Vishwajeet Kumar, Nitish Joshi, Arijit Mukherjee, Ganesh Ramakrishnan, and Preethi Jyothi. 2019. Cross-lingual training for automatic question generation. *CoRR*, abs/1906.02525.

Tom Kwiatkowski, Jennimaria Palomaki, Olivia Redfield, Michael Collins, Ankur Parikh, Chris Alberti, Danielle Epstein, Illia Polosukhin, Matthew Kelcey, Jacob Devlin, Kenton Lee, Kristina N. Toutanova, Llion Jones, Ming-Wei Chang, Andrew Dai, Jakob Uszkoreit, Quoc Le, and Slav Petrov. 2019. Natural questions: a benchmark for question answering research. *Transactions of the Association of Computational Linguistics*.

Patrick Lewis, Ethan Perez, Aleksandra Piktus, Fabio Petroni, Vladimir Karpukhin, Naman Goyal, Heinrich Küttler, Mike Lewis, Wen-tau Yih, Tim Rocktäschel, et al. 2020. Retrieval-augmented generation for knowledge-intensive nlp tasks. *Advances in Neural Information Processing Systems*, 33:9459–9474.

Patrick S. H. Lewis, Barlas Oguz, Ruty Rinott, Sebastian Riedel, and Holger Schwenk. 2019. MLQA: evaluating cross-lingual extractive question answering. *CoRR*, abs/1910.07475.

Jiahua Liu, Yankai Lin, Zhiyuan Liu, and Maosong Sun. 2019. XQA: A cross-lingual open-domain question answering dataset. In *Proceedings of the 57th Annual Meeting of the Association for Computational Linguistics*, pages 2358–2368, Florence, Italy. Association for Computational Linguistics.

S. Longpre, Yi Lu, and Joachim Daiber. 2021. Mkqa: A linguistically diverse benchmark for multilingual open domain question answering. *Transactions of the Association for Computational Linguistics*, 9:1389–1406.

Yingqi Qu, Yuchen Ding, Jing Liu, Kai Liu, Ruiyang Ren, Xin Zhao, Daxiang Dong, Hua Wu, and Haifeng Wang. 2020. Rocketqa: An optimized training approach to dense passage retrieval for open-domain question answering. *CoRR*, abs/2010.08191.

Pranav Rajpurkar, Robin Jia, and Percy Liang. 2018. Know what you don't know: Unanswerable questions for squad. In *Proceedings of the 56th Annual Meeting of the Association for Computational Linguistics (Volume 2: Short Papers)*, pages 784–789.

Matthew Richardson, Christopher J.C. Burges, and Erin Renshaw. 2013. MCTest: A challenge dataset for the open-domain machine comprehension of text. In *Proceedings of the 2013 Conference on Empirical Methods in Natural Language Processing*, pages 193–203, Seattle, Washington, USA. Association for Computational Linguistics.

Siamak Shakeri, Noah Constant, Mihir Sanjay Kale, and Linting Xue. 2020. Multilingual synthetic question and answer generation for cross-lingual reading comprehension. *CoRR*, abs/2010.12008.

Linting Xue, Noah Constant, Adam Roberts, Mihir Kale, Rami Al-Rfou, Aditya Siddhant, Aditya Barua, and Colin Raffel. 2021. mT5: A massively multilingual pre-trained text-to-text transformer. In *Proceedings of the 2021 Conference of the North American Chapter of the Association for Computational Linguistics: Human Language Technologies*, pages 483–498, Online. Association for Computational Linguistics.

MIA 2022 Shared Task Submission: Leveraging Entity Representations, Dense-Sparse Hybrids, and Fusion-in-Decoder for Cross-Lingual Question Answering

Zhucheng Tu and Sarguna Janani Padmanabhan
Apple
{zhucheng_tu, jananip}@apple.com

Abstract

We describe our two-stage system for the Multilingual Information Access (MIA) 2022 Shared Task on Cross-Lingual Open-Retrieval Question Answering. The first stage consists of multilingual passage retrieval with a hybrid dense and sparse retrieval strategy. The second stage consists of a reader which outputs the answer from the top passages returned by the first stage. We show the efficacy of using entity representations, sparse retrieval signals to help dense retrieval, and Fusion-in-Decoder. On the development set, we obtain 43.46 F1 on XOR-TyDi QA and 21.99 F1 on MKQA, for an average F1 score of 32.73. On the test set, we obtain 40.93 F1 on XOR-TyDi QA and 22.29 F1 on MKQA, for an average F1 score of 31.61. We improve over the official baseline by over 4 F1 points on both the development and test sets.[1]

1 Introduction

This paper describes our submission to the Multilingual Information Access (MIA) 2022 Shared Task on Cross-Lingual Open-Retrieval Question Answering. Cross-lingual open-retrieval question answering is the task of finding an answer to a knowledge-seeking question in the same language as the question from a collection of documents in many languages. The answer may not necessarily exist in a document that's in the same language as the question, and hence a system need to find the answer across relevant documents in a different language. The shared task at Multilingual Information Access 2022 evaluates cross-lingual open-retrieval question answering systems using two datasets, XOR-TyDi QA (Asai et al., 2020) and MKQA (Longpre et al., 2020).[2]

We use a two stage approach, similar to the CORA (Asai et al., 2021) baseline, where the first stage performs multilingual passage retrieval and the second stage performs cross-lingual answer generation. In the first stage, we leverage mLUKE (Ri et al., 2021), a pretrained language model that models entities, to train a dual encoder that encodes the question and passage separately (Karpukhin et al., 2020). During retrieval, we perform nearest neighbor search using the query vector on an index of encoded passage vectors. We merge these dense retrieval hits with BM25 sparse retrieval hits using an algorithm we call Sparse-Corroborate-Dense. Finally, we feed the ranked list of passages into a reader based on Fusion-in-Decoder (Ri et al., 2021) and mT5 (Xue et al., 2020) to produce the final answer. We do not perform iterative training to repeat these steps multiple times.

Compared to official baseline 1, we improve the macro-averaged score by 4.1 F1 points. We perform analysis to show the effectiveness of entity representations, using sparse signals to improve dense hits, and Fusion-in-Decoder.

2 Data and Processing

2.1 Datasets

We use the official training data consisting of 76635 English questions and answers from Natural Questions (Kwiatkowski et al., 2019) and 61360 questions and answers from XOR-TyDi QA (Asai et al., 2020) to train our dual encoder model. We do not train on the development data or the subsets of the Natural Questions and TyDi QA (Clark et al., 2020) data, which are used to create MKQA or XOR-TyDi QA data. For training the reader, we leverage Wikipedia language links, which is detailed in Section 3.3.

XOR-TyDi QA consists of annotated questions and short answers across seven typologically diverse languages. It can be broken down into two subsets, questions where the answer can be found in a passage in the same language as the question

[1]Our submission team name is Team Utah: https://eval.ai/challenge/1638/leaderboard/3933.

[2]https://mia-workshop.github.io/shared_task.html.

Proceedings of the Workshop on Multilingual Information Access (MIA), pages 100 - 107
July 15, 2022

("in-language"), which just come from answerable questions in TyDi QA (Karpukhin et al., 2020), and questions where the answer is unanswerable from a passage in the same language as the question and can only be found in an English passage ("cross-lingual"), which are newly added answers in XOR-TyDi QA. A system should be able to succeed at both monolingual retrieval and cross-lingual retrieval.

MKQA (Longpre et al., 2020) consists of 10K parallel questions and answers across 26 typologically diverse locales. The original question is taken from Natural Questions (Kwiatkowski et al., 2019) in English and translated to 25 different locales. MKQA does not contain any data for training and is only used for evaluation.

2.2 Passage Corpus

We directly use the passages corpus provided by the shared task, with the addition of Tamil (`ta`) and Tagalog (`tl`) which are not included in the baseline's passage data. Following the other languages, we use the `20190201` snapshot of the Wikipedia dumps. We follow the same preprocessing steps as the baseline passages data.[3] We manually split the data into language-specific files, which are later used to build language-specific dense and sparse indices. Final passage retrieval results are aggregated among different indices. The number of passages in each language is shown in Table 1.

Language	Passages	% of Total Passages
Arabic (`ar`)	1304828	2.83
Bengali (`bn`)	179936	0.39
English (`en`)	18003200	39.00
Spanish (`es`)	5738484	12.43
Finnish (`fi`)	886595	1.92
Japanese (`ja`)	5116905	11.09
Khmer (`km`)	63037	0.14
Korean (`ko`)	638865	1.38
Malaysian (`ms`)	397396	0.86
Russian (`ru`)	4545634	9.85
Swedish (`sv`)	4525695	9.81
Tamil (`ta`)	219356	0.48
Telugu (`te`)	274230	0.59
Tagalog (`tl`)	69228	0.15
Turkish (`tr`)	798368	1.73
Chinese (`zh`)	3394943	7.36
Total	**46156700**	**100.0**

Table 1: Number of passages in corpus for each language.

3 System Architecture and Pipeline

Our system differs from the baseline in three ways. First, in the passage retrieval step, we replace mBERT (Devlin et al., 2019) with mLUKE (Ri et al., 2021). Second, we construct sparse indices from which we will retrieve passages to augment dense retriever-retrieved passages, inspired by Zhang et al. (2021) but uses a different dense-sparse hybrid approach. Finally, we encode each question and passage independently as opposed to all passages together following the Fusion-in-Decoder (Izacard and Grave, 2020) approach.

3.1 Entity Representations

For dense retrieval, we use a multilingual pretrained language model with entity representations, mLUKE (Ri et al., 2021), to initialize the dual encoder in DPR (Karpukhin et al., 2020). We use the same training objective as DPR and also use the last layer's hidden state of the first input token as the representation for both the question and passage. mLUKE is a multilingual extension of LUKE (Yamada et al., 2020), a pretrained contextualized representation of words and entities based on the Transformer (Vaswani et al., 2017). Words and entities are treated as different types of tokens and the entity-aware self-attention mechanism leads to improved effectiveness. We use the Hugging Face transformers (Wolf et al., 2020) versions of `mluke-base` and `bert-base-multilingual-uncased`. Only in-batch negatives are used to train the dual encoder.

3.2 Dense-Sparse Hybrids

In order to effectively retrieve passages in a multilingual setting, the retrieval component needs to do well in both monolingual retrieval and cross-lingual retrieval. Monolingual retrieval is the setting where we want to retrieve passages in the same language as the question. For more than half of the questions in the XOR-TyDi QA dataset, for example, the answer is found in a passage that's in the same language as the question. Cross-lingual retrieval is the setting where we want to retrieve relevant passages in different language from the question. We use both sparse retrieval (i.e. BM25) and dense

[3] `https://github.com/mia-workshop/MIA-Shared-Task-2022/commits/main/baseline/wikipedia_preprocess/build_dpr_w100_data.py`

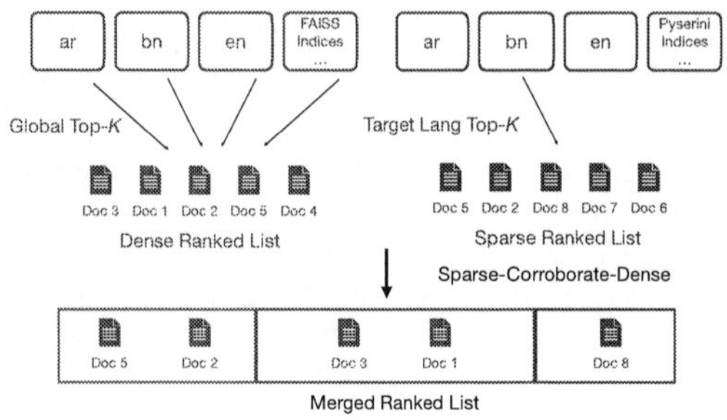

Figure 1: An illustration of the Sparse-Dense-Corroborate algorithm, running with $K = 5$ and $max\_frac = 0.6$ for a Bengali (bn) question. We first retrieve the 5 passages with the highest scores from the dense indices, and the top 5 passages from the Bengali sparse index. For the first output slice, we take passages in both lists, ordered by same order as in the dense list, which are doc 5 and doc 2. For the second slice, we add the top remaining passages from the dense list, which are doc 3 and doc 1. For the third slice, we take the top remaining passages from the sparse list, which is doc 8. The max number of sparse results that is allowed to influence the final list is $0.6 \times 5 = 3$, which are docs 5, 2, and 8.

retrieval together in our system. Experiments in Mr. TyDi (Zhang et al., 2021) indicate BM25 outperforms DPR (Karpukhin et al., 2020) for the languages in XOR-TyDi QA in the monolingual retrieval setting, but combining the sparse score and DPR score in sparse-dense hybrids perform even better. At the same time, sparse retrieval rely on lexical token matches and cannot do cross-lingual retrieval effectively without translating the query to the same language as the passage. To remove the need to use a machine translation system for simplicity, we rely on multilingual dense passage retrieval for cross-lingual retrieval.

For dense retrieval, we use FAISS (Johnson et al., 2019) with `IndexFlatIP`. For sparse retrieval, we use Pyserini (Yang et al., 2017; Lin et al., 2021) with BM25 with default parameters. We build separate indices for each language for both the dense and sparse setting. For each query, where we want to return K passage, we search for the top K passages globally in the dense indices in all languages, and search for the top K passages in the sparse index in the same language as the question.

We combine results from dense retrieval and sparse retrieval using the following algorithm, which we call Sparse-Corroborate-Dense. Our final ranked list consists of three ordered slices. The first slice consists of passages that are present in both dense and sparse retrieved lists, ranked in the same order as they appear in dense retrieval. The second slice consists of passages that are only in the dense ranked list and not in the sparse ranked list. The last slice consists of top passages in the sparse ranked list. The number of passages from the sparse hits that are allowed to influence the final ranked list is no more than $\lfloor max\_frac * K \rfloor$. We find this works better than the score normalization and combining approach in Mr. TyDi (Zhang et al., 2021) for cross-lingual retrieval. Figure 1 has an illustration of this algorithm running with $K = 5$ and $max\_frac = 0.6$ for a Bengali (bn) question. Please refer to Appendix A for code of the algorithm.

3.3 Reader

Instead of concatenating the question and all the passages in the input to the encoder like in the baseline, which we will call Fusion-in-Encoder, we use the Fusion-in-Decoder (FiD) approach (Izacard and Grave, 2020). In Fusion-in-Decoder, the encoder processes each of the *ctxs* passages independently adding special tokens *question: lang: title:* and *context:* before the question, title and text of each passage, while the decoder performs attention over the concatenation of the resulting representations of all the retrieved passages.

Independent processing of passages in the encoder allows to scale linearly to large number of contexts, while processing passages jointly in the decoder helps better aggregate evidence from multiple passages.

In order to semantically ground the entities across different languages together, we use Wikipedia language links to augment the data from retriever while training FiD based reader, like the CORA baseline. First, for each question in the MIA training set that comes from Natural Questions, we use the answer to search for the corresponding Wikipedia page using the Wikipedia API. Generally, only answers that are entities will have a result. This returns the titles of the Wikipedia articles in different languages, which we use as the answer in different languages. We use the DPR checkpoint trained with adversarial examples to retrieve English passages from the index.[4] For each English question-answer pair, we find corresponding entries in other

[4]`https://github.com/facebookresearch/DPR#new-march-2021-retrieval-model`

languages being evaluated in the task and generate $[Query_{eng}, Lang_{target}, Answer_{target}, Passages]$ tuples for training FiD. This data is augmented to the original training data provided by the retriever.

4 Results

For training the dual encoder, we use the official training data without any hard negatives with the same hyperparameters as the baseline dual encoder (Asai et al., 2021). For training Fusion-in-Decoder, we combine the all of the retrieval results with sampled Wikipedia language link augmented passages such that the total percentage of training examples from either source is 50%. We use the baseline retrieval results instead of mLUKE-retrieved results to develop the retriever and reader in parallel. We use learning rate of 0.00005 with linear learning schedule with a weight decay of 0.01 using the AdamW optimizer. The context size (number of passages) in the final submission is 20 passages. Note for retrieval we use $K = 60$ to use the same retrieval results for different context size experiments, but in the final submitted system take the top 20 from this list for the reader. We use $max\_frac = 0.2$ for Sparse-Corroborate-Dense. We use the best checkpoint on the development set for both components.

4.1 Main Results

We first report end-to-end results using our best system compared to the baseline in Table 2 for the development set and Table 3 for the test set. On the development set, we obtain macro-averaged F1 score of 43.46 across all languages on XOR-TyDi QA, an improvement of 3.70 F1 points over 39.76 obtained by baseline 1. We obtain macro-averaged F1 score of 21.99 across all languages on MKQA, an improvement of 4.61 F1 points over 17.38 obtained by baseline 1. On the test set, we observe fairly consistent results compared to the development set. On XOR-TyDi QA, our system and baseline 1 obtains 40.93 and 37.95 respectively, an improvement of 2.98 F1 points. On MKQA, our system and baseline 1 obtains 22.29 and 17.14 respectively, an improvement of 5.15 F1 points. On both the development set and test set, we outperform the baseline on all languages except for Khmer (`km`) on MKQA.

We observe our system frequently retrieves irrelevant passages for Khmer through qualitatively sampling some passages retrieved for Khmer questions, providing little chance for the reader to find the answer. mLUKE uses 24 languages for pretraining and does not include Khmer, making it difficult to align entities in Khmer. Furthermore, even if we use the baseline retrieval results, we still see a large drop in reader effectiveness when we switch to Fusion-in-Decoder from row (iii) to (ii) in Table 4. We only have 3101 rows in the training data for Khmer for our reader all from Wikipedia language links, out of 275990 rows in total.

On the surprising languages Tagalog (`tl`) and Tamil (`ta`), we outperform the baseline by a large margin. Perhaps surprisingly, this large improvement cannot be attributed to the presence of Tagalog and Tamil passages in our corpus, since in our best submission, for example, out of the 350 Tamil questions, only one question has a retrieved passage in Tamil in the top results that are fed to the reader. Instead, the system is able to generate correct answers from English passages.

4.2 Analysis

Ablation Studies We conduct ablation studies on our system in Table 4. We find the biggest gain comes from switching Fusion-in-Encoder (FiE) in the baseline to Fusion-in-Decoder (FiD) from row (iii) to row (ii), even though we did not increase the number of passages for Fusion-in-Decoder and kept it at 20 for the final system. The second largest gain comes from switching mBERT to mLUKE from row (ii) to row (i). Finally, the smaller gain comes from switching dense retrieval only to Sparse-Corroborate-Dense, from row (i) to mLUKE + SP + FiD. We study each of the components in greater detail below.

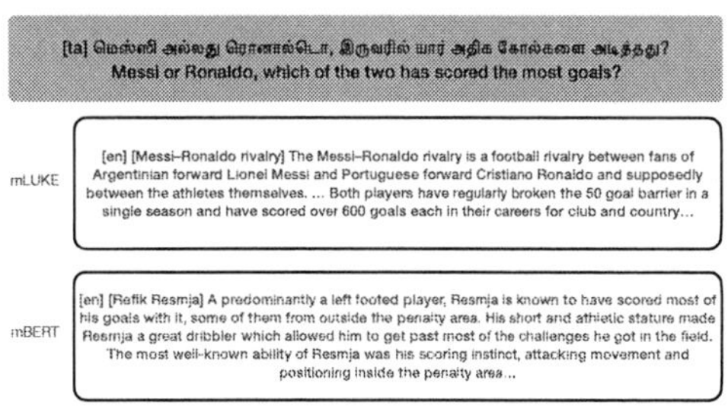

Figure 2: The top passage for a Tamil question retrieved by mBERT and mLUKE. We see mLUKE is able to find English passages related to entities Messi and Ronaldo, but mBERT struggles and only finds a general passage related to another unrelated soccer player related to goal scoring.

System	XOR-TyDi QA F1 ar	bn	fi	ja	ko	ru	te	Avg	MKQA F1 ar	en	es	fi	ko	ms	ja	km	ru	sv	tr	zh_cn	Avg
Baseline 1	51.29	28.72	44.35	43.21	29.84	40.68	40.19	39.76	8.77	27.86	24.92	23.25	8.28	22.64	15.18	**5.73**	14.00	24.13	20.60	13.14	17.38
Our submission	**54.84**	**30.68**	**47.41**	**47.29**	**33.90**	**43.13**	**47.00**	**43.46**	**13.34**	**39.57**	**29.74**	**24.73**	**12.14**	**27.44**	**18.97**	2.57	**19.36**	**28.26**	**25.52**	**22.29**	**21.99**

Table 2: End-to-end development set results. Baseline 1 and our submission obtain overall macro-averaged F1 scores of 28.57 and 32.73 respectively. Our submission outperforms the baseline on all languages except Khmer (km) on MKQA.

System	XOR-TyDi QA F1 ar	bn	fi	ja	ko	ru	te	Avg	MKQA F1 ar	en	es	fi	ko	ms	ja	km	ru	sv	tr	zh_cn	Avg	Sup ta	tl
Baseline 1	49.66	33.99	39.54	39.72	25.59	40.98	36.16	37.95	9.52	36.34	27.23	22.70	7.68	25.11	15.89	**6.00**	14.60	26.69	21.66	13.78	17.14	0.00	12.78
Our submission	**55.33**	30.48	**41.01**	**43.45**	**31.21**	**42.62**	**42.40**	**40.93**	**12.67**	**39.63**	**30.85**	**25.22**	**12.18**	**29.09**	**20.49**	2.36	**18.82**	**29.62**	**26.16**	**22.60**	**22.29**	**20.75**	**20.95**

Table 3: End-to-end test set results. Baseline 1 and our submission obtain overall macro-averaged F1 scores of 27.55 and 31.61 respectively. "Sup" indicates the surprise languages. Our submission outperforms the baseline on all languages except Khmer (km) on MKQA.

Entity Representations To evaluate the passage retrieval component for XOR-TyDi QA, we measure MRR@60 and Recall@60. We picked 60 because it is the near the maximum number of passages we can feed into Fusion-in-Decoder bound by the GPU memory. For each question, to determine if a passage is relevant, we use a heuristic. First, we find the universe set of answers for the questions, which not only contain answers in the same language, but also possibly answers in English using the English answer in the XOR-English Span task (Asai et al., 2020). We check if the normalized answer is a substring of the passage text, and if so, we mark the passage as relevant. Note that this is a proxy for measuring passage relevance, since answers may not necessarily be exact spans / substrings or the same answer may appear as a substring in a non-relevant passage, but we found it to correlate well with end-to-end effectiveness. We see from Table 5 that overall using mLUKE improves passage retrieval effectiveness. Qualitatively, we also find examples where the dual encoder trained with mLUKE can find passages cross-lingually with the relevant entity whereas that trained with mBERT could not. In Figure 2, we see mLUKE can retrieve an English top passage about the soccer players Messi and Ronaldo asked in Tamil, but mBERT returns just an English passage about another soccer player not relevant to the question.

Dense-Sparse Hybrids Next, we evaluate the benefits of using dense retrieval in conjunction with sparse retrieval as opposed to using only dense retrieval in Table 6. The dense retriever here is mLUKE. We see that dense retrieval always works better than sparse retrieval when used independently, and the score combination approach used

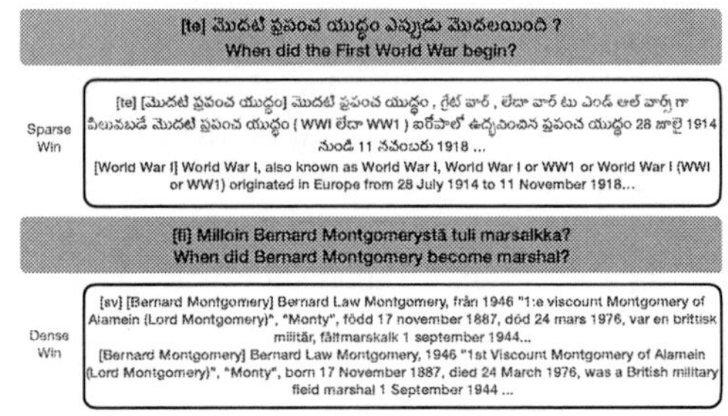

Figure 3: Here we see a highly relevant passage found by sparse monolingual retrieval that is not found by dense retrieval, and a relevant passage found by dense retrieval cross-lingually that is not found by sparse retrieval.

in Mr. TyDi (Zhang et al., 2021) does not outperform dense retrieval in recall, but does improve the MRR. We use Sparse-Corroborate-Dense, which piggybacks on dense retrieval results, but boosts the ranking of some passages in dense retrieval, and add in additional passages not found by dense retrieval to the end of the top-K list. Compared to dense only, it is better on both MRR and recall. When both dense and sparse retrieval finds the same passage, it is a strong signal the passage is relevant. Nonetheless, sparse retrieval can still find passages that dense retrieval cannot find, and adding these to the candidate passage list passed to the reader can provide additional relevant evidence passages. In Figure 3, we see sparse retrieval can find a highly relevant passage related to World War I in Telugu (te) to the Telugu question that cannot be found by dense retrieval, and dense retrieval can find a passage related to Bernard Montgomery cross-lingually in Swedish (sv) to a Finnish (fi) question that cannot be found by sparse retrieval – they can complement each other.

	XOR-TyDi QA F1								MKQA F1												
System	ar	bn	fi	ja	ko	ru	te	Avg	ar	en	es	fi	ko	ms	ja	km	ru	sv	tr	zh_cn	Avg
mLUKE + SP + FiD	54.84	**30.68**	**47.41**	**47.29**	**33.90**	**43.13**	**47.00**	**43.46**	**13.34**	**39.57**	**29.74**	24.73	**12.14**	**27.44**	**18.97**	**2.57**	**19.36**	**28.26**	**25.52**	**22.29**	**21.99**
(i) mLUKE + FiD	**54.93**	29.56	46.88	45.76	33.16	42.03	46.28	42.66	13.23	38.01	29.57	**25.36**	11.45	27.28	18.37	2.53	18.59	28.22	25.43	21.98	21.67
(ii) mBERT + FiD	53.19	29.25	46.97	43.25	30.38	42.79	44.22	41.44	10.94	37.42	28.18	21.89	9.63	27.20	15.00	2.11	16.41	26.96	21.86	20.24	19.82
(iii) mBERT + FiE	49.71	29.15	42.72	41.20	30.64	40.16	38.57	38.88	8.95	33.87	25.08	21.15	6.72	24.55	15.27	6.05	15.60	25.53	20.44	13.71	18.07

Table 4: Ablation studies on the development sets. mLUKE + SP + FiD is our submission with mLUKE + Sparse-Corroborate-Dense. (i) mLUKE + FiD only relies on dense retrieval, and we observe a slight decrease in the F1 score of most languages compared with our submission. (ii) mBERT + FiD changes the retriever to mBERT, and we observe a larger drop in F1 score compared to mLUKE in row (i). (iii) mBERT + FiE changes Fusion-in-Decoder to Fusion-in-Encoder as in the baseline and we see an even larger drop in F1 score compared with row (ii).

	MRR@60							
Model	ar	bn	fi	ja	ko	ru	te	Avg
mBERT (Devlin et al., 2019)	0.106	0.026	0.069	0.031	0.023	0.057	**0.050**	0.362
mLUKE (Ri et al., 2021)	0.106	**0.028**	**0.076**	**0.035**	**0.027**	**0.122**	0.042	**0.372**
	Recall@60							
Model	ar	bn	fi	ja	ko	ru	te	Avg
mBERT (Devlin et al., 2019)	0.185	0.057	0.130	0.073	0.050	**0.118**	0.075	0.689
mLUKE (Ri et al., 2021)	**0.189**	**0.065**	**0.133**	**0.078**	**0.056**	0.056	**0.079**	**0.723**

Table 5: MRR@60 and Recall@60 of passage retrieval for XOR-TyDi QA dev set for different pretrained language models.

	MRR@60							
Methodology	ar	bn	fi	ja	ko	ru	te	Avg
Sparse Only	0.088	0.023	0.640	0.024	0.018	0.051	0.032	0.299
Dense Only	0.106	0.028	0.076	0.035	0.027	0.058	0.042	0.372
Combine Score (Zhang et al., 2021)	0.113	0.029	0.076	0.032	0.023	0.060	0.048	**0.382**
Sparse-Corroborate-Dense	0.110	0.029	0.074	0.032	0.026	0.063	0.049	**0.382**
	Recall@60							
Methodology	ar	bn	fi	ja	ko	ru	te	Avg
Sparse Only	0.172	0.045	0.120	0.063	0.044	0.098	0.070	0.611
Dense Only	0.189	0.065	0.133	0.078	0.056	0.122	0.079	0.723
Combine Score (Zhang et al., 2021)	0.178	0.059	0.118	0.070	0.046	0.107	0.076	0.652
Sparse-Corroborate-Dense	0.192	0.065	0.136	0.078	0.057	0.124	0.080	**0.733**

Table 6: Comparison of various dense-sparse hybrid strategies for original XOR-TyDi QA dev set. The dense retrieval dual encoder used is mLUKE. max_frac used for Sparse-Corroborate-Dense is 0.2.

Fusion-in-Decoder We want to understand the effect of increasing the number of passages sent to the reader by comparing the effectiveness of the reader when there are 20 passages versus 60 passages. Intuitively, there could be relevant passages found in positions 21-60, which should strengthen the evidence needed to output the final answer. From Table 7 we observe using more evidence passages consistently improve results, and this scaling advantage is key over Fusion-in-Encoder. However, due to time limitations, we only used the 20 passages setting for the final shared task submission.

5 Conclusion

We describe our submission for the MIA 2022 Shared Task and detail some experiments we perform to improve specific components of the system. We find that using mLUKE (Ri et al., 2021), a pretrained language model that models entities, combing dense and sparse results using Sparse-Corroborate-Dense, and Fusion-in-Decoder, are effective for improving the effectiveness for cross-lingual question answering over the baseline.

	XOR-TyDi QA		MKQA	
Number of Passages	EM	F1	EM	F1
20	31.63	38.06	16.15	20.21
60	33.74	41.29	17.31	21.51

Table 7: Exact Match (EM) and F1 score for different number of passages on the development sets from mLUKE retrieved passages.

6 Acknowledgement

We thank Yinfei Yang, Wei Wang, and Jinhao Lei for their insightful discussions and feedback on early versions of the paper.

References

Akari Asai, Jungo Kasai, Jonathan H Clark, Kenton Lee, Eunsol Choi, and Hannaneh Hajishirzi. 2020. XOR QA: Cross-lingual open-retrieval question answering. *arXiv preprint arXiv:2010.11856*.

Akari Asai, Xinyan Yu, Jungo Kasai, and Hannaneh Hajishirzi. 2021. One question answering model for many languages with cross-lingual dense passage retrieval. In *NeurIPS*.

Jonathan H Clark, Jennimaria Palomaki, Vitaly Nikolaev, Eunsol Choi, Dan Garrette, Michael Collins, and Tom Kwiatkowski. 2020. TyDi QA: A benchmark for information-seeking question answering in typologically diverse languages. *Transactions of the Association for Computational Linguistics*, 8:454–470.

Jacob Devlin, Ming-Wei Chang, Kenton Lee, and Kristina Toutanova. 2019. BERT: Pre-training of deep bidirectional transformers for language understanding. In *Proceedings of the 2019 Conference of the North American Chapter of the Association for Computational Linguistics: Human Language Technologies, Volume 1 (Long and Short Papers)*, pages 4171–4186.

Gautier Izacard and Edouard Grave. 2020. Leveraging passage retrieval with generative models for open domain question answering.

Jeff Johnson, Matthijs Douze, and Hervé Jégou. 2019. Billion-scale similarity search with GPUs. *IEEE Transactions on Big Data*, 7(3):535–547.

Vladimir Karpukhin, Barlas Oğuz, Sewon Min, Ledell Wu, Sergey Edunov, Danqi Chen, and Wen-tau Yih. 2020. Dense passage retrieval for open-domain question answering. In *Proc. of EMNLP*.

Tom Kwiatkowski, Jennimaria Palomaki, Olivia Redfield, Michael Collins, Ankur Parikh, Chris Alberti, Danielle Epstein, Illia Polosukhin, Jacob Devlin, Kenton Lee, et al. 2019. Natural Questions: a benchmark for question answering research. *Transactions of the Association for Computational Linguistics*, 7:452–466.

Jimmy Lin, Xueguang Ma, Sheng-Chieh Lin, Jheng-Hong Yang, Ronak Pradeep, and Rodrigo Nogueira. 2021. Pyserini: An easy-to-use python toolkit to support replicable ir research with sparse and dense representations. *arXiv preprint arXiv:2102.10073*.

Shayne Longpre, Yi Lu, and Joachim Daiber. 2020. MKQA: A linguistically diverse benchmark for multilingual open domain question answering. *arXiv preprint arXiv:2007.15207*.

Ryokan Ri, Ikuya Yamada, and Yoshimasa Tsuruoka. 2021. mLUKE: The power of entity representations in multilingual pretrained language models. *arXiv preprint arXiv:2110.08151*.

Ashish Vaswani, Noam Shazeer, Niki Parmar, Jakob Uszkoreit, Llion Jones, Aidan N Gomez, Łukasz Kaiser, and Illia Polosukhin. 2017. Attention is all you need. *Advances in neural information processing systems*, 30.

Thomas Wolf, Lysandre Debut, Victor Sanh, Julien Chaumond, Clement Delangue, Anthony Moi, Pierric Cistac, Tim Rault, Rémi Louf, Morgan Funtowicz, Joe Davison, Sam Shleifer, Patrick von Platen, Clara Ma, Yacine Jernite, Julien Plu, Canwen Xu, Teven Le Scao, Sylvain Gugger, Mariama Drame, Quentin Lhoest, and Alexander M. Rush. 2020. Transformers: State-of-the-art natural language processing. In *Proceedings of the 2020 Conference on Empirical Methods in Natural Language Processing: System Demonstrations*, pages 38–45, Online. Association for Computational Linguistics.

Linting Xue, Noah Constant, Adam Roberts, Mihir Kale, Rami Al-Rfou, Aditya Siddhant, Aditya Barua, and Colin Raffel. 2020. mT5: A massively multilingual pre-trained text-to-text transformer. *arXiv preprint arXiv:2010.11934*.

Ikuya Yamada, Akari Asai, Hiroyuki Shindo, Hideaki Takeda, and Yuji Matsumoto. 2020. LUKE: Deep contextualized entity representations with entity-aware self-attention. In *Proceedings of the 2020 Conference on Empirical Methods in Natural Language Processing (EMNLP)*. Association for Computational Linguistics.

Peilin Yang, Hui Fang, and Jimmy Lin. 2017. Anserini: Enabling the use of lucene for information retrieval research. In *Proceedings of the 40th international ACM SIGIR conference on research and development in information retrieval*, pages 1253–1256.

Xinyu Zhang, Xueguang Ma, Peng Shi, and Jimmy Lin. 2021. Mr. TyDi: A multi-lingual benchmark for dense retrieval. *arXiv:2108.08787*.

A Sparse-Corroborate-Dense Algorithm

Here is the precise algorithm for Sparse-Corroborate-Dense.

```
def sparse_corroborate_dense(
dense_hits: List[Tuple[str, float]],
sparse_hits: List[Tuple[str, float]],
max_frac: float, K: int):
  dense_docid_to_idx = {
    tup[0]: idx for idx, tup in enumerate(dense_hits)
  }

  RESERVED_SPARSE_SLOTS = min(
    int(max_frac * K),
    len(sparse_hits)
  )
  final_hits = []
  docids_added = set()
  backfill_sparse_hits = []

  # Go through top sparse results, if sparse hit is also in dense, push it to front, else, put it in backfill
  for docid, sparse_score in sparse_hits:
    if docid in dense_docid_to_idx:
      final_hits.append(
        dense_hits[dense_docid_to_idx[docid]]
      )
      docids_added.add(docid)
      RESERVED_SPARSE_SLOTS -= 1
    else:
      backfill_sparse_hits.append([docid, sparse_score])

  # Add rest of dense ids
  i = 0
  while len(final_hits) < K - RESERVED_SPARSE_SLOTS and i < len(dense_hits):
    if dense_hits[i][0] not in docids_added:
      final_hits.append(dense_hits[i])
      docids_added.add(
        dense_hits[i][0]
      )
    i += 1

  final_hits.extend(
    backfill_sparse_hits[:K - len(final_hits)]
  )

  return final_hits
```

MIA 2022 Shared Task: Evaluating Cross-lingual Open-Retrieval Question Answering for 16 Diverse Languages

Akari Asai♣, Shayne Longpre♠, Jungo Kasai♣, Chia-Hsuan Lee♣, Rui Zhang♦, Junjie Hu♡, Ikuya Yamada★◊, Jonathan H. Clark‡, Eunsol Choi†

♣University of Washington ♠Massachusetts Institute of Technology ♦Penn State University
♡University of Wisconsin-Madison ★Studio Ousia ◊RIKEN
‡Google Research †The University of Texas at Austin
mia.nlp.workshop@gmail.com

Abstract

We present the results of the Workshop on Multilingual Information Access (MIA) 2022 Shared Task, evaluating cross-lingual open-retrieval question answering (QA) systems in 16 typologically diverse languages. In this task, we adapted two large-scale cross-lingual open-retrieval QA datasets in 14 typologically diverse languages, and newly annotated open-retrieval QA data in 2 underrepresented languages: Tagalog and Tamil. Four teams submitted their systems. The best *constrained* system uses entity-aware contextualized representations for document retrieval, thereby achieving an average F1 score of 31.6, which is 4.1 F1 absolute higher than the challenging baseline. The best system obtains particularly significant improvements in Tamil (20.8 F1), whereas most of the other systems yield nearly zero scores. The best *unconstrained* system achieves 32.2 F1, outperforming our baseline by 4.5 points. The official leaderboard[1] and baselines[2] models are publicly available.

1 Introduction

Open-retrieval[3] question answering (QA) is a task of answering questions in diverse domains given large-scale document collections such as Wikipedia (Chen and Yih, 2020). Despite the rapid progress in this area (Chen et al., 2017; Karpukhin et al., 2020; Lewis et al., 2020b), the systems have primarily been evaluated in English, yet open-retrieval QA in non-English languages has been understudied (Longpre et al., 2021; Asai et al., 2021a). Moreover, due to the task complexity, cross-lingual open-retrieval QA has unique challenges such as multi-step inference (retrieval and answer selection) and cross-lingual pattern matching (Lewis et al., 2020a; Schäuble and Sheridan, 1997), whereas other multilingual NLP tasks have their inputs specified at once (e.g. natural language inference) and typically only need to perform inference on one language at a time.

In this work, we introduce the MIA 2022 shared task on cross-lingual open-retrieval QA, which tests open-retrieval QA systems across typologically diverse languages. Compared to previous efforts on multilingual open-retrieval QA (Forner et al., 2008, 2010), this shared task covers a wider set of languages (i.e., 16 topologically diverse languages) and orders of magnitude more passages in retrieval targets (i.e., 40 million passages in total), and constitutes the first shared task for massive-scale cross-lingual open-retrieval QA. Four teams submitted systems, three of which significantly improve the baseline system based on a state-of-the-art multilingual open-retrieval QA system (Asai et al., 2021b).

Our analysis reveals that the system performance varies across languages even when the questions are parallel (as in one of our two settings), and several findings from the submitted systems shed light on the importance on entity-enhanced representations, leveraging more passages and data augmentation for future research in multilingual knowledge-intensive NLP. Our analysis suggests that (i) it is still challenging to retrieve passages cross-lingually, (ii) generating answers in the target language whose script differs from the script of evidence document is nontrivial, (iii) and potential answer overlaps in existing datasets may overestimate models' performance.

We formally introduce our task in Section 2, followed by data collection process for 16 languages in Section 3. We then introduce our baseline systems in Section 4 and the submitted systems. Section 5 presents our meta analysis of the systems performances, and we conclude by suggesting future improvements in this area.

[1] https://eval.ai/web/challenges/challenge-page/1638/leaderboard

[2] https://github.com/mia-workshop/MIA-Shared-Task-2022

[3] Also sometimes referred to as *open-domain* QA; we use *open-retrieval* as it is not ambiguous with the sense of "covering many domains."

Proceedings of the Workshop on Multilingual Information Access (MIA), pages 108 - 120
July 15, 2022 ©2022 Association for Computational Linguistics

2 Task Descriptions

We first formulate cross-lingual open-retrieval QA and introduce metrics used to evaluate systems' performance. We then present two submission tracks: constrained and unconstrained tracks.

2.1 Task Formulation

Cross-lingual open-retrieval QA is a challenging multilingual NLP task, where given questions written in a user's preferred language, a system needs to find evidence from large-scale document collections written in many different languages. The final answer needs to be in the user's preferred language which is indicated by their question, as in real-world applications. We follow the general definition of Asai et al. (2021b), where a system can retrieve evidence from documents in *any* languages, not limiting the retrieval target to certain languages as in Forner et al. (2008). For instance, a system needs to answer in Arabic to an Arabic question, but it can use evidence passages written in any language included in a large-document corpus such as English, German, Japanese and so on. In real-world applications, the issues of information asymmetry and information scarcity (Roy et al., 2022; Blasi et al., 2022; Asai et al., 2021a; Joshi et al., 2020) arise in many languages, hence the need to source answer contents from other languages—yet we often do not know *a priori* in which language the evidence can be found to answer a question.

2.2 Evaluation Metrics

Systems are evaluated using automatic metrics: token-level F1 and exact match (EM). Although EM is often used as the primary evaluation metric for English, the risk of surface-level mismatching (Min et al., 2020a) can be more pervasive in cross-lingual settings. Therefore, we use F1 as the primary metric and rank systems using the F1 scores. Evaluation is conducted using language-specific tokenization and evaluation scripts provided in the MIA shared task repository.[4] We use data from XOR-TyDi QA and MKQA (detailed in Section 3), and due to different characteristics these datasets have, we macro-average scores per language set on each dataset, and then macro-average those scores to produce an F1 score for XOR-TyDi QA and an F1 score for MKQA to compute the final scores for ranking.

2.3 Tracks

For the shared task, we defined two tracks based on the resource used to train systems: *constrained* and *unconstrained* settings. Systems trained only on the official training data qualify for the constrained track, while systems trained with additional data sources participate in the unconstrained track.

Constrained Track. To qualify as a constrained track submission, participants are required to use the official training corpus, which consists of examples pooled from XOR-TyDi QA and Natural Questions (Kwiatkowski et al., 2019). See more data collection details in Section 3. No other QA data may be used for training. We allow participants to use off-the-shelf tools for linguistic annotations (e.g. POS taggers, syntactic parsers), as well as any publicly available unlabeled data and models derived from these (e.g. word vectors, pre-trained language models). In the constrained setup, participants may not use external blackbox APIs such as Google Search API and Google Translate API for inference, as those models are often trained on additional data, but they are permitted to use them for offline data augmentation or training.

Unconstrained track. Any model submissions using APIs or training data beyond the scope of the constrained track are considered for the *unconstrained* setting. Participants are required to report the details of their additional resources used for training, for transparency. For instance, a submission might use publicly available QA datasets, such as CMRC 2018 (Cui et al., 2019) and FQuAD (d'Hoffschmidt et al., 2020), to create larger-scale training data.

3 Shared Task Data

The MIA shared task data is derived from two large-scale multilingual evaluation sets: XOR-TyDi QA (Asai et al., 2021a) and MKQA (Longpre et al., 2021). We first discuss the source datasets, and then discuss how the target languages are selected, and how the data is split into training and evaluation sets. Table 1 shows the included languages, their language groups, the size of training, development and test data, and the number of Wikipedia passages available in each language.

[4]For non-spacing languages (i.e., Japanese, Khmer, and Chinese), we use off-the-shelf tokenizers including Mecab, khmernltk and jieba to tokenize both predictions and ground-truth answers.

Language	Language Family		# of examples			# Wiki. passages
	Family	Branch	Train	Development	Test	
Arabic (ar)	Afro-Asiatic	Semitic	18,402	3,145	5,590	1,304,828
Bengali (bn)	Indo-European	Indo-Iranian	5,007	2,248	5,203	179,936
English (en)	Indo-European	Germanic	76,635	1,758	5,000	18,003,200
Spanish (es)	Indo-European	Italic	0	1,758	5,000	5,738,484
Finnish (fi)	Uralic	Finnic	9,762	2,732	1,368	886,595
Japanese (ja)	Japonic	Japonic	7,815	2,451	6,056	5,116,905
Khmer (km)	Austroasiatic	Khmer	0	1,758	5,000	63,037
Korean (ko)	Koreanic	Han	4,319	2,231	6,048	638,864
Malay (ms)	Austronesian	Malayo-Poly.	0	1,758	5,000	397,396
Russian (ru)	Indo-European	Balto-Slavic	9,290	2,776	6,910	4,545,635
Swedish (sv)	Indo-Europea	Germanic	0	1,758	5,000	4,525,695
Chinese (zh)	Sino-Tibetan	Sinitic	0	1,758	5,000	3,394,943
Telugu (te)	Dravidian	South-Central	6,759	2,322	6,873	274,230
Surprise Languages						
Tagalog (tl)	Austronesian	Malayo-Poly.	0	0	350	–
Tamil (ta)	Dravidian	Southern	0	0	350	–

Table 1: List of the languages, their families and amount of data available in the MIA shared task data. The last two languages are surprise languages hidden from the participants.

3.1 Source Datasets

XOR-TyDi QA (Asai et al., 2021a) is a cross-lingual open-retrieval QA dataset covering 7 languages built upon TyDi QA (Clark et al., 2020). Asai et al. (2021a) collect answers for questions in TyDi QA that are *unanswerable* using the same-language Wikipedia. As the questions are inherited from TyDi QA, they are written by native speakers to better reflect their own interests and linguistic phenomena, and they are not parallel across languages. We use data for the XOR-full setting, where some questions can be answered based on the target language's Wikipedia (monolingual) while others require evidence only presented in English Wikipedia (cross-lingual). We use all of the 7 languages covered by XOR-TyDi QA: Arabic (ar), Bengali (bn), Finnish (fi), Japanese (ja), Korean (ko), Russian (ru), Telugu (te).

MKQA (Longpre et al., 2021) comprises the largest set of languages and dialects (26) for open-retrieval QA, spanning 14 language families. There are 10k question and answer pairs per language. The questions are human-translated from English Natural Questions (Kwiatkowski et al., 2019) and the answers are re-annotated for higher quality – chosen independently of any web pages or document corpora. From MKQA, we sample the 6,758 parallel examples which are answerable. We select 12 of the 26 languages to lower the computational barrier: Arabic (ar), English (en), Spanish (es), Finnish (fi), Japanese (ja), Khmer (km), Korean (ko), Malay (ms), Russian (ru), Swedish (sv), Turkish (tr), and traditional Chinese (zh-cn).

3.2 Language Selection

We select a subset of languages from each resource (i) to cover a wide range of languages and typological features with a sufficient scale, and (ii) to compare participating model performance between questions that are translated from English and ones that are naturally generated by native speakers. The natively-written questions from XOR-TyDi QA allow measuring systems' quality on questions that are likely to serve information need expressed by speakers of each language, whereas the human-translated questions of MKQA allow measuring the performance on the target script and language, holding constant the question content. For this reason, we include 5 languages present in both XOR-TyDi QA and MKQA to compare the gap between cultural and linguistic model generalization: Arabic, Finnish, Japanese, Korean, and Russian.

Surprise languages. In addition, we newly annotated data in Tagalog (tl) and Tamil (ta), where little work studies open-retrieval QA (Liu et al., 2019). For each language, we sample 350 MKQA English examples, where the answer entities have an Wikipedia article in the target language. The 350 questions are all translated using Gengo's human translation,[5] but the answers are automatically translated using Wikidata. This annotation results in 350 well-formed examples in Tagalog (tl) and Tamil (ta). Surprise languages are released two

[5] https://gengo.com/

weeks before the system submission deadline to test systems' ability to perform zero-shot transfer (Hu et al., 2020) to unseen languages that are substantially different from the languages they are trained on. Except for one system, all of the submissions directly apply their systems to the new languages without any training or adding new target languages' Wikipedia.

3.3 Data Statistics

Table 1 presents the list of the languages and statistics of the train, development and test set data in each target language.

Training data. Our training data consists of Natural Questions (Kwiatkowski et al., 2019) for English and XOR-TyDi QA for the other languages in the shared task.[6] In the constrained track (Section 2.3) only this data source is permitted for providing QA supervision, though other tools are permissible for data augmentation.

Evaluation data. Our evaluation sets span 16 languages: 7 from XOR-TyDi QA and 12 from MKQA with an overlap of five languages and two surprise languages newly annotated for this shared task following MKQA annotation schema. We found that the original XOR-TyDi QA validation and test splits have different proportions of the in-language and cross-lingual questions, resulting in large performance gaps between dev and test subsets as reported by Asai et al. (2021b). We re-split XOR-TyDi QA so that the validation and test sets have similar ratios of the two question types of in-language and cross-lingual questions. In-language questions are answerable from Wikipedia in the question's language, and are often easier to answer while the other category requires cross-lingual retrieval between the target language and English, and are more challenging. Further, we add aliases that can be retrieved via the Wikimedia API to the gold answers, following MKQA, thereby avoiding penalizing models for generating correct answers with surface-level differences. For MKQA we split the answerable examples into a validation set of 1,758 questions and a test set of 5,000 question. We add the newly annotated data for the surprise languages (Tamil and Tagalog) to the test set only.

3.4 Limitations

False negatives in evaluations. First, because the original source questions and answers are from TyDi QA or Natural Questions, their answers are annotated based on a single Wikipedia article in English or the question language. MKQA answers are re-labeled by English speakers without any Wikipedia or web corpus, but small portion of the answers can be geographically incorrect for that regions of the languages the data is translated into (e.g., when the first harry potter movie was released?). As we generalize the task setting to *cross-lingual open retrieval*, there are inconsistent contents across articles in different languages leading to many possible answers. However, because we only have one answer, this can penalize correct answers (Palta et al., 2022). It is a common issue that open-retrieval QA datasets do not comprehensively cover all valid answers (Min et al., 2020a; Asai and Choi, 2021), and this can be more prevalent in multilingual settings due to transliteration of entities or diverse ways to express numeric in some languages (Al-Onaizan and Knight, 2002).

English American-centric biases. Second, the MKQA questions as well as the new data annotated for this shared task are translated from English. This annotation scheme enables us to scale up to many typologically diverse languages, but the resulting questions are likely to be Western- or specifically American-centric, rather than reflecting native speakers' interests and unique linguistic phenomena (Clark et al., 2020). We try to reduce such English-centric bias by only using the questions whose answer entities are also included in Tamil or Tagalog Wikipedia, though this constrains the distribution to simple factoid questions. We also found that in some languages, MKQA answers have high overlap with their English counterparts.

4 Baseline Models

We use a state-of-the-art open-retrieval QA model as our baseline. We open source the code, trained checkpoints, training data, and intermediate/final prediction results.[7]

4.1 Modeling

Our baseline model is based on CORA (Asai et al., 2021b), which has two components: mDPR for

[6]See the training data linked at `https://github.com/mia-workshop/MIA-Shared-Task-2022#training-data`

[7]`https://github.com/mia-workshop/MIA-Shared-Task-2022`

document retrieval and mGEN for answer generation. Both mDPR and mGEN are based on multilingual pretrained models to process data written in many different languages without relying on external translation modules.

Given a question q^L written in a language L, mDPR $\mathcal{R}$ retrieves top N passages: $\mathbf{P} = p_1, \ldots, p_N = \mathcal{R}(q^L)$. mDPR includes all of the target languages' Wikipedias as its retrieval target, except for the two surprise languages. mGEN $\mathcal{G}$ takes as input q and $\mathbf{P}$ and generates an answer a^L in the target language: $a^L = \mathcal{G}(q, \mathbf{P})$. mDPR is a multilingual extension of DPR (Karpukhin et al., 2020), which employs a dual-encoder architecture based on BERT (Devlin et al., 2019) and retrieves top passages based on the dot-product similarities between encoded representations. During training, mDPR optimizes the loss function as the negative log likelihood of the positive passages. mGEN simply concatenates the question and a set of top K passages, and the fine-tuned multilingual encoder-decoder model generates a final answer in the target language. Unlike some prior work in English conducting end-to-end training of the retriever and reader (Lewis et al., 2020c; Guu et al., 2020), we train mDPR and mGEN independently. Note that during mGEN training, we use the passages retrieved by the trained mDPR, as in Izacard and Grave (2021a).

4.2 Training and Hyperparameters

We use the official training data for training. We also leverage the long answer annotations in the Natural Questions dataset and the gold paragraph annotations of XOR-TyDi QA to create mDPR training data, released at the shared task repository.[8] After training mDPR, we run it on the shared task training data questions to obtain top passages, and then use those retrieved passages to train the mGEN model: mGEN is trained to generate the gold answer given an input query and top retrieved passages.

mDPR uses multilingual BERT-base uncased (Devlin et al., 2019), and mGEN is fine-tuned from mT5-base (Xue et al., 2021). For mDPR, we use the same hyperparameters as in DPR (Karpukhin et al., 2020), and train it for 30 epochs, and take the last checkpoint. For mGEN, we follow Asai et al. (2021b) hyperparameters.

4.3 Pre-processing Knowledge Corpus.

Following DPR and mDPR, we split each article into 100-token chunks based on whitespace. For non-spacing languages (e.g., Japanese, Thai), we tokenize the articles using off-the-shelf tokenizers (i.e., MeCab for Japanese[9] and Thai NLP for Thai[10]). We exclude passages with less than 20 tokens. Total numbers of passages for each language are listed in Table 1.

5 Shared Task Submissions

Four teams submitted their final systems to our EvalAI (Yadav et al., 2019) leaderboard,[11] three of which significantly outperformed the original baseline described in Section 4. We summarize the submitted systems here and refer readers to their system description paper for details.

5.1 Constrained Systems

mLUKE+FiD. Tu and Padmanabhan (2022) adapt the retrieve-then-read baseline system with several improvements, including (a) using an mLUKE encoder (Ri et al., 2022) for dense retrieval, (b) combining sparse and dense retrieval, (c) using a fusion-in-decoder reader (Izacard and Grave, 2021b), and (d) leveraging Wikipedia links to augment the training data with additional target language labels.

For retrieval, Tu and Padmanabhan (2022) use the 2019/02/01 Wikipedia snapshot as their document corpora, matching the baseline. They include the Wikipedia snapshots for Tamil and Tagalog to evaluate on the surprise languages. Their sparse retriever searches the monolingual corpora only, while their dense retriever searches all corpora.

CMUmQA. Agarwal et al. (2022) build a four-stage pipeline for a retrieve-then-read approach, based on the CORA open-retrieval system (Asai et al., 2021b) that searches evidence documents in any language for target questions (many-to-many QA; Asai et al., 2021b), without relying on translation. They first apply an mBERT-based DPR retrieval model, followed by a reranker (Qu et al., 2021) with XLM-RoBERTA (Conneau et al., 2020). While it is computationally intractable to use for

[8] https://github.com/mia-workshop/MIA-Shared-Task-2022#training-data

[9] https://taku910.github.io/mecab/.

[10] https://github.com/PyThaiNLP/pythainlp.

[11] https://eval.ai/web/challenges/challenge-page/1638/leaderboard

System	Macro F1			Language F1						
	Total	XOR	MKQA	Arabic	Bengali	Finnish	Japanese	Korean	Russian	Telugu
(a) mLUKE-FID	31.61	40.93	22.29	45.33	30.48	41.01	43.45	31.21	42.62	42.40
(b) CMUmQA	31.53	40.20	**22.87**	55.06	30.56	41.25	42.44	28.76	42.56	40.75
(c) ZusammenQA	27.00	37.95	16.04	49.66	33.99	39.54	39.72	25.59	40.98	36.16
(d) Baseline	27.55	37.95	17.14	51.66	31.96	38.68	40.89	25.35	39.87	37.26
(e) Texttron	**32.02**	**45.50**	18.54	**56.37**	**42.43**	**43.13**	**44.71**	**34.37**	**47.79**	**49.72**

Table 2: Final results on the XOR-TyDi QA subsets of the MIA 2022 shared task. The grayed entry indicates an unconstrained setting.

sys	Language F1													
	ar	en	es	fi	ko	ma	ja	km	ru	sv	tr	zh	tm	ta
(a)	12.67	39.63	30.85	25.22	12.81	29.09	20.49	2.36	18.82	29.62	26.16	**22.60**	**20.75**	20.95
(b)	**13.94**	**42.58**	**32.11**	**26.75**	**14.59**	**31.13**	**22.72**	**8.71**	**22.36**	**31.48**	26.59	18.00	2.74	**26.42**
(c)	8.73	35.32	25.54	20.42	6.78	24.10	14.27	6.06	12.01	25.97	20.27	13.95	0.00	11.14
(d)	9.52	36.34	27.23	22.70	7.68	25.11	15.89	6.00	14.60	26.69	21.66	13.78	0.00	12.78
(e)	13.62	33.24	28.98	25.26	13.07	29.04	23.11	3.96	20.11	29.75	**28.15**	11.30	0.00	0.00

Table 3: Final results on the MKQA subsets of the MIA 2022 shared task. The grayed entry indicates an unconstrained setting.

retrieval, the reranker has the advantage of encoding a question and a passage together, rather than independently. An mT5-based fusion-in-decoder is then applied to generate an answer. As the final step of their pipeline, Wikidata is used to translate English entities in the answer into the target language, if any.

ZusammenQA. Hung et al. (2022) follow the retrieve-then-read system, but with the expansion of several components, along with training methods and data augmentation. Their retriever ensembles supervised models (mDPR and mDPR with a MixCSE loss; Wang et al., 2022) along with unsupervised sparse (Oracle BM-25) and unsupervised dense models (DISTIL, LaBSE, MiniLM, MPNet).

The reader system is based on mGEN, but with domain adaptation by continued masked language modeling on the document corpora, to better adapt to Wikipedia and the target languages. The training data is augmented using Dugan et al. (2022) that generates question-answer pairs from raw document corpora and translates them into multiple languages.

5.2 Unconstrained Systems

Texttron. This unconstrained submission also follows the retrieve-then-read structure: the retrieval model performs dense passage retrieval with XLM-RoBERTa Large (Conneau et al., 2020), and the reading model uses mt5 large. The retrieval text is split into paragraphs (as opposed to 100-word text segments) extracted by the WikiExtractor package. The retrieval model is trained on a combination of three types of custom training data: target-to-target (both the query and retrieved paragraphs are in the target language), target-to-English (the query is in the target language and the retrieval paragraphs are in English), and English-to-English (both the query and retrieved paragraphs are in English). These data are created based on BM25 retrieval and query translation.

Texttron also used multiple stages of training and negative sample mining to tune their final dense retriever with hard negatives: a combination of BM25 and examples from the previous iteration of retrieval that had low token overlap with the gold answers. No system description was available.

6 Main Results

Tables 2 and 3 show final results on XOR-TyDi QA and MKQA subsets, respectively. Three systems are submitted in the constrained setting, while Texttron is an unconstrained submission.

Macro performance. Texttron, mLUKE + mFiD, and CMUmQA significantly improve the baseline performance. Among the constraint submissions, mLUKE + mFiD yields the best performance. While several systems achieve higher than 40 average F1 on XOR-TyDi QA, only two systems achieve higher than 20 average F1 on MKQA, demonstrating how difficult it is to build a system that performs well in many languages without language-specific supervision. Texttron significantly outperforms other baselines on XOR-TyDi QA while CMUmQA shows the best MKQA performance among the submitted systems.

Language-wise performance. The performance varies across different languages. Among XOR-TyDi QA, all of the systems struggle in Korean and Bengali, while in Arabic, Japanese and Russian, they generally show relatively high F1 scores.

On MKQA, where all of the questions are parallel, the performance still significantly differs across languages. Almost all of the systems report lower than 10 F1 in Khmer and Tamil, which are less represented in existing pretraining corpora (Xue et al., 2021) and use their own script systems—with the notable exception of mLUKE + FiD, which achieves 20.8 F1 on Tamil. mLUKE+FiD achieves substantially better performance than other systems in Tamil. This is partially because they also include the Tamil Wikipedia passages for passage retrieval, while other systems, including the baseline, do not. As discussed in Asai et al. (2021b), all systems show lower scores in the languages that are distant from English and use non-Latin scripts (e.g., Cyrillic for Russian, Hangul for Korean).

7 Analysis

We provide further analysis on the submitted systems. In Section 7.1 we provide a brief summary of the findings from the submitted system descriptions. Section 7.2 provides performance comparison over answer-type, and answer overlap with English or training data. We then analyze the degree of answer agreements among the submitted systems to understand which questions remain challenging in Section 7.3. We further conduct manual error analysis in five languages in Section 7.4.

7.1 Summary of Findings

In this section, we highlight several effective techniques from the submitted systems. Overall, a surprisingly wide range of complementary, and potentially additive, methods all reported strong benefits, including: (i) larger and longer pre-trained models for retrieving and reading, (ii) a reranking step with fusion-in-decoder multi-passage cross-encodings, (iii) iterative dense retrieval tuning with progressively harder negative example mining, (iv) using entity-aware retrieval encodings, (v) combining dense and sparse retrievers, (vi) data augmentation, and (vii) leveraging Wikidata answer post-processing for language localization. We discuss some of these below.

These findings highlight various techniques migrating the performances in English retrieval systems. And most of all, they emphasize that cross-lingual retrieval still poses the major bottleneck to the end-to-end task, while large multilingual fusion-in-decoder reader systems can operate well when given sufficient evidence. These findings suggest multilingual retrieval is the most important avenue for future research, especially on questions not easily answered by English Wikipedia. Moreover, retrieving evidence cross-lingually is keys for other knowledge intensive NLP tasks such as fact verification (Thorne et al., 2018) and knowledge-grounded dialogues (Dinan et al., 2019) beyond open-retrieval QA.

Entity representations. Using entity-aware representations for the passage retriever's encoders gives a large performance improvement; As shown in analysis by Team Utah (Tu and Padmanabhan, 2022), replacing mBERT encoders in DPR with mLUKE improves by 1.22 F1 on XOR macro-average and 1.85 MKQA macro F1. We hypothesize that the mLUKE may capture better cross-lingual entity alignment than mBERT as it leverages inter-language links in Wikipedia during pre-training. This sheds light on the potential effectiveness of multilingual entity contextualized representations for cross-lingual passage representations, which is an under-explored direction.

Combining dense and sparse retrievers & hard negatives. Texttron and Team Utah combine both BM25 and mDPR, while ZusammenQA explore a diverse set of unsupervised and supervised retrieval approaches including BM25 and LaBSE (Feng et al., 2022). Team Utah shows that combining BM25 with mDPR helps, while ZusammenQA shows that only using BM25 gives significantly lower scores than the original baseline (Hung et al., 2022), as BM25 does not have cross-lingual phrase matching capabilities. Texttron iteratively trained their dense retriever, mining increasingly hard negative examples using BM25 and query translation, filtered using simple heuristics.

Fusion-in-Decoder and passage reranking. Team Utah and CMUmQA demonstrate that

Fusion-in-Decoder architectures outperform simply concatenating passages as in mGEN (Fusion-in-Encoder). While Fusion-in-Encoder simply concatenates retrieved passages in a retrieved order, Fusion-in-Decoder encodes each of the retrieved passages independently and then concatenate them. This may help the model to pay more attentions to the passages that are ranked lower by the retriever but indeed provides evidence to answer. Recent work in open domain QA also demonstrates that the Fusion-in-Decoder architecture is more competitive than prior systems that simply concatenate passages (Fajcik et al., 2021; Asai et al., 2022).

Team Utah show increasing the number of passages improves performance, while CMUmQA show that cross-encoder reranking is particularly beneficial for Fusion-in-Decoder.

Data augmentation. ZusammenQA introduces data augmentation using Google Translate to translate the training data into target languages. **AUG-QA** translates question-answer pairs into target languages, while **AUG-QAP** translates question, answer and the original training data passages into the target languages. They found that the AUG-QAP and AUG-QA both improve performance from their direct counterpart without data augmentation.

Wikipedia answer localization. CMUmQA and others used Wikidata entity maps to localize answers to the correct target script following Longpre et al. (2021). This process was particularly effective for localizing short answers into a target language from English due to the overwhelming English bias of retrieval and generative systems finetuned on English. As a result, CMUmQA obtains the best MKQA performance among the submitted systems.

7.2 Performance Comparison

In this section, we group questions based on several factors (e.g., answer types) and compare the models' performance across different sub-groups.

Answer types. MKQA provides answer categories for each question. We analyze the per-category model performance to understand what types of questions remain challenging. The original MKQA source data except for the unanswerable subsets has the following answer type distributions: Entity (42%), Date (12%), Number (5%), Number with Unit (4%), Short Phrase (3%), Boolean (yes, no; 1%), Unanswerable (14%), and Long Answers (13%). The Unanswerable and Long Answers categories are excluded from the MIA 2022 shared task evaluation data.

	en	es	ja	zh
Number with units	7.77	3.56	1.94	3.88
Entity	**58.18**	**53.19**	34.42	15.75
Number	27.07	29.83	21.27	25.70
Date	28.14	28.49	6.10	11.37
Short phrases	8.60	7.81	5.08	5.08
Binary	32.99	31.96	**79.38**	**75.25**

Table 4: The percentage of the exact match per answer types in English (en), Spanish (es), Japanese (ja) and Chinese (zh).

We present the percentage of the questions where any of the submitted system predictions match the annotated gold answers in English, Spanish, Japanese and Chinese in Table 4. In all of the languages, the systems show relatively higher exact matching rate in Entity types questions except for Chinese and Japanese. In those languages, many of the entity names are written in their own script systems (e.g., Chinese characters, katakana), which is challenging to be generated from the evidence passages written in other languages; it is known to be challenging to translate an entity name from one language to another using different script systems (Wang et al., 2017). In English and Spanish, the systems show significantly higher accuracy on entity and date than in Japanese or Chinese, while the systems struggle in Boolean questions. XOR-TyDi QA Japanese subset shows higher percentage of boolean questions than other subsets, which potentially helps the systems in Japanese and Chinese MKQA boolean questions. All of the systems show significantly lower performance in short phrase questions, indicating the difficulty of generating phrase length answers beyond simple factoid questions with entity or date answers.

Answer overlaps with English. We analyze performances across languages by examining the relationship between the final performance and the number of the questions whose answers are the same as English answers. Figure 1a shows the performance of the best constrained track submission, mLUKE + FiD and answer overlap with the English subsets for each MKQA language except for Khmer and two surprise languages. We observe a clear correlation between the answer overlap and final performance among those languages. The model performs well on the languages where

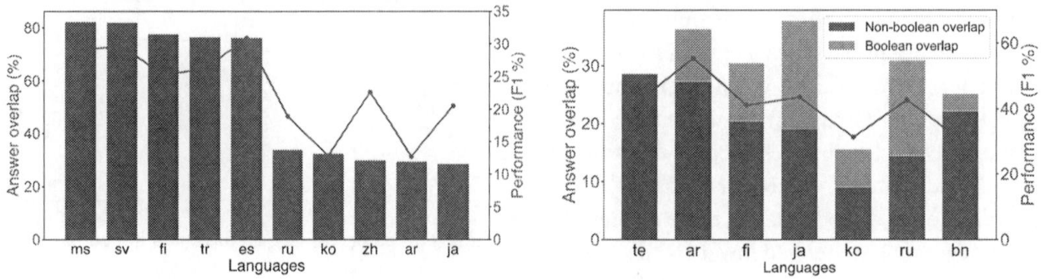

(a) MKQA performance vs. answer overlap with English answers.

(b) XOR-TyDi QA performance vs. answer overlap between train and test sets.

Figure 1: Performance vs. answer overlap between train and test sets.

many answers are the same as English answers. Finnish, on the other hand, shows relatively lower performance compared to other languages with high answer overlap (i.e., Malay, Swedish, Spanish). Among the languages with low answer overlap, on the Japanese and Chinese sets, the system shows relatively high F1 scores compared to the other languages with lower than 40% overlap (i.e., Russian, Korean, Arabic). This is likely because Chinese and Japanese show higher accuracy on Boolean type questions than other languages as discussed above.

Answer overlap with training data. Prior work shows that the high overlap between train and test data can result in the overestimated performance of the systems (Lewis et al., 2021). In XOR-TyDi QA, the questions are annotated by native speakers of the target languages, so the percentage of the train-test overlap can vary across languages. We calculate the percentage of the answers for the test data questions that also appear as gold answers in XOR-TyDi QA training data. We then check whether the degree of the answer overlap between the train and test sets correlate with the final XOR-TyDi QA test performance.

Figure 1b shows the performance and train-test overlap percentage. Although we can see the percentage of overlap between train and test data varies across languages, it is not particularly correlated with the final performance. For instance, Bengali actually shows relatively high overlap between train and test data (over 25% answer overlap), but the performance is much lower than Telugu, whose answer overlap ratio is close to that of Bengali. We also found that the percentage of the Boolean questions (yes, no) significantly differs across languages: in Japanese, around 10% of the questions are Boolean questions, while in Telugu, almost no questions are Boolean. The original TyDi QA data is annotated by different groups of annotators for each language, and thus such question distributions can differ (Clark et al., 2020).

XOR-TyDi QA vs. MKQA. Arabic, Japanese, Korean, and Finnish are included both in MKQA and XOR-TyDi QA, but their performance on the two subsets significantly differ; In general, the XOR-TyDi QA F1 scores are much higher than MKQA (e.g., Japanese: 44.71 vs. 23.11). We hypothesize that this happens because we do not have training data for MKQA and all MKQA questions tend to require cross-lingual retrieval as the questions are translated from English and answers are American-centric. In contrast, half of the questions in XOR-TyDi QA are from TyDi QA, and the answers are grounded to their own languages' Wikipedia. Cross-lingual retrieval is generally more challenging than monolingual retrieval (Zhang et al., 2021). In addition, all of the XOR-TyDi QA cross-lingual questions are labeled "unanswerable" in TyDi QA, and can be more difficult to answer than its monolingual counterparts.

To further test this hypothesis, we evaluate the submitted systems' performance on XOR-TyDi QA's cross-lingual and monolingual subsets in Table 5. We can clearly see that all of the baseline's performance deteriorates on the cross-lingual subsets, while they show high F1 scores across languages on the monolingual subsets.

7.3 Prediction Agreement

We analyze how often all of the systems agree on the same answers on the MKQA test data in five languages. In particular, we compare all of the four system predictions on the English, Japanese, Chinese, Spanish and Turkish subsets of the MKQA test data, and check the prediction agreements

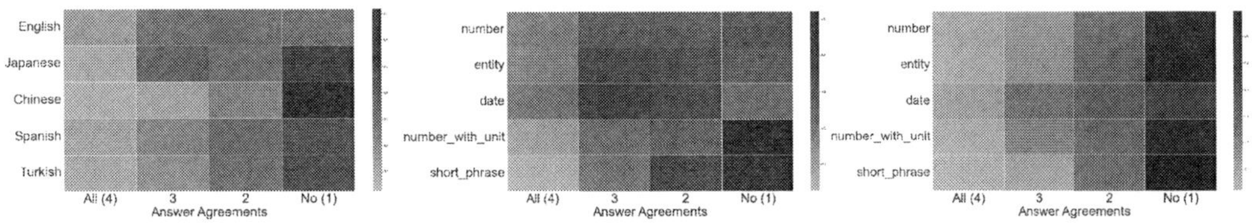

(a) MKQA Answer agreement. (b) Per-category agreement (En). (c) Per-category agreement (Ja).

Figure 2: Answer agreements of the four submitted systems.

	Avg.		Arabic		Bengali		Finnish		Japanese		Korean		Russian		Telugu	
Sys.	cl	m	cl	m	cl	m	cl	m	cl	m	cl	m	cl	m	cl	m
(a)	27.2	58.8	28.3	64.8	29.4	63.3	30.3	51.3	29.5	55.9	22.2	53.2	24.9	55.8	25.9	67.6
(b)	21.4	54.2	22.2	65.2	21.7	44.6	24.1	51.7	27.4	55.2	19.5	49.3	19.1	50.8	16.0	62.2
(c)	20.3	52.5	21.5	64.6	20.5	42.3	25.5	50.9	26.3	53.1	17.6	44.9	16.0	51.2	14.7	60.3
(d)	19.5	49.7	22.4	59.0	19.0	51.5	23.8	46.9	25.2	50.2	15.3	38.8	16.9	47.0	14.0	54.2

Table 5: Final results on MIA 2022 Shared Task XOR-TyDi QA cross-lingual ("cl") / monolingual subsets ("m"). Systems (a), (b), (c) and (d) are Texttron, mLUKE-FID, CMUmQA, and ZusammenQA, respectively.

based on the number of the unique predictions among the union of the predictions. We can see that in English and Spanish, the agreement is high (e.g., in 40% of the questions, all or three of the four systems agree on the same answers), while the agreement is lower in other languages, particularly in Japanese and Chinese.

To understand the phenomena, we breakdown the prediction agreement statistics in English and Japanese into different answer categories. Figure 2b and Figure 2c show per-category prediction agreements in English and Japanese, respectively. While in English, systems show high agreements in date, entity and number type questions, in Japanese, the agreement rate is lower across category, potentially because of their diverse formats of number and dates, as well as the transliteration of the entity names.

7.4 Error Analysis

We conduct a set of error analysis in five languages (i.e., English, Japanese, Korean, Chinese and Telugu) on randomly sampled 30 questions, where none of the submission systems' predictions exactly match any of the ground truth answers.

Error types. We classify the errors into following categories: (i) incorrect predictions, (ii) answers are semantically correct in different languages (incorrect languages), (iii) incorrect gold answers, (iv) semantically-equivalent predictions in the target language but are penalized because gold answers do not cover all of the potential gold answers (not comprehensive gold answers), (v) questions are open-ended or ambiguous (e.g., entity ambiguity), (vi) questions' granularity is unclear (unclear question granularity; e.g., year v.s. month, kilometers v.s. meters), (vii) questions are highly subjective (e.g., who is the best singer ever), (viii) temporal or geographical dependency in questions.

The first two error types, (i) and (ii), reveal the limitations of models. The error type (iii) and (iv) are considered answer annotation errors (Min et al., 2020a; Asai and Choi, 2021). The last four error types (v), (vi), (vii) and (viii) requires some specifications or context (Zhang and Choi, 2021; Min et al., 2020b).

Error analysis schema. We recruit native speakers of the five target languages and ask them to classify the errors into the aforementioned categories. We present the predictions of all of the systems as well as the intermediate retrieval results of the top constrained system (Team Utah).

Error analysis results. Table 6 provides the error analysis result. Besides modeling errors, we found that the original annotations themselves exhibit some issues, which underestimates models' performance. Across languages, annotators found non-negligible proportion of the errors happen as the original gold answers do not cover all of the possible answer aliases or the answer granularity is unclear. For instance, an English question asks "what is the temperature at the center of earth" and the gold answer is 6000 °C. Several systems answer in Fahrenheit or Kelvin, and got zero F1 score. Several questions are also temporal or geographical de-

	English	Arabic	Japanese	Korean	Chinese
(i) incorrect predictions	12	9	23	16	12
(ii) incorrect languages	0	2	3	0	2
(iii) incorrect gold answers	2	4	5	1	0
(iv) not comprehensive gold answers	10	1	7	5	6
(v) ambiguous question	3	7	6	15	5
(vi) unclear question granularity	3	2	1	2	0
(vii) subjective question	0	0	0	0	0
(viii) temporal or geographical dependency in questions	4	4	1	4	5

Table 6: Error analysis on sampled questions where all of the submissions unanimously fail to predict the correct answers. We show the percentage of the errors in each category.

pendent such as "who was the last person appointed to the u.s. supreme court" or クリミナル・マインドの新シーズンが公開されるのはいつか (when is the next season of Criminal Minds will be released?). Although situation-grounded QA has been recently studied (Zhang and Choi, 2021), there's little work that analyzes this phenomena in multilingual settings, where the particularly geographical dependence can be even more prevalent. Question ambiguity is also common in multilingual QA.

8 Conclusion and Discussions

We have presented the MIA 2022 Shared Task on cross-lingual open-retrieval QA systems in 16 typologically diverse languages, many of which are unseen during training. Several submissions improved significantly over our baseline based on a state-of-the-art cross-lingual open-retrieval QA system and investigated a wide range of techniques. Those results shed light on the effectiveness of several techniques in this challenging task, such as entity-enhanced representations, sparse-dense retrieval, and better interactions between passages. We further conducted detailed performance analysis on different subsets of the datasets, such as languages, answer types, the necessity of cross-lingual retrieval as well as detailed error analysis. We also suggest several bottlenecks in the area.

Acknowledgements

We would like to acknowledgments and Noah A. Smith for serving as our steering committee. We are grateful to Google for providing funding for our workshop. We thank GENGO translators to translate questions into Tamil and Tagalog. we thank the EvalAI team, particularly Ram Ramrakhya, for their help with hosting the shared task submission site. We thank Maraim Masoud for her help in error analysis.

References

Sumit Agarwal, Suraj Tripathi, Teruko Mitamura, and Carolyn Penstein Rose. 2022. Zero-shot cross-lingual open domain question answering. In *Proc. of MIA*.

Yaser Al-Onaizan and Kevin Knight. 2002. Translating named entities using monolingual and bilingual resources. In *Proc. of ACL*.

Akari Asai and Eunsol Choi. 2021. Challenges in information-seeking QA: Unanswerable questions and paragraph retrieval. In *Proc. of ACL*.

Akari Asai, Matt Gardner, and Hannaneh Hajishirzi. 2022. Evidentiality-guided generation for knowledge-intensive nlp tasks. In *In Proc. of NAACL*.

Akari Asai, Jungo Kasai, Jonathan H Clark, Kenton Lee, Eunsol Choi, and Hannaneh Hajishirzi. 2021a. XOR QA: Cross-lingual open-retrieval question answering. In *Proc. of NAACL*.

Akari Asai, Xinyan Yu, Jungo Kasai, and Hannaneh Hajishirzi. 2021b. One question answering model for many languages with cross-lingual dense passage retrieval. In *Proc. of NeurIPS*.

Damian Blasi, Antonios Anastasopoulos, and Graham Neubig. 2022. Systematic inequalities in language technology performance across the world's languages. In *Proc. of ACL*.

Danqi Chen, Adam Fisch, Jason Weston, and Antoine Bordes. 2017. Reading Wikipedia to answer open-domain questions. In *Proc. of ACL*.

Danqi Chen and Wen-tau Yih. 2020. Open-domain question answering. In *Proc. of ACL: Tutorial Abstracts*.

Jonathan H. Clark, Eunsol Choi, Michael Collins, Dan Garrette, Tom Kwiatkowski, Vitaly Nikolaev, and Jennimaria Palomaki. 2020. TyDi QA: A benchmark for information-seeking question answering in typologically diverse languages. *TACL*.

Alexis Conneau, Kartikay Khandelwal, Naman Goyal, Vishrav Chaudhary, Guillaume Wenzek, Francisco Guzmán, Edouard Grave, Myle Ott, Luke Zettlemoyer, and Veselin Stoyanov. 2020. Unsupervised cross-lingual representation learning at scale. In *Proc. of ACL*.

Yiming Cui, Ting Liu, Wanxiang Che, Li Xiao, Zhipeng Chen, Wentao Ma, Shijin Wang, and Guoping Hu. 2019. A span-extraction dataset for Chinese machine reading comprehension. In *Proc. of EMNLP*.

Jacob Devlin, Ming-Wei Chang, Kenton Lee, and Kristina Toutanova. 2019. BERT: Pre-training of deep bidirectional transformers for language understanding. In *Proc. of NAACL*.

Martin d'Hoffschmidt, Wacim Belblidia, Quentin Heinrich, Tom Brendlé, and Maxime Vidal. 2020. FQuAD: French question answering dataset. In *Findings of EMNLP*.

Emily Dinan, Stephen Roller, Kurt Shuster, Angela Fan, Michael Auli, and Jason Weston. 2019. Wizard of wikipedia: Knowledge-powered conversational agents. In *Proc. of ICLR*.

Liam Dugan, Eleni Miltsakaki, Shriyash Upadhyay, Etan Ginsberg, Hannah Gonzalez, DaHyeon Choi, Chuning Yuan, and Chris Callison-Burch. 2022. A feasibility study of answer-unaware question generation for education. In *Findings of ACL*.

Martin Fajcik, Martin Docekal, Karel Ondrej, and Pavel Smrz. 2021. R2-D2: A modular baseline for open-domain question answering. In *Findings of EMNLP*.

Fangxiaoyu Feng, Yinfei Yang, Daniel Cer, Naveen Arivazhagan, and Wei Wang. 2022. Language-agnostic BERT sentence embedding. In *Proc. of ACL*.

Pamela Forner, Danilo Giampiccolo, Bernardo Magnini, Anselmo Peñas, Álvaro Rodrigo, and Richard Sutcliffe. 2010. Evaluating multilingual question answering systems at CLEF. In *Proc. of LREC*.

Pamela Forner, Anselmo Peñas, Eneko Agirre, Iñaki Alegria, Corina Forăscu, Nicolas Moreau, Petya Osenova, Prokopis Prokopidis, Paulo Rocha, Bogdan Sacaleanu, Richard Sutcliffe, and Erik Tjong Kim Sang. 2008. Overview of the clef 2008 multilingual question answering track. In *Proc. of CLEF*.

Kelvin Guu, Kenton Lee, Zora Tung, Panupong Pasupat, and Ming-Wei Chang. 2020. REALM: Retrieval-augmented language model pre-training.

Junjie Hu, Sebastian Ruder, Aditya Siddhant, Graham Neubig, Orhan Firat, and Melvin Johnson. 2020. XTREME: A massively multilingual multi-task benchmark for evaluating cross-lingual generalisation. In *Proc. of ICML*.

Chia-Chien Hung, Tommaso Green, Robert Litschko, Tornike Tsereteli, Sotaro Takeshita, Marco Bombieri, Goran Glavaš, and Simone Paolo Ponzetto1. 2022. ZusammenQA: Data augmentation with specialized models for cross-lingual open-retrieval question answering system. In *Proc. of MIA*.

Gautier Izacard and Edouard Grave. 2021a. Distilling knowledge from reader to retriever for question answering. In *Proc. of ICLR*.

Gautier Izacard and Edouard Grave. 2021b. Leveraging passage retrieval with generative models for open domain question answering. In *Proc. of EACL*.

Pratik Joshi, Sebastin Santy, Amar Budhiraja, Kalika Bali, and Monojit Choudhury. 2020. The state and fate of linguistic diversity and inclusion in the NLP world. In *Proc. of ACL*.

Vladimir Karpukhin, Barlas Oguz, Sewon Min, Patrick Lewis, Ledell Wu, Sergey Edunov, Danqi Chen, and Wen-tau Yih. 2020. Dense passage retrieval for open-domain question answering. In *Proc. of EMNLP*.

Tom Kwiatkowski, Jennimaria Palomaki, Olivia Redfield, Michael Collins, Ankur Parikh, Chris Alberti, Danielle Epstein, Illia Polosukhin, Jacob Devlin, Kenton Lee, et al. 2019. Natural questions: a benchmark for question answering research. *TACL*.

Patrick Lewis, Barlas Oguz, Ruty Rinott, Sebastian Riedel, and Holger Schwenk. 2020a. MLQA: Evaluating cross-lingual extractive question answering. In *Proc. of ACL*.

Patrick Lewis, Ethan Perez, Aleksandra Piktus, Fabio Petroni, Vladimir Karpukhin, Naman Goyal, Heinrich Küttler, Mike Lewis, Wen-tau Yih, Tim Rocktäschel, Sebastian Riedel, and Douwe Kiela. 2020b. Retrieval-augmented generation for knowledge-intensive nlp tasks. In *Proc. of NeurIPS*.

Patrick Lewis, Ethan Perez, Aleksandra Piktus, Fabio Petroni, Vladimir Karpukhin, Naman Goyal, Heinrich Küttler, Mike Lewis, Wen-tau Yih, Tim Rocktäschel, et al. 2020c. Retrieval-augmented generation for knowledge-intensive NLP tasks. In *Proc. of NeurIPS*.

Patrick Lewis, Pontus Stenetorp, and Sebastian Riedel. 2021. Question and answer test-train overlap in open-domain question answering datasets. In *Proc. of EACL*.

Jiahua Liu, Yankai Lin, Zhiyuan Liu, and Maosong Sun. 2019. XQA: A cross-lingual open-domain question answering dataset. In *Proc. of ACL*.

Shayne Longpre, Yi Lu, and Joachim Daiber. 2021. MKQA: A linguistically diverse benchmark for multilingual open domain question answering. *TACL*.

Sewon Min, Jordan Boyd-Graber, Chris Alberti, Danqi Chen, Eunsol Choi, Michael Collins, Kelvin Guu, Hannaneh Hajishirzi, Kenton Lee, Jennimaria Palomaki, Colin Raffel, Adam Roberts, Tom Kwiatkowski, Patrick Lewis, Yuxiang Wu, Heinrich Küttler, Linqing Liu, Pasquale Minervini, Pontus Stenetorp, Sebastian Riedel, Sohee Yang, Minjoon Seo, Gautier Izacard, Fabio Petroni, Lucas Hosseini, Nicola De Cao, Edouard Grave, Ikuya Yamada, Sonse Shimaoka, Masatoshi Suzuki, Shumpei

Miyawaki, Shun Sato, Ryo Takahashi, Jun Suzuki, Martin Fajcik, Martin Docekal, Karel Ondrej, Pavel Smrz, Hao Cheng, Yelong Shen, Xiaodong Liu, Pengcheng He, Weizhu Chen, Jianfeng Gao, Barlas Oguz, Xilun Chen, Vladimir Karpukhin, Stan Peshterliev, Dmytro Okhonko, Michael Schlichtkrull, Sonal Gupta, Yashar Mehdad, and Wen-tau Yih. 2020a. NeurIPS 2020 efficientQA competition: Systems, analyses and lessons learned. In *Proc. of NeurIPS 2020 Competition and Demonstration Track*.

Sewon Min, Julian Michael, Hannaneh Hajishirzi, and Luke Zettlemoyer. 2020b. AmbigQA: Answering ambiguous open-domain questions. In *Proc. of EMNLP*.

Shramay Palta, Haozhe An, Yifan Yang, Shuaiyi Huang, and Maharshi Gor. 2022. Investigating information inconsistency in multilingual open-domain question answering.

Yingqi Qu, Yuchen Ding, Jing Liu, Kai Liu, Ruiyang Ren, Wayne Xin Zhao, Daxiang Dong, Hua Wu, and Haifeng Wang. 2021. RocketQA: An optimized training approach to dense passage retrieval for open-domain question answering. In *Proc. of NAACL*.

Ryokan Ri, Ikuya Yamada, and Yoshimasa Tsuruoka. 2022. mLUKE: The power of entity representations in multilingual pretrained language models. In *Proc. of ACL*.

Dwaipayan Roy, Sumit Bhatia, and Prateek Jain. 2022. Information asymmetry in wikipedia across different languages: A statistical analysis. *JASIST*.

Peter Schäuble and Páraic Sheridan. 1997. Cross-language information retrieval (CLIR) track overview. In *Proc. of TREC*.

James Thorne, Andreas Vlachos, Christos Christodoulopoulos, and Arpit Mittal. 2018. FEVER: a large-scale dataset for fact extraction and VERification. In *Proc. of NAACL*.

Zhucheng Tu and Sarguna Janani Padmanabhan. 2022. MIA 2022 shared task submission: Leveraging entity representations, dense-sparse hybrids, and fusion-in-decoder for cross-lingual question. In *Proc. of MIA*.

Hao Wang, Yangguang Li, Zhen Huang, Yong Dou, Lingpeng Kong, and Jing Shao. 2022. SNCSE: Contrastive learning for unsupervised sentence embedding with soft negative samples.

Yuguang Wang, Shanbo Cheng, Liyang Jiang, Jiajun Yang, Wei Chen, Muze Li, Lin Shi, Yanfeng Wang, and Hongtao Yang. 2017. Sogou neural machine translation systems for WMT17. In *Proc. of WMT*.

Linting Xue, Noah Constant, Adam Roberts, Mihir Kale, Rami Al-Rfou, Aditya Siddhant, Aditya Barua, and Colin Raffel. 2021. mT5: A massively multilingual pre-trained text-to-text transformer. In *Proc. of NAACL*.

Deshraj Yadav, Rishabh Jain, Harsh Agrawal, Prithvijit Chattopadhyay, Taranjeet Singh, Akash Jain, Shiv Baran Singh, Stefan Lee, and Dhruv Batra. 2019. EvalAI: Towards better evaluation systems for ai agents.

Michael Zhang and Eunsol Choi. 2021. SituatedQA: Incorporating extra-linguistic contexts into QA. In *Proc. of EMNLP*.

Xinyu Zhang, Xueguang Ma, Peng Shi, and Jimmy Lin. 2021. Mr. TyDi: A multi-lingual benchmark for dense retrieval. In *Proc. of MRL*.

Author Index

Association for Computational Linguistics
209 N. Eighth Street
Stroudsburg, Pennsylvania 18360

ISBN 978-1-7138-5635-1

CURRAN ASSOCIATES INC.
proceedings.com